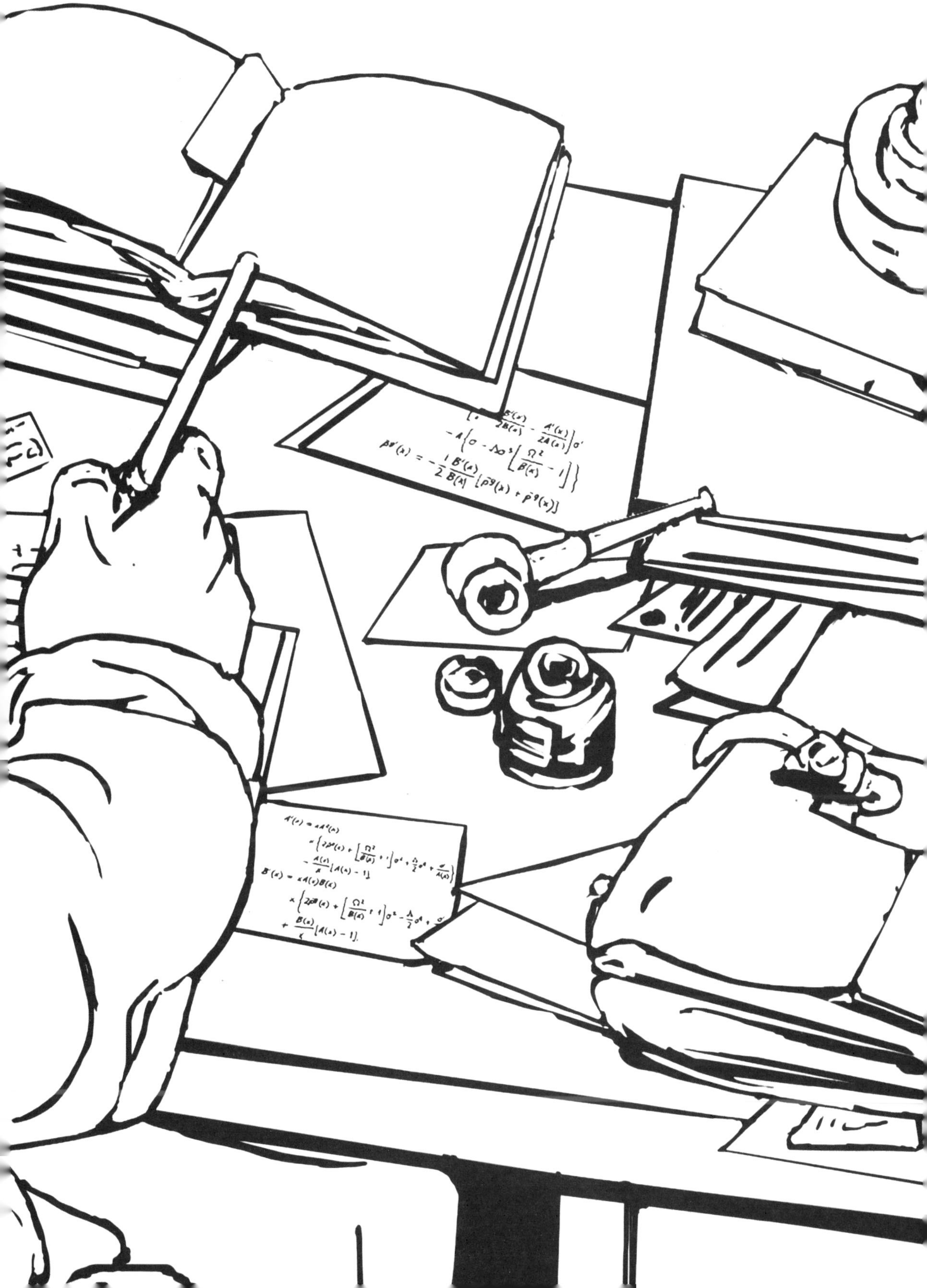

A. Einstein
THE POETRY OF REAL
ART • MANUEL GARCÍA IGLESIAS   WRITER • MARWAN KAHIL

"IF I HAVE SEEN FURTHER IT IS BY STANDING ON THE SHOULDERS OF GIANTS." ISAAC NEWTON

nbm GRAPHIC NOVELS
Nantier • Beall • Minoustchine
N E W   Y O R K

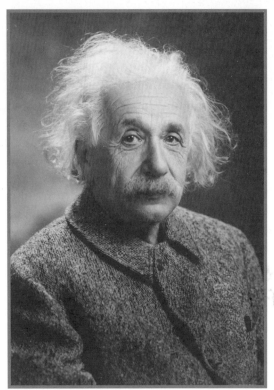

ALBERT EINSTEIN (1879-1955)
PHOTO : ORREN JACK TURNER, 1947 - LIBRARY OF CONGRESS

Marwan Kahil would like to thank Manuel for his talent and patience, Jean-Paul for his confidence and his keen eye, Aloysia for her presence and for her re-readings, his mother Laure for everything she's brought him, Diana for her support, Angela for her passion for history.
A salute to all the Alumni of Jamhour and for the instructors at this prestigious establishment who pursue their mission of offering a rigorous world class education that encourages autonomy and curiosity. Parcticularly Mr. Ayoud, Mr. Bark and Mr. Irani for the transmission of their understanding of mathematics and physics. Also for Mr. Salamé who introduced him to philosophy in the most beautiful way possible.
Finally, Marwan Kahil would like to thank Eddy, Miche and Sami for their advice and for always supporting his decisions.

Manuel Garcia Iglesias would like to thank Marwan for his friendship, his creativity and for the serenity with which he undertook this project, and Jean-Paul for his presence. He would also like to thank his precious friends with all his heart for their unfailing support under all manner of circumstances, particularly Félix Ruiz, who helped give birth to this project.

Certain illustrations were inspired by news images taken barring involuntary error, from the public domain. The example of the elevator on pages 66 and 67 is in part inspired by an illustration by L. Hindryckx that appeared in the magazine Science & Vie N°273 dedicated to Einstein and his theories of relativity.

ISBN 9781681122021
© 2017 Blue Lotus Prod.
Initially published in France under the 21g imprint - www.21g.fr
© 2019 NBM for the English translation
Library of Congress Control Number 2019940465
Translation by Peter Russella
Lettering by Ortho
Printed in China
1st printing August 2019

This book is also available wherever e-books are sold

GRAPHIC NOVELS
Comics Biographies

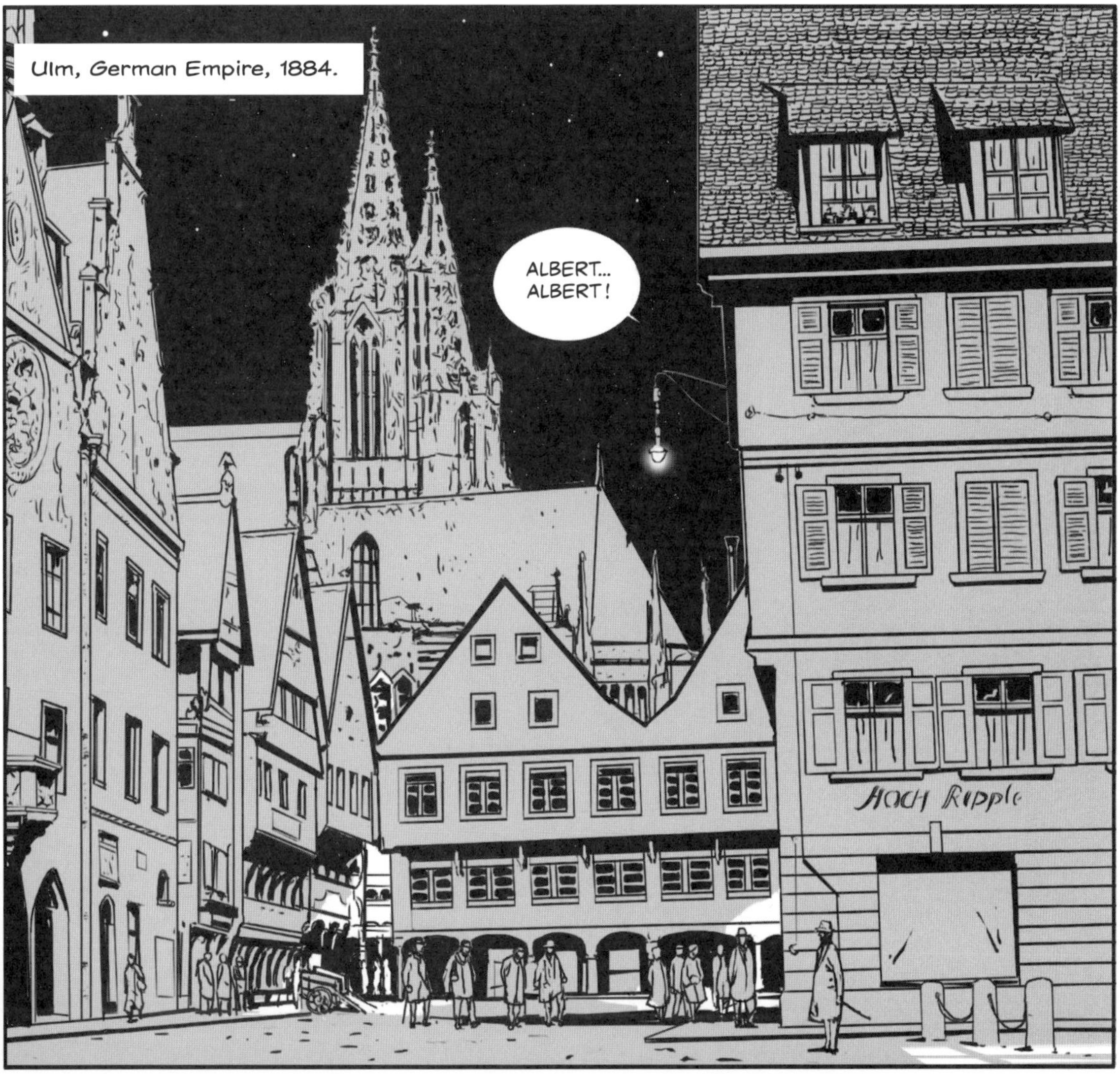
Ulm, German Empire, 1884.
ALBERT... ALBERT!
Hoch Ripple

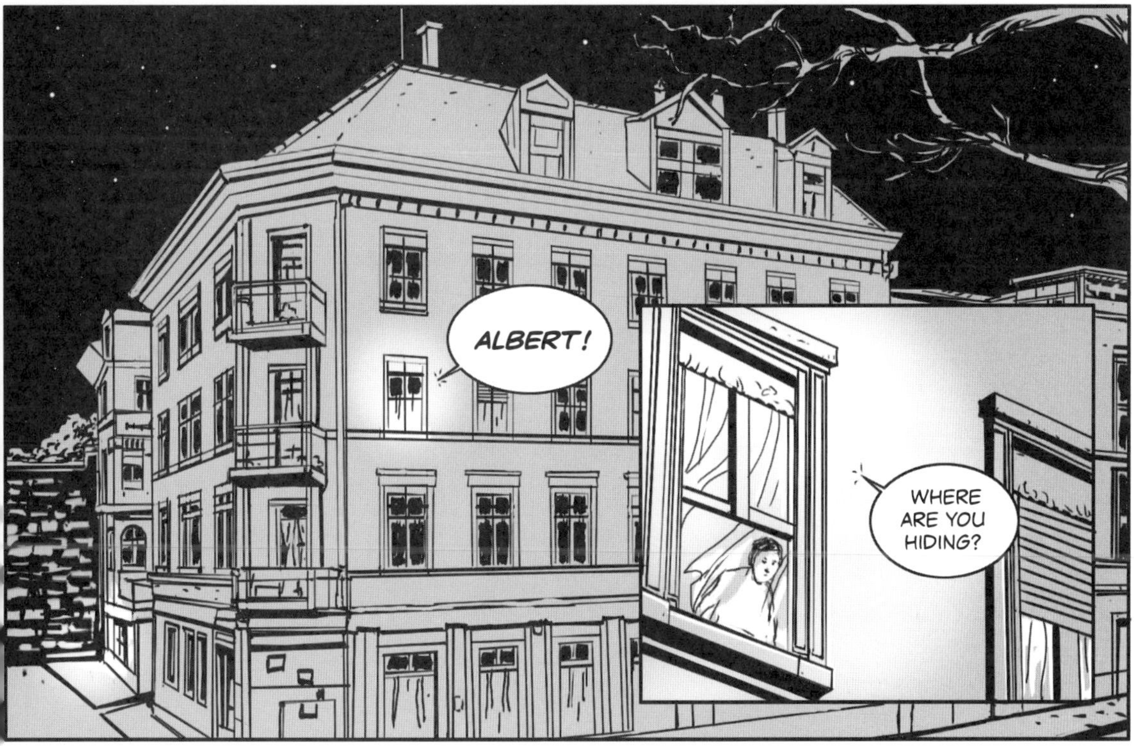
ALBERT!
WHERE ARE YOU HIDING?

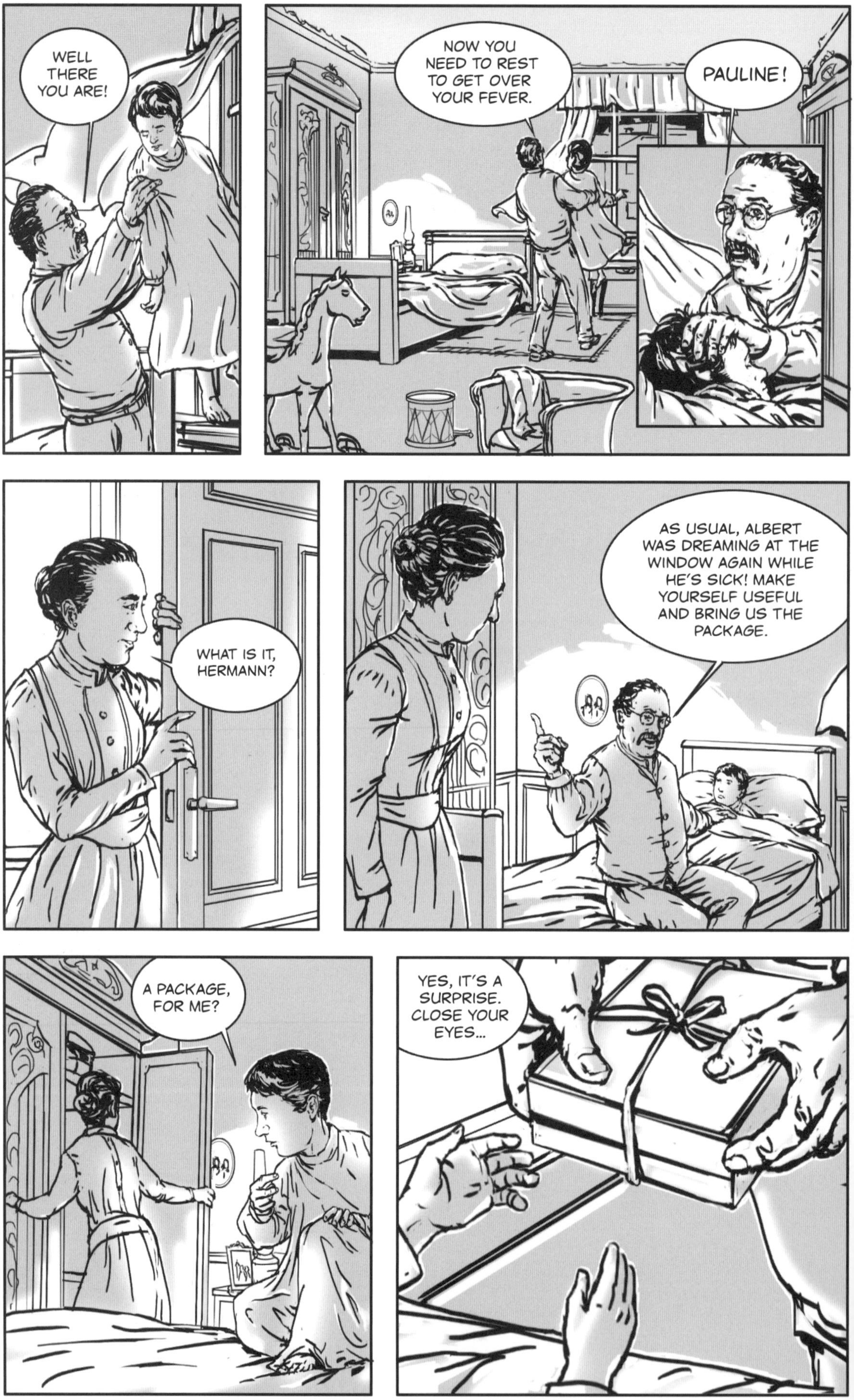
WELL THERE YOU ARE!
NOW YOU NEED TO REST TO GET OVER YOUR FEVER.
PAULINE!
WHAT IS IT, HERMANN?
AS USUAL, ALBERT WAS DREAMING AT THE WINDOW AGAIN WHILE HE'S SICK! MAKE YOURSELF USEFUL AND BRING US THE PACKAGE.
A PACKAGE, FOR ME?
YES, IT'S A SURPRISE. CLOSE YOUR EYES...

I REMEMBER IT LIKE IT WAS YESTERDAY, MARK!

THE DAY MY FATHER GAVE ME THAT COMPASS...

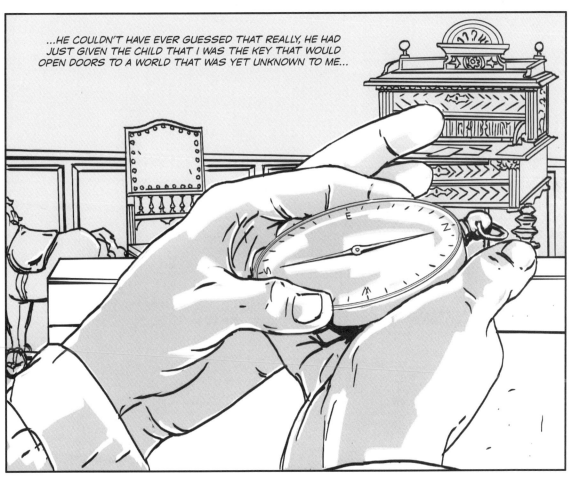

...HE COULDN'T HAVE EVER GUESSED THAT REALLY, HE HAD JUST GIVEN THE CHILD THAT I WAS THE KEY THAT WOULD OPEN DOORS TO A WORLD THAT WAS YET UNKNOWN TO ME...

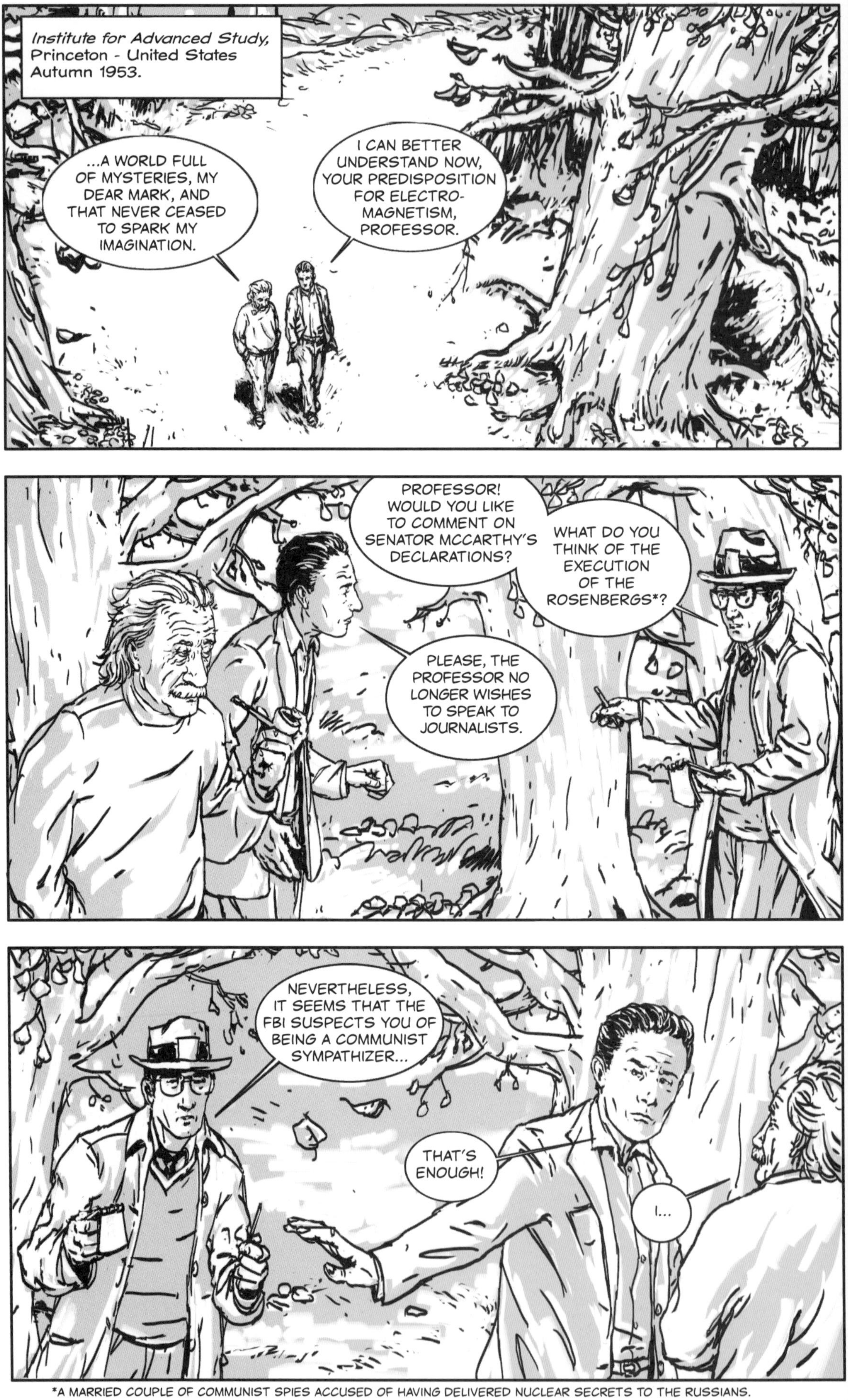
Institute for Advanced Study, Princeton - United States Autumn 1953.
...A WORLD FULL OF MYSTERIES, MY DEAR MARK, AND THAT NEVER CEASED TO SPARK MY IMAGINATION.
I CAN BETTER UNDERSTAND NOW, YOUR PREDISPOSITION FOR ELECTRO-MAGNETISM, PROFESSOR.
PROFESSOR! WOULD YOU LIKE TO COMMENT ON SENATOR MCCARTHY'S DECLARATIONS?
WHAT DO YOU THINK OF THE EXECUTION OF THE ROSENBERGS*?
PLEASE, THE PROFESSOR NO LONGER WISHES TO SPEAK TO JOURNALISTS.
NEVERTHELESS, IT SEEMS THAT THE FBI SUSPECTS YOU OF BEING A COMMUNIST SYMPATHIZER...
THAT'S ENOUGH!
I...

*A MARRIED COUPLE OF COMMUNIST SPIES ACCUSED OF HAVING DELIVERED NUCLEAR SECRETS TO THE RUSSIANS.

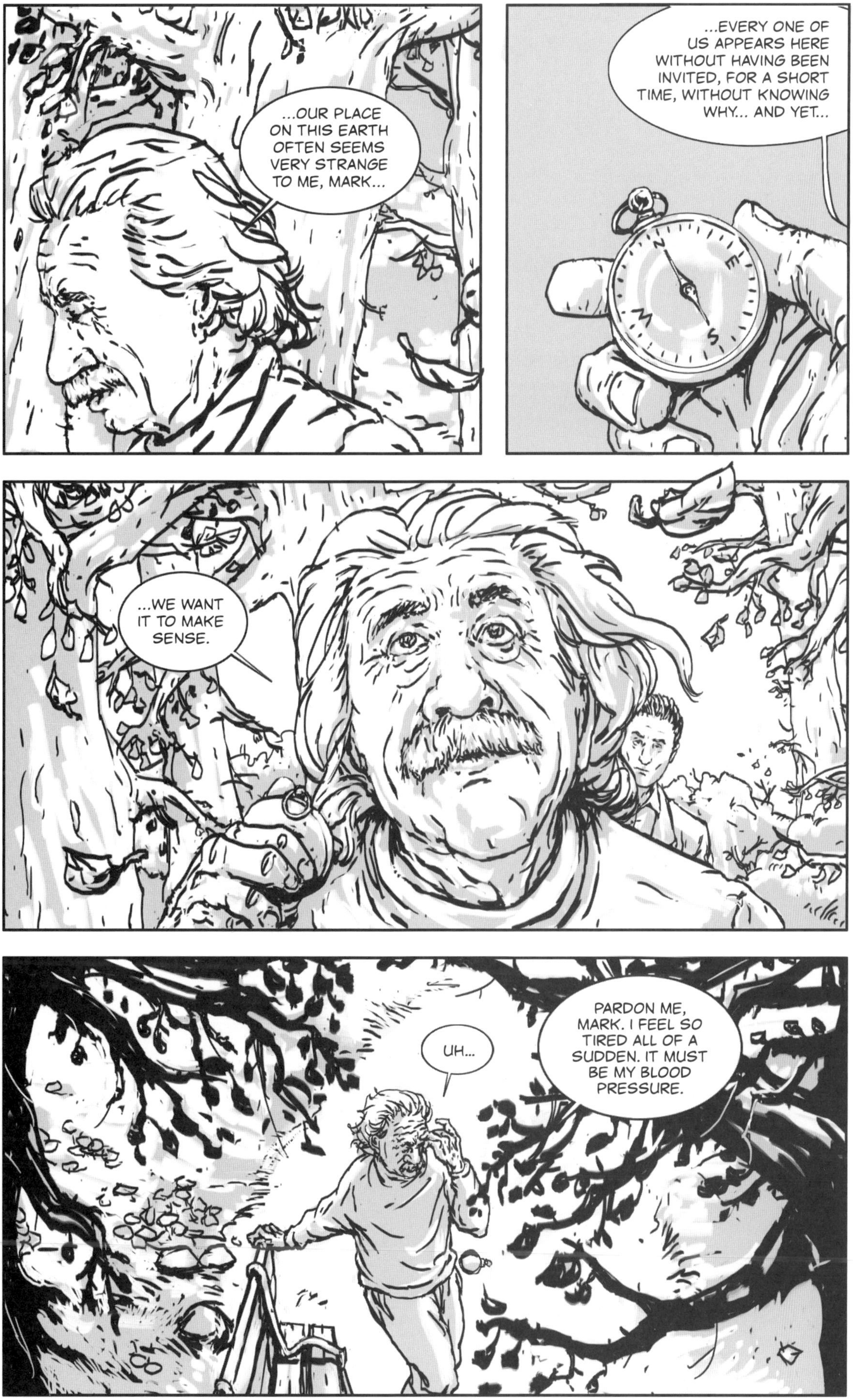
...OUR PLACE ON THIS EARTH OFTEN SEEMS VERY STRANGE TO ME, MARK...
...EVERY ONE OF US APPEARS HERE WITHOUT HAVING BEEN INVITED, FOR A SHORT TIME, WITHOUT KNOWING WHY... AND YET...
N
E
S
W
...WE WANT IT TO MAKE SENSE.
UH...
PARDON ME, MARK. I FEEL SO TIRED ALL OF A SUDDEN. IT MUST BE MY BLOOD PRESSURE.

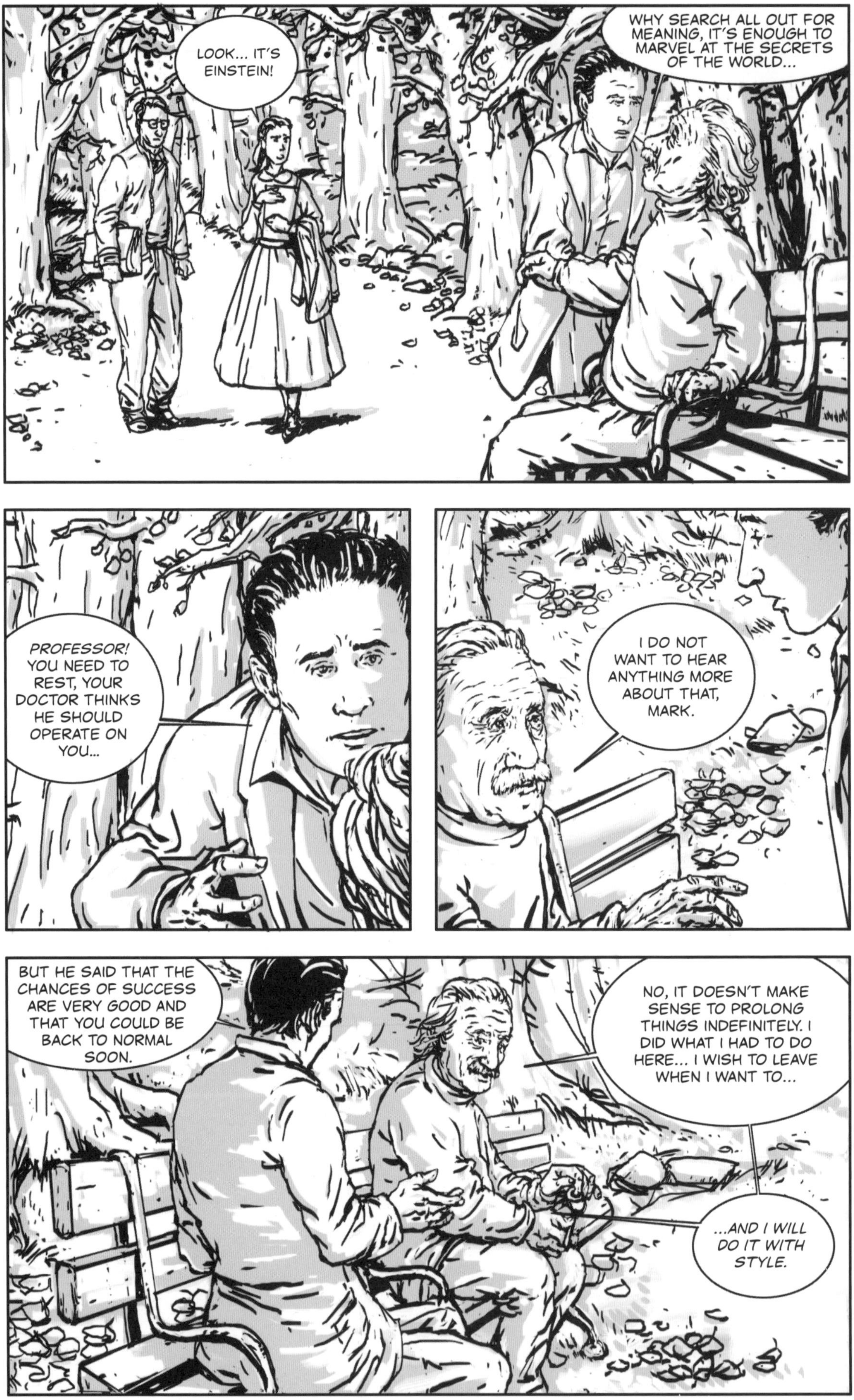
LOOK... IT'S EINSTEIN!
WHY SEARCH ALL OUT FOR MEANING, IT'S ENOUGH TO MARVEL AT THE SECRETS OF THE WORLD...
PROFESSOR! YOU NEED TO REST, YOUR DOCTOR THINKS HE SHOULD OPERATE ON YOU...
I DO NOT WANT TO HEAR ANYTHING MORE ABOUT THAT, MARK.
BUT HE SAID THAT THE CHANCES OF SUCCESS ARE VERY GOOD AND THAT YOU COULD BE BACK TO NORMAL SOON.
NO, IT DOESN'T MAKE SENSE TO PROLONG THINGS INDEFINITELY. I DID WHAT I HAD TO DO HERE... I WISH TO LEAVE WHEN I WANT TO...
...AND I WILL DO IT WITH STYLE.

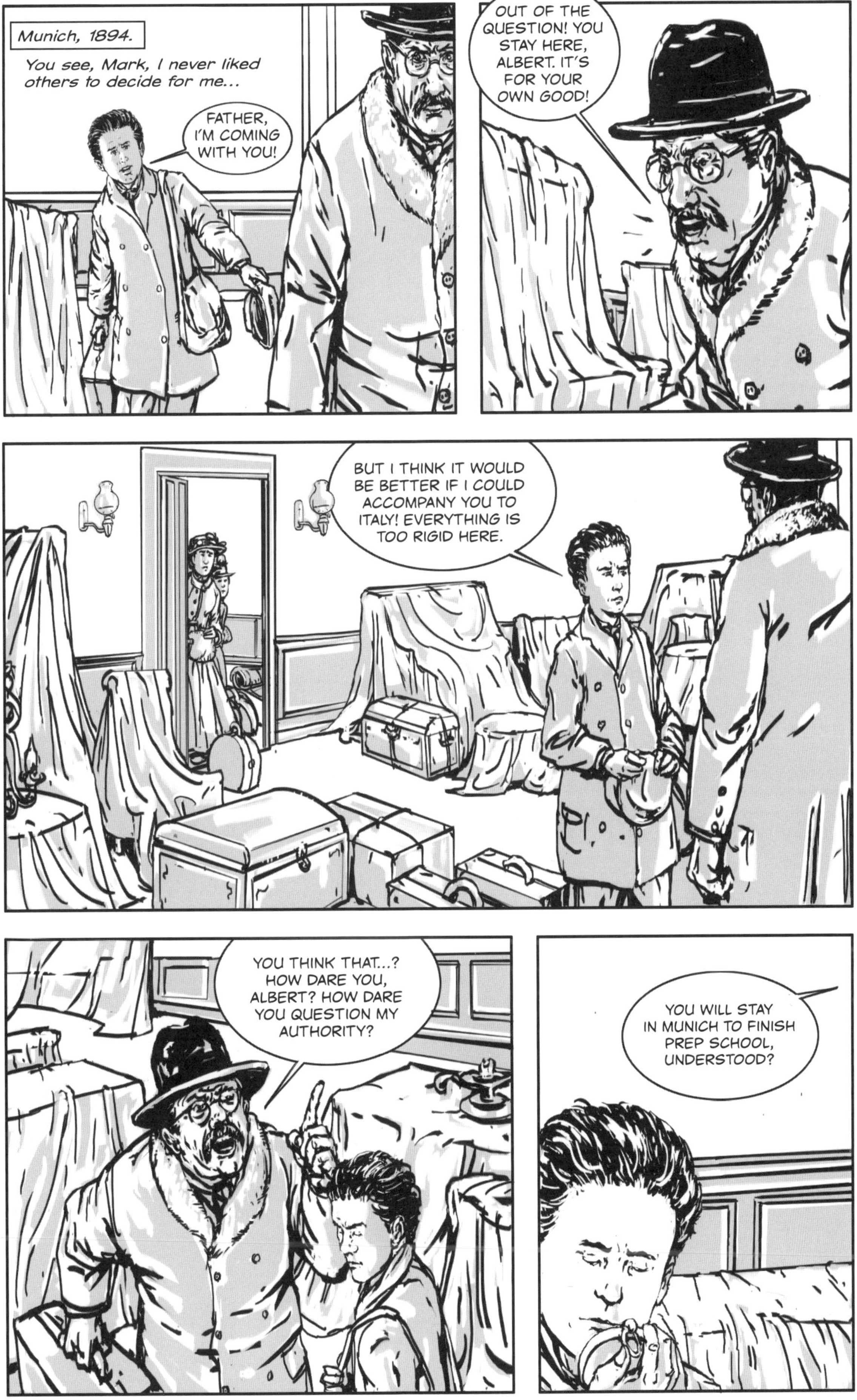

Munich, 1894.
You see, Mark, I never liked others to decide for me...
FATHER, I'M COMING WITH YOU!
OUT OF THE QUESTION! YOU STAY HERE, ALBERT. IT'S FOR YOUR OWN GOOD!
BUT I THINK IT WOULD BE BETTER IF I COULD ACCOMPANY YOU TO ITALY! EVERYTHING IS TOO RIGID HERE.
YOU THINK THAT...? HOW DARE YOU, ALBERT? HOW DARE YOU QUESTION MY AUTHORITY?
YOU WILL STAY IN MUNICH TO FINISH PREP SCHOOL, UNDERSTOOD?

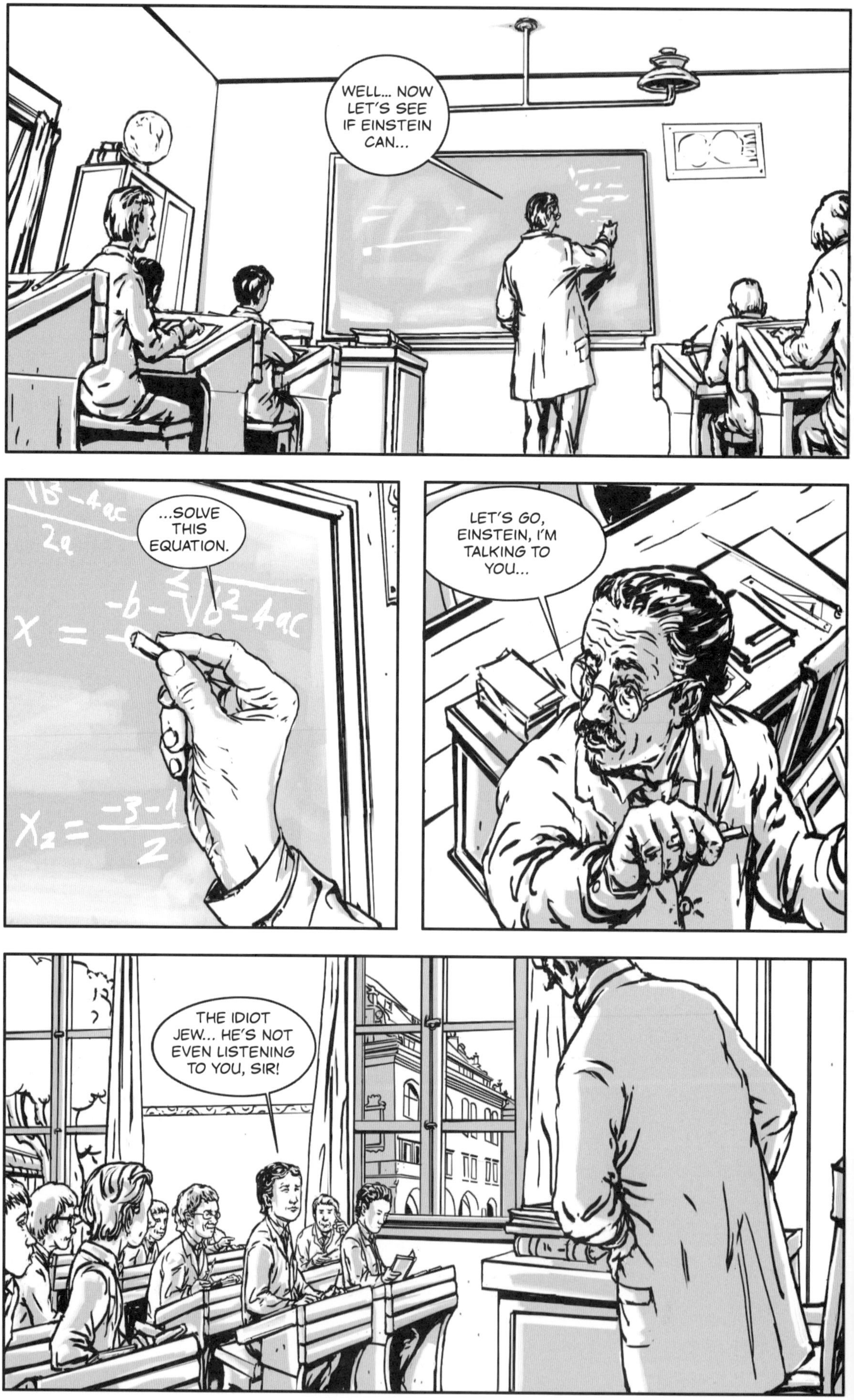
WELL... NOW LET'S SEE IF EINSTEIN CAN...
...SOLVE THIS EQUATION.
LET'S GO, EINSTEIN, I'M TALKING TO YOU...
THE IDIOT JEW... HE'S NOT EVEN LISTENING TO YOU, SIR!

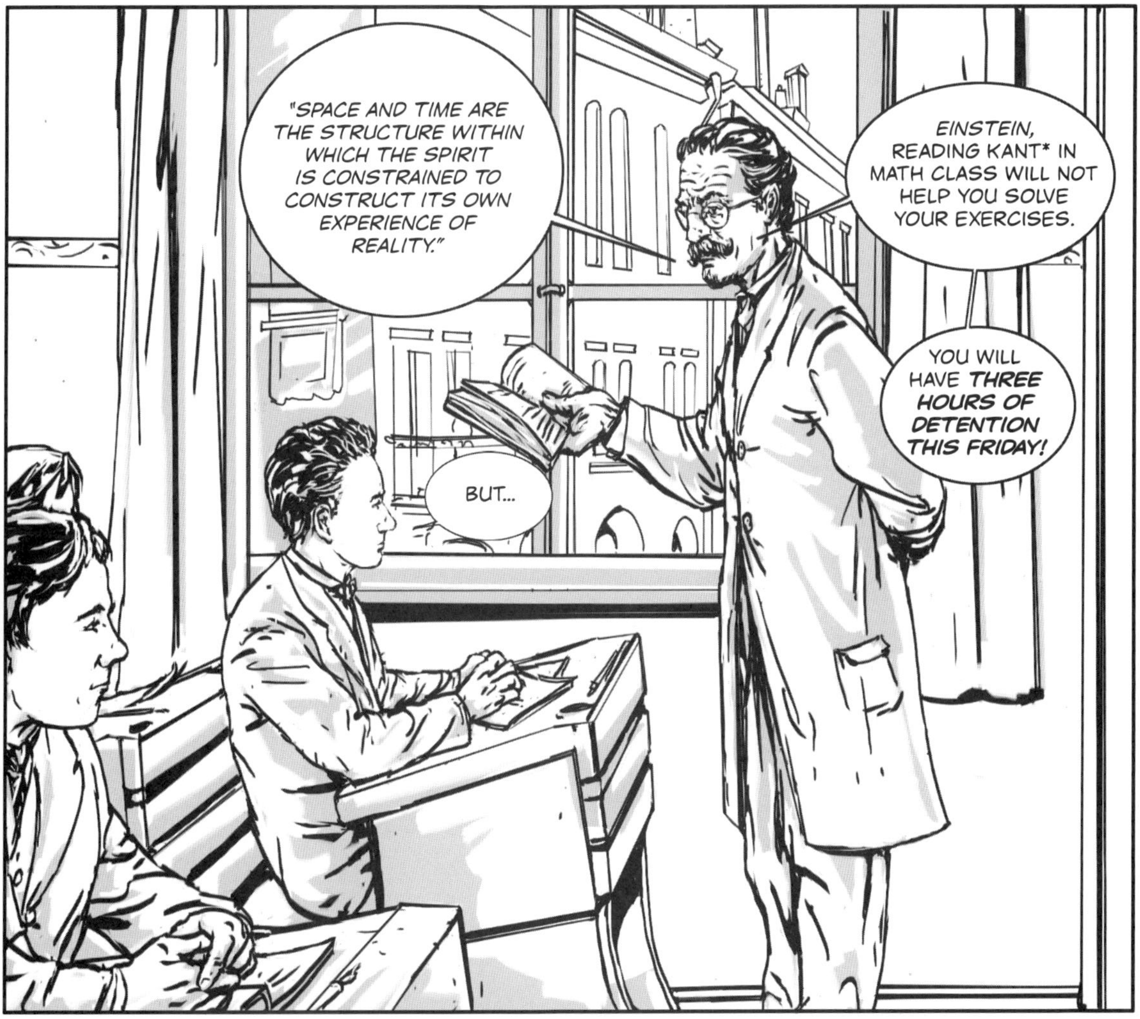
"SPACE AND TIME ARE THE STRUCTURE WITHIN WHICH THE SPIRIT IS CONSTRAINED TO CONSTRUCT ITS OWN EXPERIENCE OF REALITY."
EINSTEIN, READING KANT* IN MATH CLASS WILL NOT HELP YOU SOLVE YOUR EXERCISES.
YOU WILL HAVE THREE HOURS OF DETENTION THIS FRIDAY!
BUT...

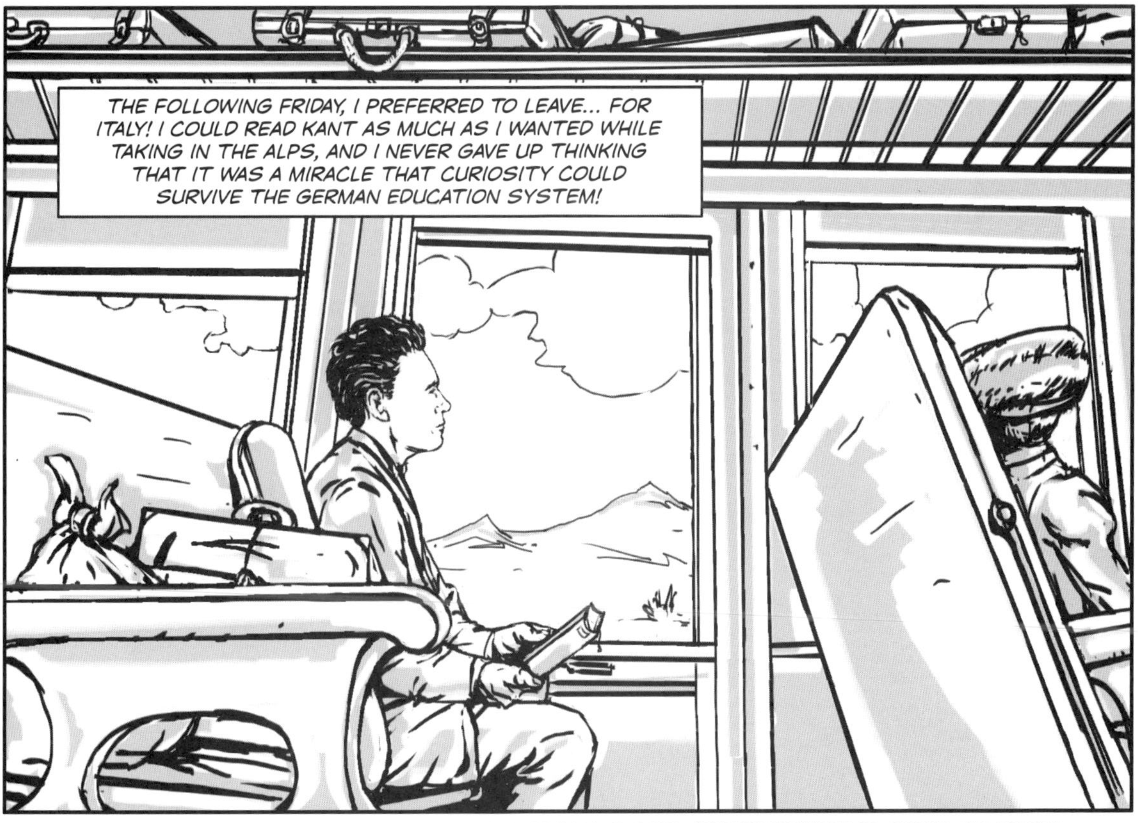
THE FOLLOWING FRIDAY, I PREFERRED TO LEAVE... FOR ITALY! I COULD READ KANT AS MUCH AS I WANTED WHILE TAKING IN THE ALPS, AND I NEVER GAVE UP THINKING THAT IT WAS A MIRACLE THAT CURIOSITY COULD SURVIVE THE GERMAN EDUCATION SYSTEM!

* GERMAN PHILOSOPHER FROM THE 18TH CENTURY, FOUNDER OF CRITICAL PHILOSOPHY

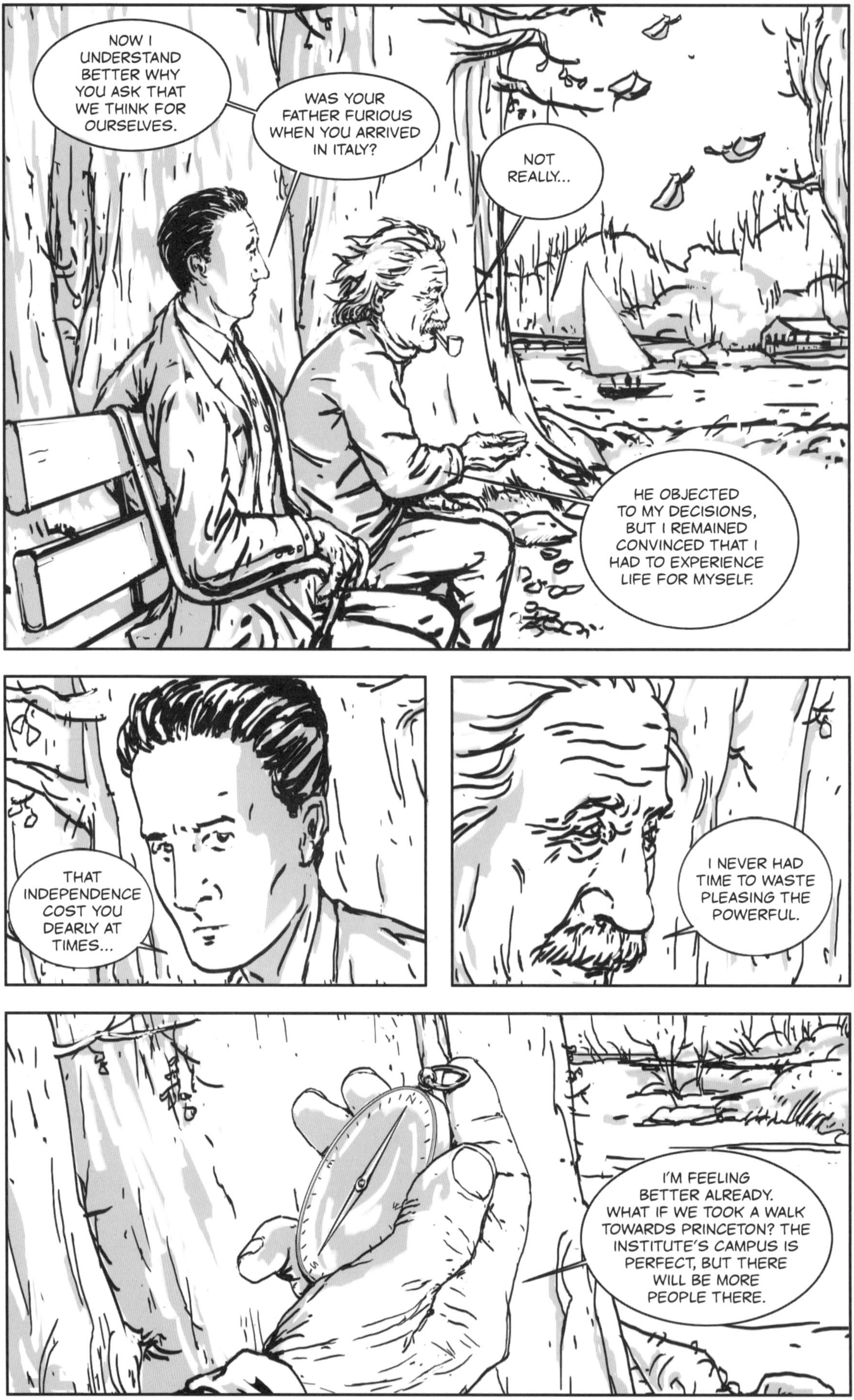
NOW I UNDERSTAND BETTER WHY YOU ASK THAT WE THINK FOR OURSELVES.
WAS YOUR FATHER FURIOUS WHEN YOU ARRIVED IN ITALY?
NOT REALLY...
HE OBJECTED TO MY DECISIONS, BUT I REMAINED CONVINCED THAT I HAD TO EXPERIENCE LIFE FOR MYSELF.
THAT INDEPENDENCE COST YOU DEARLY AT TIMES...
I NEVER HAD TIME TO WASTE PLEASING THE POWERFUL.
I'M FEELING BETTER ALREADY. WHAT IF WE TOOK A WALK TOWARDS PRINCETON? THE INSTITUTE'S CAMPUS IS PERFECT, BUT THERE WILL BE MORE PEOPLE THERE.

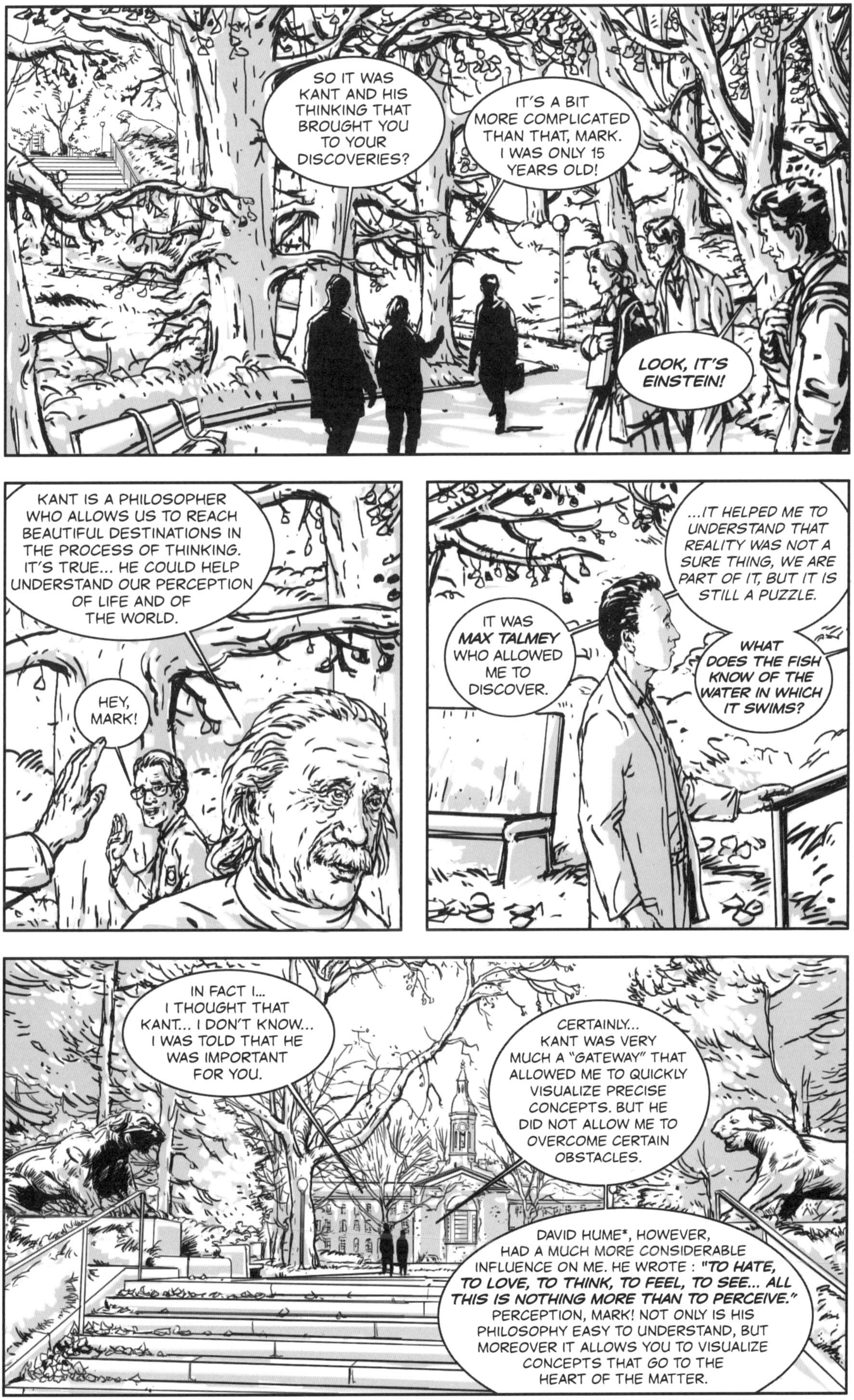
SO IT WAS KANT AND HIS THINKING THAT BROUGHT YOU TO YOUR DISCOVERIES?
IT'S A BIT MORE COMPLICATED THAN THAT, MARK. I WAS ONLY 15 YEARS OLD!
LOOK, IT'S EINSTEIN!
KANT IS A PHILOSOPHER WHO ALLOWS US TO REACH BEAUTIFUL DESTINATIONS IN THE PROCESS OF THINKING. IT'S TRUE... HE COULD HELP UNDERSTAND OUR PERCEPTION OF LIFE AND OF THE WORLD.
HEY, MARK!
IT WAS MAX TALMEY WHO ALLOWED ME TO DISCOVER.
...IT HELPED ME TO UNDERSTAND THAT REALITY WAS NOT A SURE THING, WE ARE PART OF IT, BUT IT IS STILL A PUZZLE.
WHAT DOES THE FISH KNOW OF THE WATER IN WHICH IT SWIMS?
IN FACT I... I THOUGHT THAT KANT... I DON'T KNOW... I WAS TOLD THAT HE WAS IMPORTANT FOR YOU.
CERTAINLY... KANT WAS VERY MUCH A "GATEWAY" THAT ALLOWED ME TO QUICKLY VISUALIZE PRECISE CONCEPTS. BUT HE DID NOT ALLOW ME TO OVERCOME CERTAIN OBSTACLES.
DAVID HUME*, HOWEVER, HAD A MUCH MORE CONSIDERABLE INFLUENCE ON ME. HE WROTE : "TO HATE, TO LOVE, TO THINK, TO FEEL, TO SEE... ALL THIS IS NOTHING MORE THAN TO PERCEIVE." PERCEPTION, MARK! NOT ONLY IS HIS PHILOSOPHY EASY TO UNDERSTAND, BUT MOREOVER IT ALLOWS YOU TO VISUALIZE CONCEPTS THAT GO TO THE HEART OF THE MATTER.

* SCOTTISH PHILOSOPHER FROM THE 18TH CENTURY, FOUNDER OF MODERN EMPIRICISM.

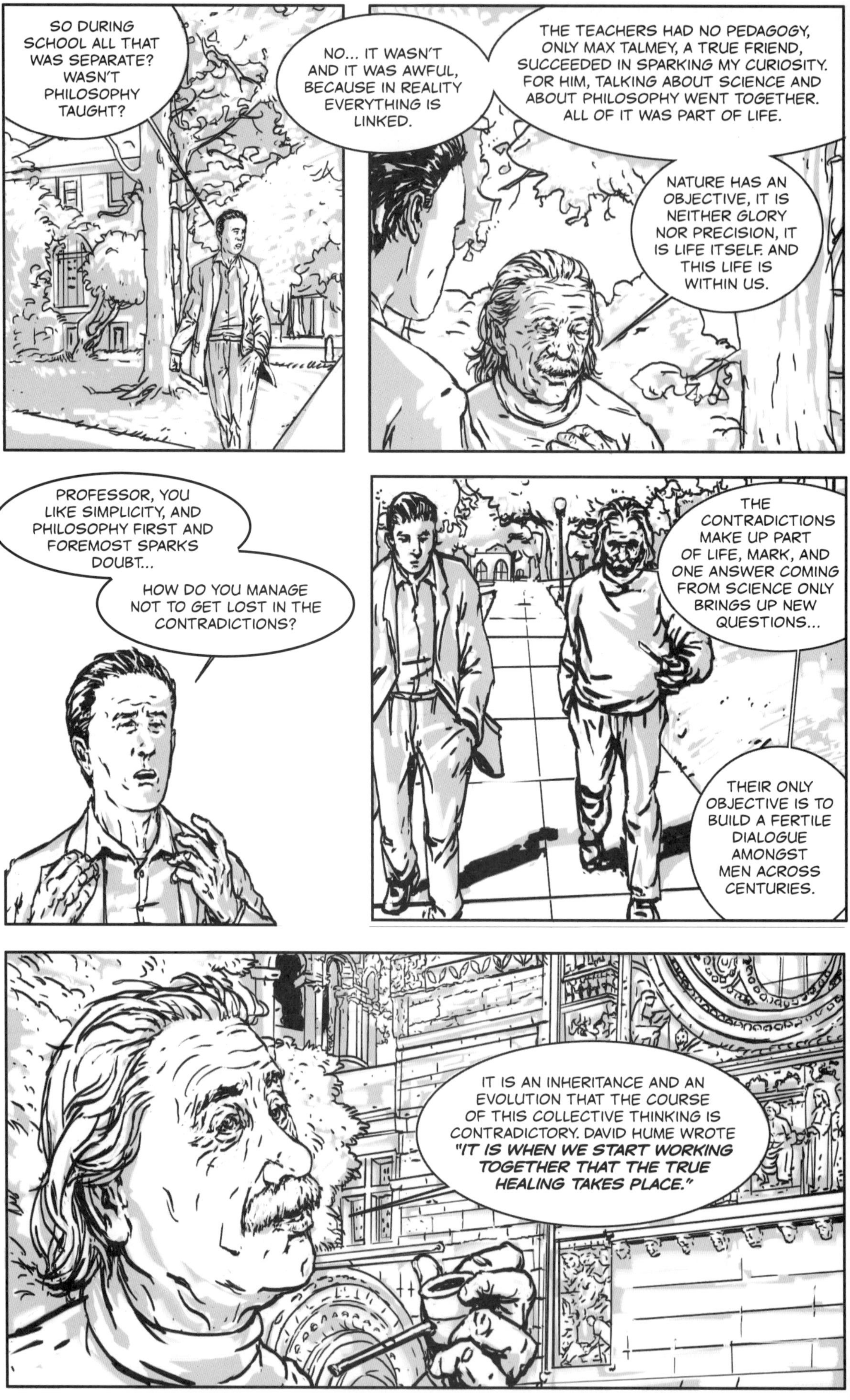
SO DURING SCHOOL ALL THAT WAS SEPARATE? WASN'T PHILOSOPHY TAUGHT?
NO... IT WASN'T AND IT WAS AWFUL, BECAUSE IN REALITY EVERYTHING IS LINKED.
THE TEACHERS HAD NO PEDAGOGY, ONLY MAX TALMEY, A TRUE FRIEND, SUCCEEDED IN SPARKING MY CURIOSITY. FOR HIM, TALKING ABOUT SCIENCE AND ABOUT PHILOSOPHY WENT TOGETHER. ALL OF IT WAS PART OF LIFE.
NATURE HAS AN OBJECTIVE, IT IS NEITHER GLORY NOR PRECISION, IT IS LIFE ITSELF. AND THIS LIFE IS WITHIN US.
PROFESSOR, YOU LIKE SIMPLICITY, AND PHILOSOPHY FIRST AND FOREMOST SPARKS DOUBT...
HOW DO YOU MANAGE NOT TO GET LOST IN THE CONTRADICTIONS?
THE CONTRADICTIONS MAKE UP PART OF LIFE, MARK, AND ONE ANSWER COMING FROM SCIENCE ONLY BRINGS UP NEW QUESTIONS...
THEIR ONLY OBJECTIVE IS TO BUILD A FERTILE DIALOGUE AMONGST MEN ACROSS CENTURIES.
IT IS AN INHERITANCE AND AN EVOLUTION THAT THE COURSE OF THIS COLLECTIVE THINKING IS CONTRADICTORY. DAVID HUME WROTE *"IT IS WHEN WE START WORKING TOGETHER THAT THE TRUE HEALING TAKES PLACE."*

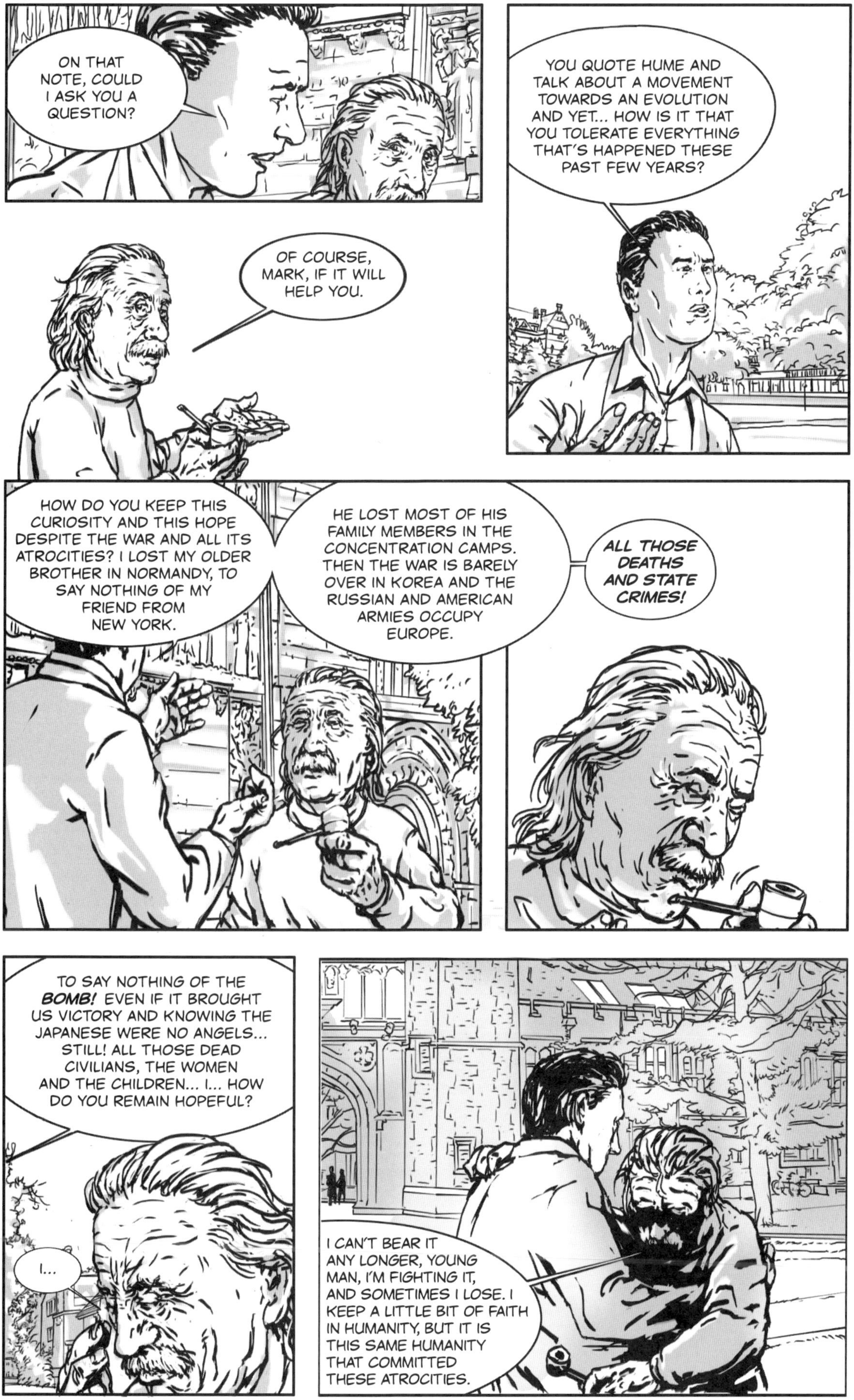

ON THAT NOTE, COULD I ASK YOU A QUESTION?
YOU QUOTE HUME AND TALK ABOUT A MOVEMENT TOWARDS AN EVOLUTION AND YET... HOW IS IT THAT YOU TOLERATE EVERYTHING THAT'S HAPPENED THESE PAST FEW YEARS?
OF COURSE, MARK, IF IT WILL HELP YOU.
HOW DO YOU KEEP THIS CURIOSITY AND THIS HOPE DESPITE THE WAR AND ALL ITS ATROCITIES? I LOST MY OLDER BROTHER IN NORMANDY, TO SAY NOTHING OF MY FRIEND FROM NEW YORK.
HE LOST MOST OF HIS FAMILY MEMBERS IN THE CONCENTRATION CAMPS. THEN THE WAR IS BARELY OVER IN KOREA AND THE RUSSIAN AND AMERICAN ARMIES OCCUPY EUROPE.
ALL THOSE DEATHS AND STATE CRIMES!
TO SAY NOTHING OF THE ***BOMB!*** EVEN IF IT BROUGHT US VICTORY AND KNOWING THE JAPANESE WERE NO ANGELS... STILL! ALL THOSE DEAD CIVILIANS, THE WOMEN AND THE CHILDREN... I... HOW DO YOU REMAIN HOPEFUL?
I...
I CAN'T BEAR IT ANY LONGER, YOUNG MAN, I'M FIGHTING IT, AND SOMETIMES I LOSE. I KEEP A LITTLE BIT OF FAITH IN HUMANITY, BUT IT IS THIS SAME HUMANITY THAT COMMITTED THESE ATROCITIES.

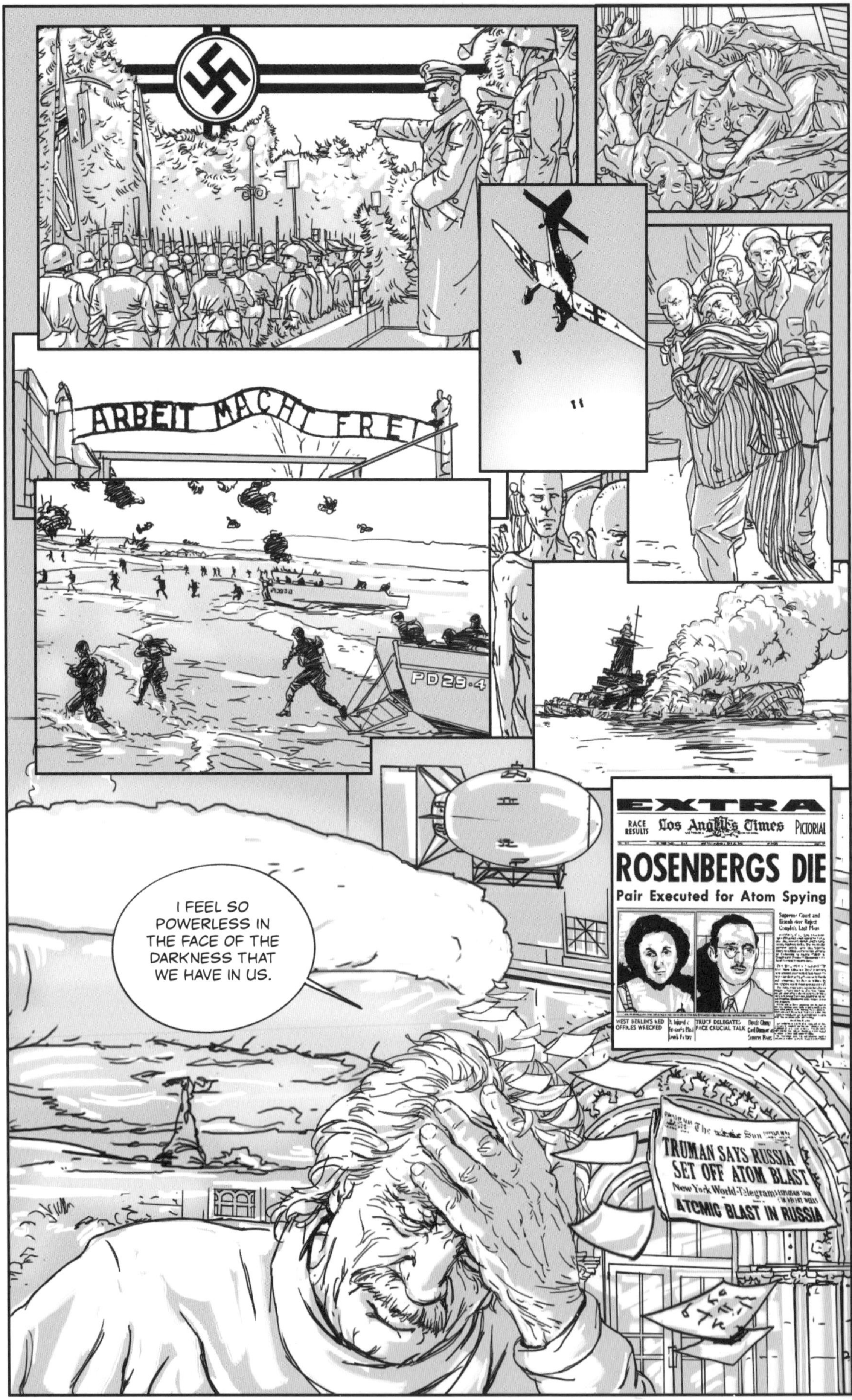
ARBEIT MACHT FREI
PD29-4
EXTRA
RACE RESULTS
Los Angeles Times
PICTORIAL
ROSENBERGS DIE
Pair Executed for Atom Spying
WEST BERLIN'S RED OFFICES WRECKED
TRUCE DELEGATES FACE CRUCIAL TALK
I FEEL SO POWERLESS IN THE FACE OF THE DARKNESS THAT WE HAVE IN US.
TRUMAN SAYS RUSSIA SET OFF ATOM BLAST
New York World-Telegram
ATOMIC BLAST IN RUSSIA

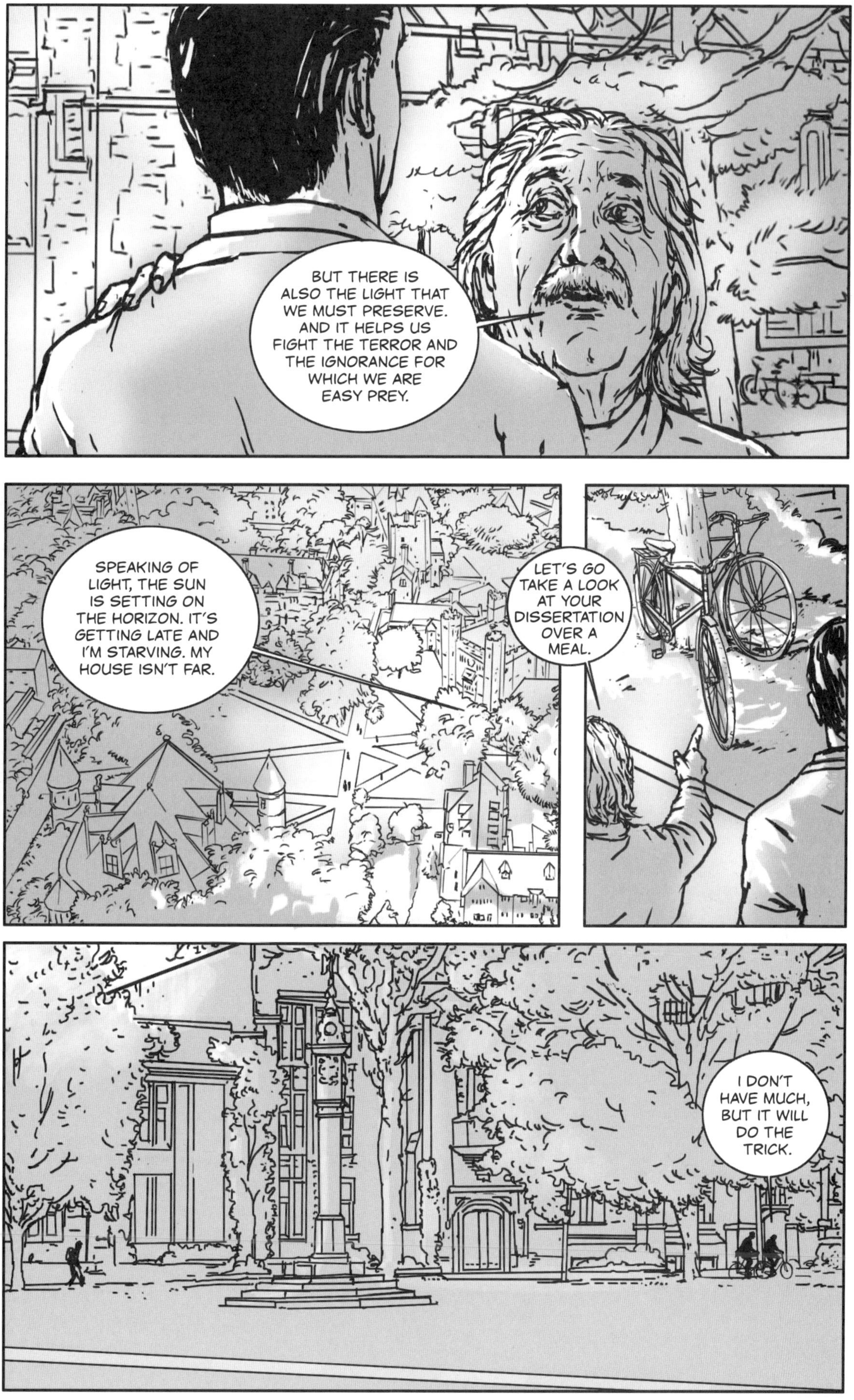
BUT THERE IS ALSO THE LIGHT THAT WE MUST PRESERVE. AND IT HELPS US FIGHT THE TERROR AND THE IGNORANCE FOR WHICH WE ARE EASY PREY.
SPEAKING OF LIGHT, THE SUN IS SETTING ON THE HORIZON. IT'S GETTING LATE AND I'M STARVING. MY HOUSE ISN'T FAR.
LET'S GO TAKE A LOOK AT YOUR DISSERTATION OVER A MEAL.
I DON'T HAVE MUCH, BUT IT WILL DO THE TRICK.

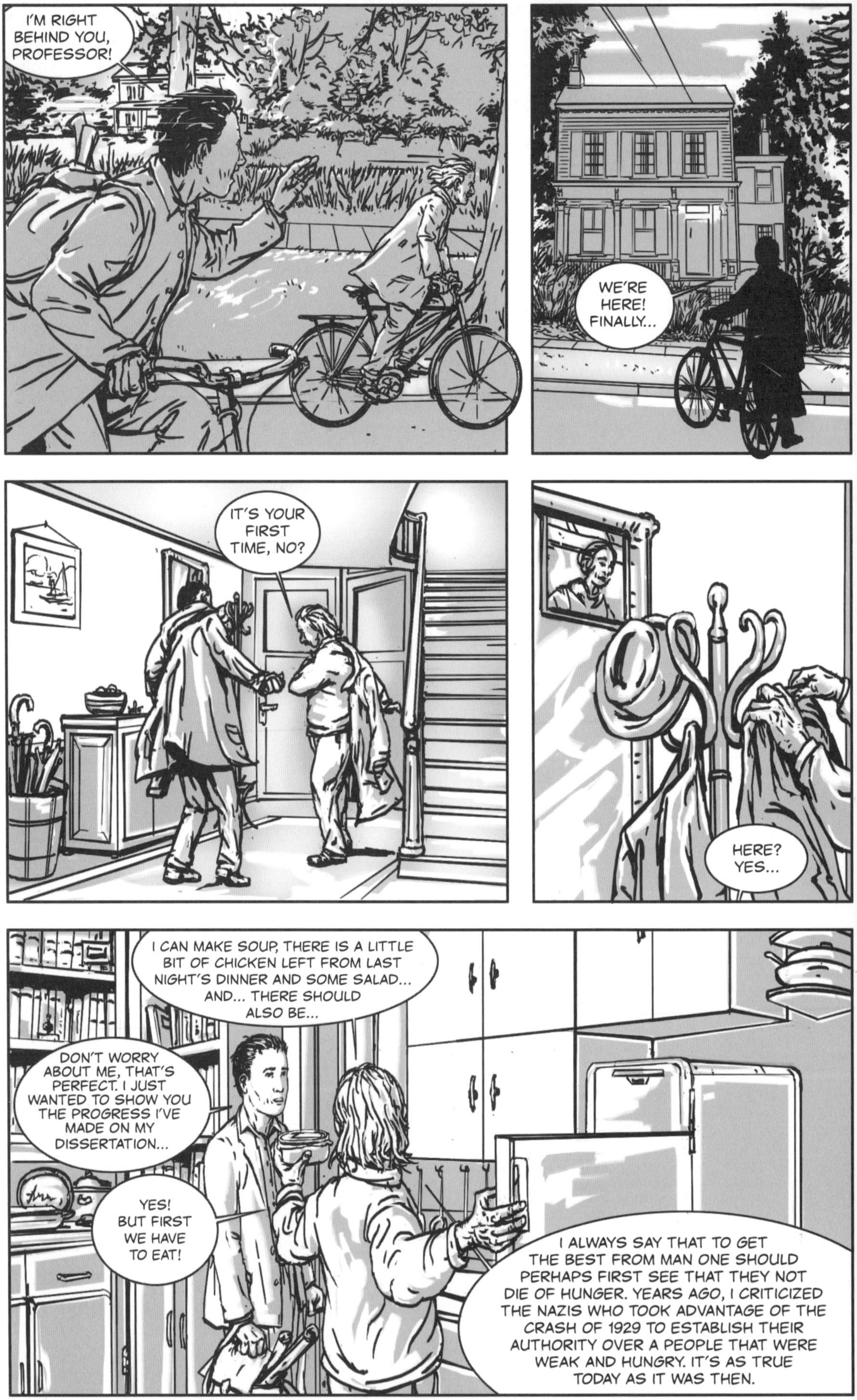
I'M RIGHT BEHIND YOU, PROFESSOR!
WE'RE HERE! FINALLY...
IT'S YOUR FIRST TIME, NO?
HERE? YES...
I CAN MAKE SOUP, THERE IS A LITTLE BIT OF CHICKEN LEFT FROM LAST NIGHT'S DINNER AND SOME SALAD... AND... THERE SHOULD ALSO BE...
DON'T WORRY ABOUT ME, THAT'S PERFECT. I JUST WANTED TO SHOW YOU THE PROGRESS I'VE MADE ON MY DISSERTATION...
YES! BUT FIRST WE HAVE TO EAT!
I ALWAYS SAY THAT TO GET THE BEST FROM MAN ONE SHOULD PERHAPS FIRST SEE THAT THEY NOT DIE OF HUNGER. YEARS AGO, I CRITICIZED THE NAZIS WHO TOOK ADVANTAGE OF THE CRASH OF 1929 TO ESTABLISH THEIR AUTHORITY OVER A PEOPLE THAT WERE WEAK AND HUNGRY. IT'S AS TRUE TODAY AS IT WAS THEN.

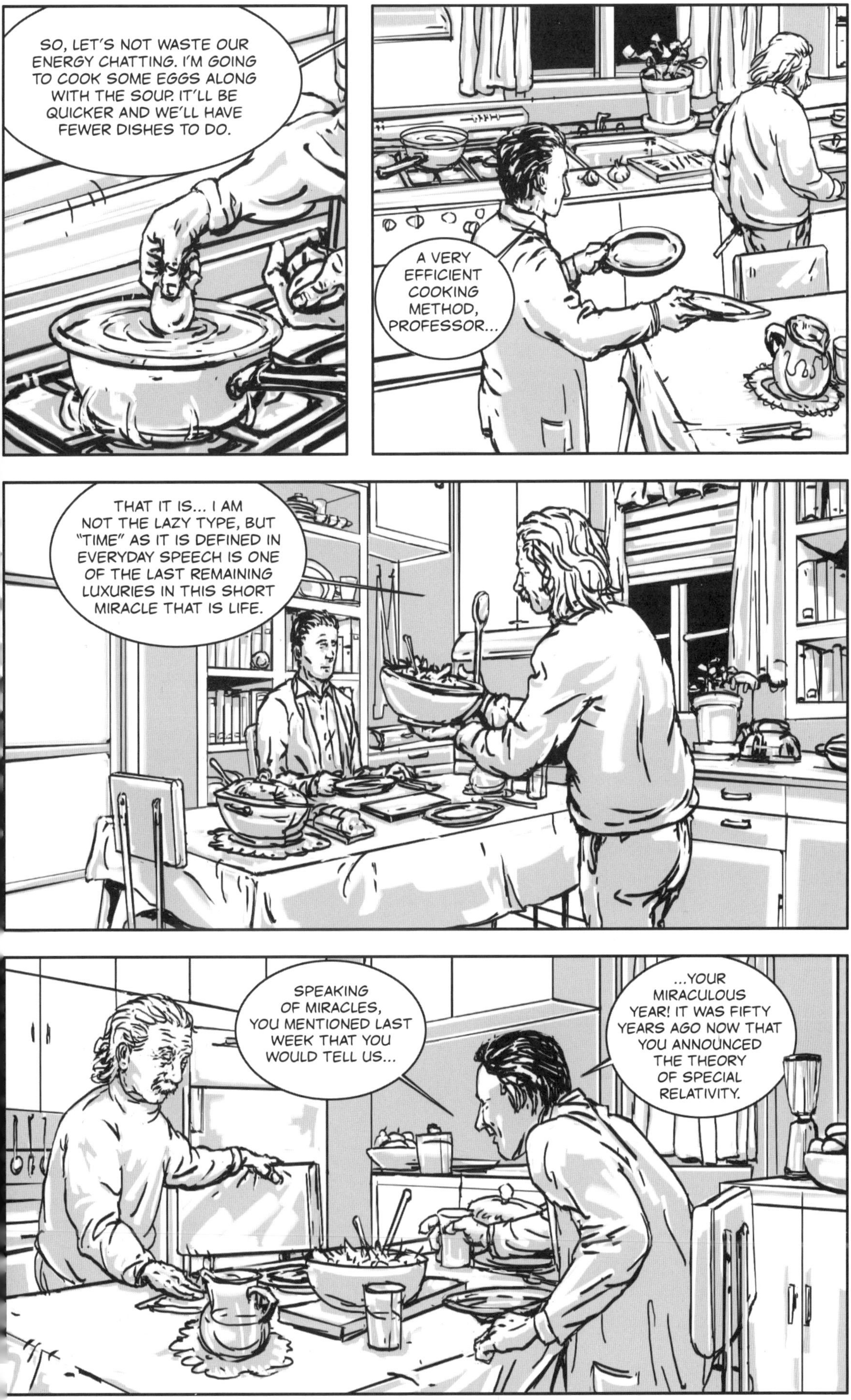
SO, LET'S NOT WASTE OUR ENERGY CHATTING. I'M GOING TO COOK SOME EGGS ALONG WITH THE SOUP. IT'LL BE QUICKER AND WE'LL HAVE FEWER DISHES TO DO.
A VERY EFFICIENT COOKING METHOD, PROFESSOR...
THAT IT IS... I AM NOT THE LAZY TYPE, BUT "TIME" AS IT IS DEFINED IN EVERYDAY SPEECH IS ONE OF THE LAST REMAINING LUXURIES IN THIS SHORT MIRACLE THAT IS LIFE.
SPEAKING OF MIRACLES, YOU MENTIONED LAST WEEK THAT YOU WOULD TELL US...
...YOUR MIRACULOUS YEAR! IT WAS FIFTY YEARS AGO NOW THAT YOU ANNOUNCED THE THEORY OF SPECIAL RELATIVITY.

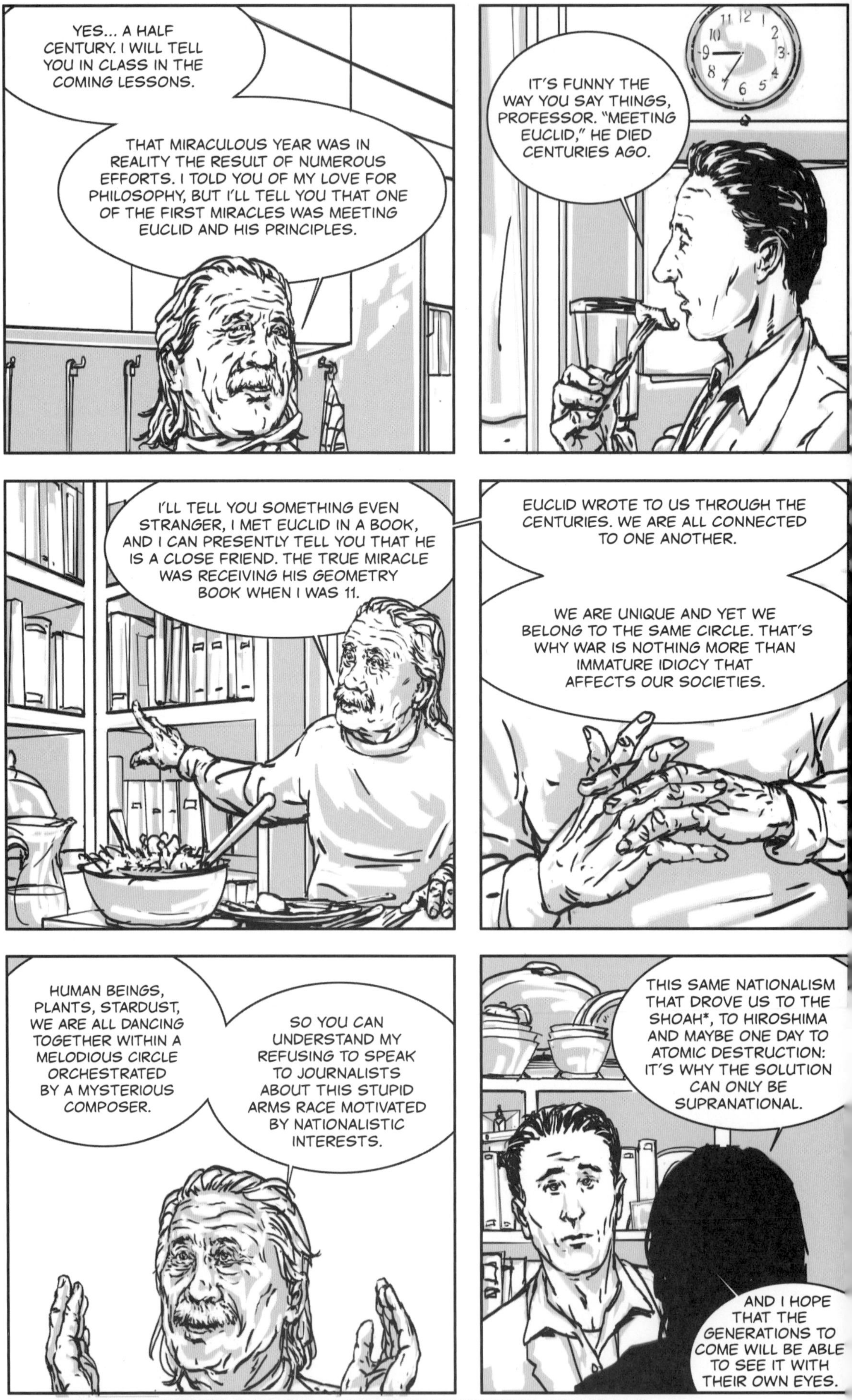
YES... A HALF CENTURY. I WILL TELL YOU IN CLASS IN THE COMING LESSONS.
THAT MIRACULOUS YEAR WAS IN REALITY THE RESULT OF NUMEROUS EFFORTS. I TOLD YOU OF MY LOVE FOR PHILOSOPHY, BUT I'LL TELL YOU THAT ONE OF THE FIRST MIRACLES WAS MEETING EUCLID AND HIS PRINCIPLES.
IT'S FUNNY THE WAY YOU SAY THINGS, PROFESSOR. "MEETING EUCLID," HE DIED CENTURIES AGO.
I'LL TELL YOU SOMETHING EVEN STRANGER, I MET EUCLID IN A BOOK, AND I CAN PRESENTLY TELL YOU THAT HE IS A CLOSE FRIEND. THE TRUE MIRACLE WAS RECEIVING HIS GEOMETRY BOOK WHEN I WAS 11.
EUCLID WROTE TO US THROUGH THE CENTURIES. WE ARE ALL CONNECTED TO ONE ANOTHER.
WE ARE UNIQUE AND YET WE BELONG TO THE SAME CIRCLE. THAT'S WHY WAR IS NOTHING MORE THAN IMMATURE IDIOCY THAT AFFECTS OUR SOCIETIES.
HUMAN BEINGS, PLANTS, STARDUST, WE ARE ALL DANCING TOGETHER WITHIN A MELODIOUS CIRCLE ORCHESTRATED BY A MYSTERIOUS COMPOSER.
SO YOU CAN UNDERSTAND MY REFUSING TO SPEAK TO JOURNALISTS ABOUT THIS STUPID ARMS RACE MOTIVATED BY NATIONALISTIC INTERESTS.
THIS SAME NATIONALISM THAT DROVE US TO THE SHOAH*, TO HIROSHIMA AND MAYBE ONE DAY TO ATOMIC DESTRUCTION: IT'S WHY THE SOLUTION CAN ONLY BE SUPRANATIONAL.
AND I HOPE THAT THE GENERATIONS TO COME WILL BE ABLE TO SEE IT WITH THEIR OWN EYES.

*CAMPAIGN TO EXTERMINATE JEWS DURING THE 2ND WORLD WAR BY THE NAZIS AND THEIR ALLIES

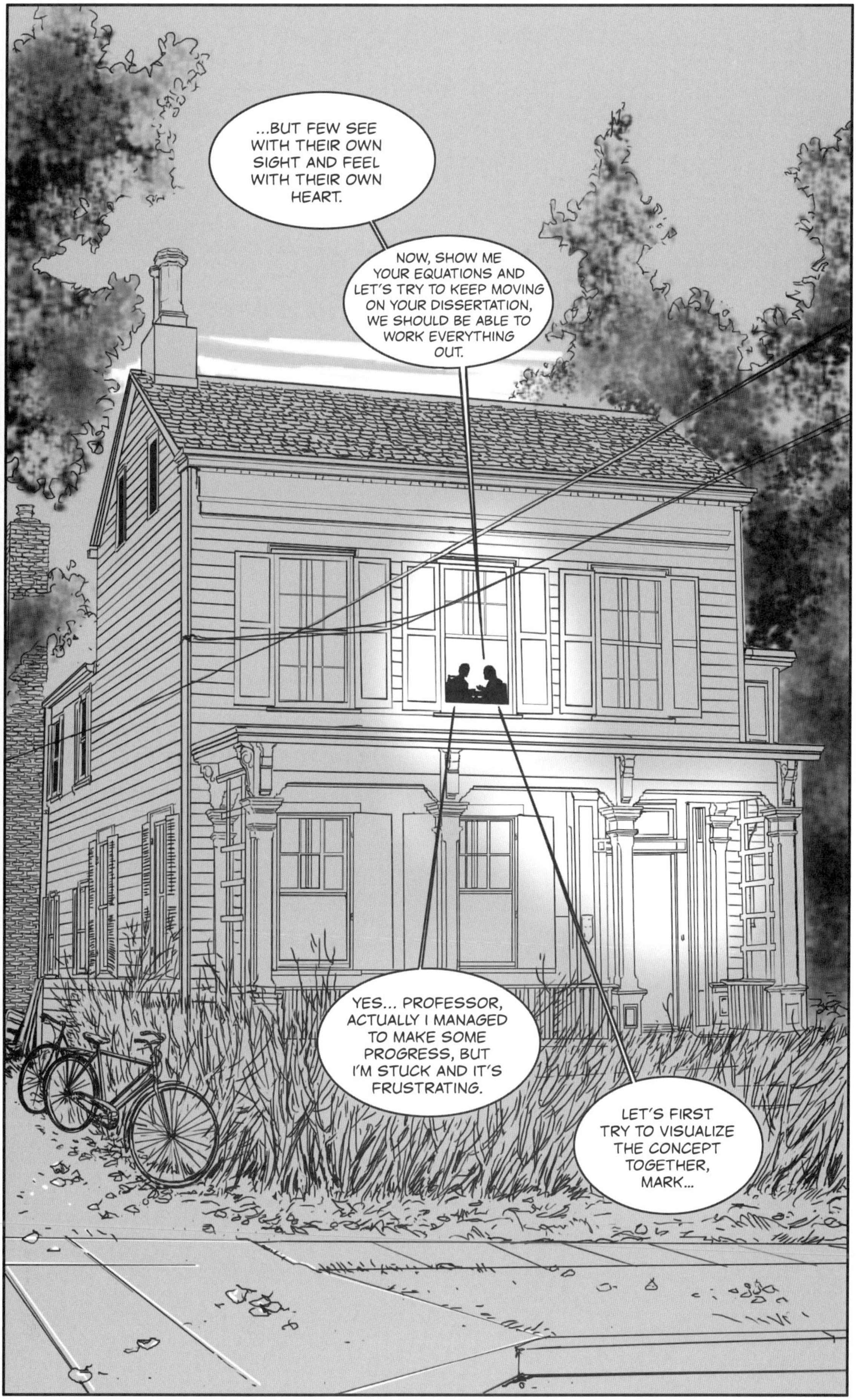
...BUT FEW SEE WITH THEIR OWN SIGHT AND FEEL WITH THEIR OWN HEART.
NOW, SHOW ME YOUR EQUATIONS AND LET'S TRY TO KEEP MOVING ON YOUR DISSERTATION, WE SHOULD BE ABLE TO WORK EVERYTHING OUT.
YES... PROFESSOR, ACTUALLY I MANAGED TO MAKE SOME PROGRESS, BUT I'M STUCK AND IT'S FRUSTRATING.
LET'S FIRST TRY TO VISUALIZE THE CONCEPT TOGETHER, MARK...

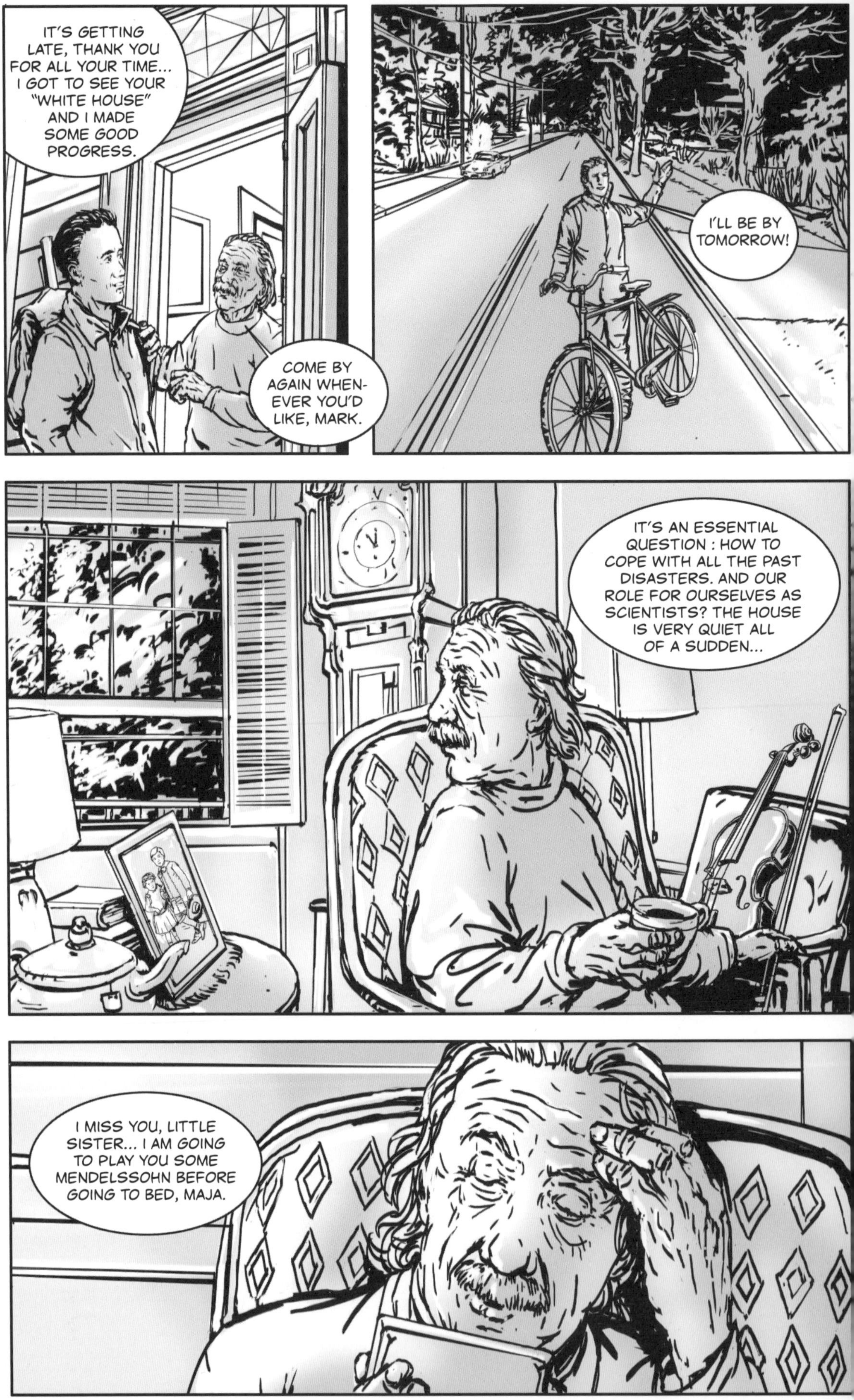
IT'S GETTING LATE, THANK YOU FOR ALL YOUR TIME... I GOT TO SEE YOUR "WHITE HOUSE" AND I MADE SOME GOOD PROGRESS.
COME BY AGAIN WHEN-EVER YOU'D LIKE, MARK.
I'LL BE BY TOMORROW!
IT'S AN ESSENTIAL QUESTION : HOW TO COPE WITH ALL THE PAST DISASTERS. AND OUR ROLE FOR OURSELVES AS SCIENTISTS? THE HOUSE IS VERY QUIET ALL OF A SUDDEN...
I MISS YOU, LITTLE SISTER... I AM GOING TO PLAY YOU SOME MENDELSSOHN BEFORE GOING TO BED, MAJA.

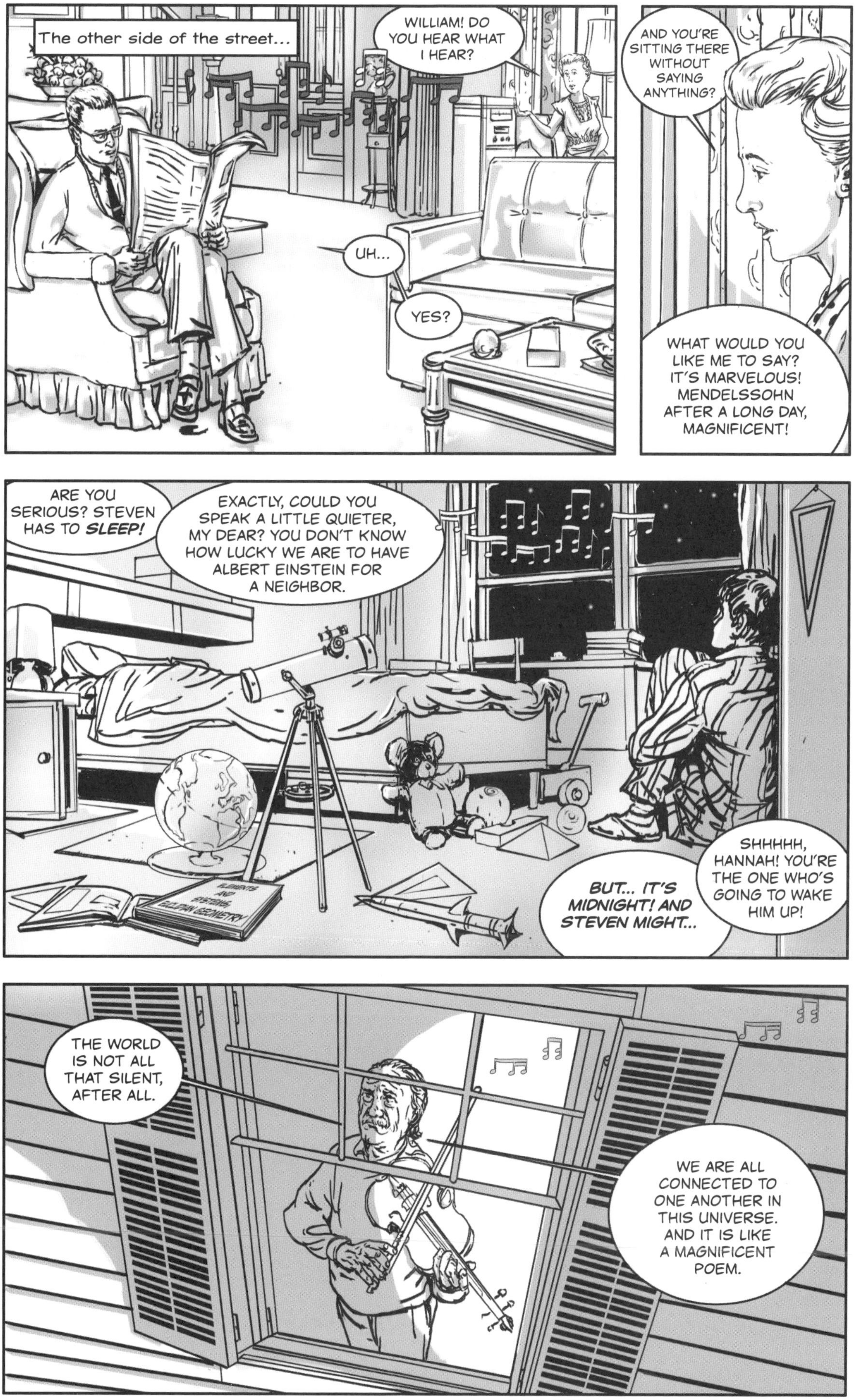
The other side of the street...
WILLIAM! DO YOU HEAR WHAT I HEAR?
UH...
YES?
AND YOU'RE SITTING THERE WITHOUT SAYING ANYTHING?
WHAT WOULD YOU LIKE ME TO SAY? IT'S MARVELOUS! MENDELSSOHN AFTER A LONG DAY, MAGNIFICENT!
ARE YOU SERIOUS? STEVEN HAS TO *SLEEP!*
EXACTLY, COULD YOU SPEAK A LITTLE QUIETER, MY DEAR? YOU DON'T KNOW HOW LUCKY WE ARE TO HAVE ALBERT EINSTEIN FOR A NEIGHBOR.
ELEMENTS AND SYSTEMS EUCLIDIAN GEOMETRY
BUT... IT'S MIDNIGHT! AND STEVEN MIGHT...
SHHHHH, HANNAH! YOU'RE THE ONE WHO'S GOING TO WAKE HIM UP!
THE WORLD IS NOT ALL THAT SILENT, AFTER ALL.
WE ARE ALL CONNECTED TO ONE ANOTHER IN THIS UNIVERSE. AND IT IS LIKE A MAGNIFICENT POEM.

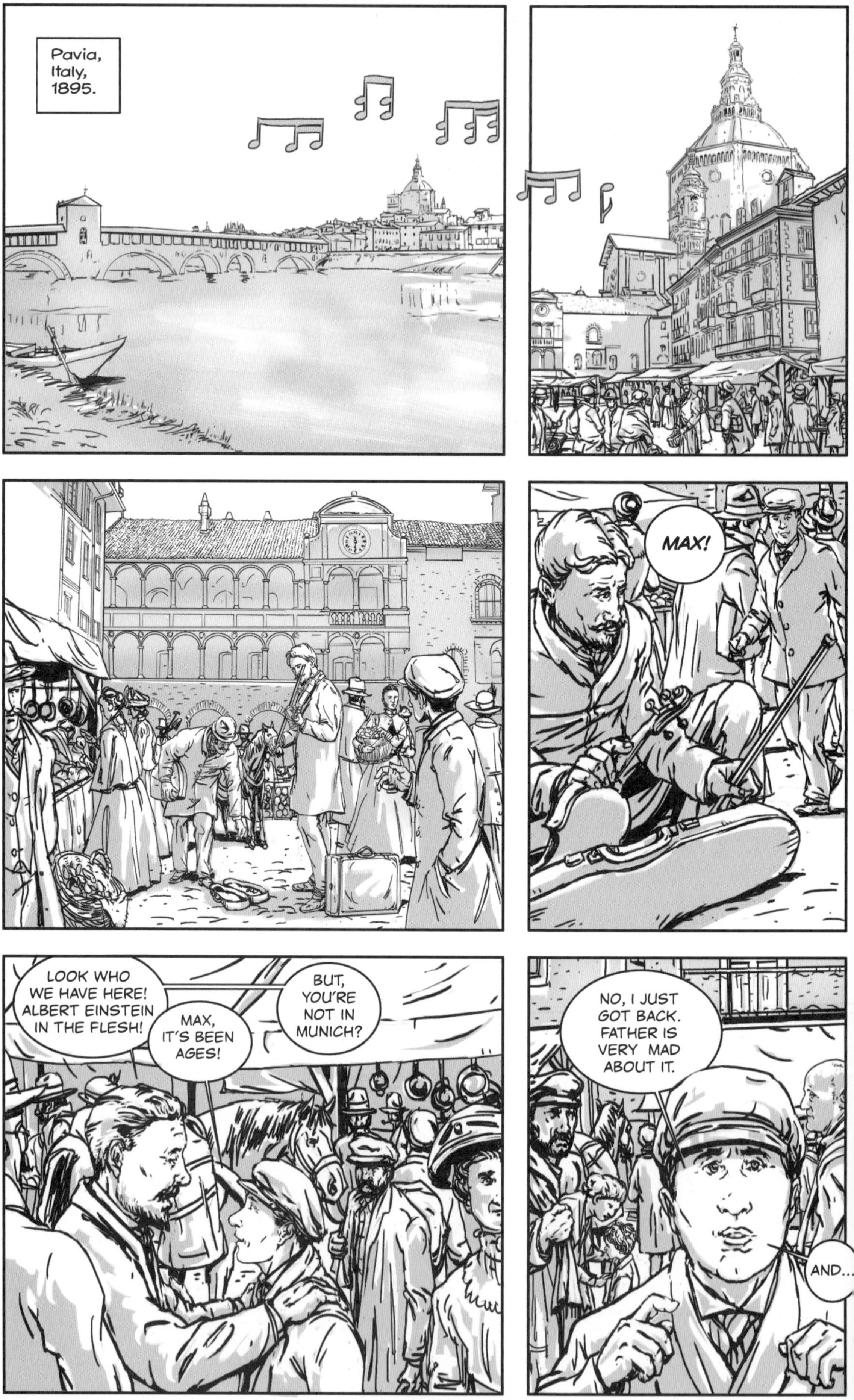
Pavia, Italy, 1895.
MAX!
LOOK WHO WE HAVE HERE! ALBERT EINSTEIN IN THE FLESH!
MAX, IT'S BEEN AGES!
BUT, YOU'RE NOT IN MUNICH?
NO, I JUST GOT BACK. FATHER IS VERY MAD ABOUT IT.
AND...

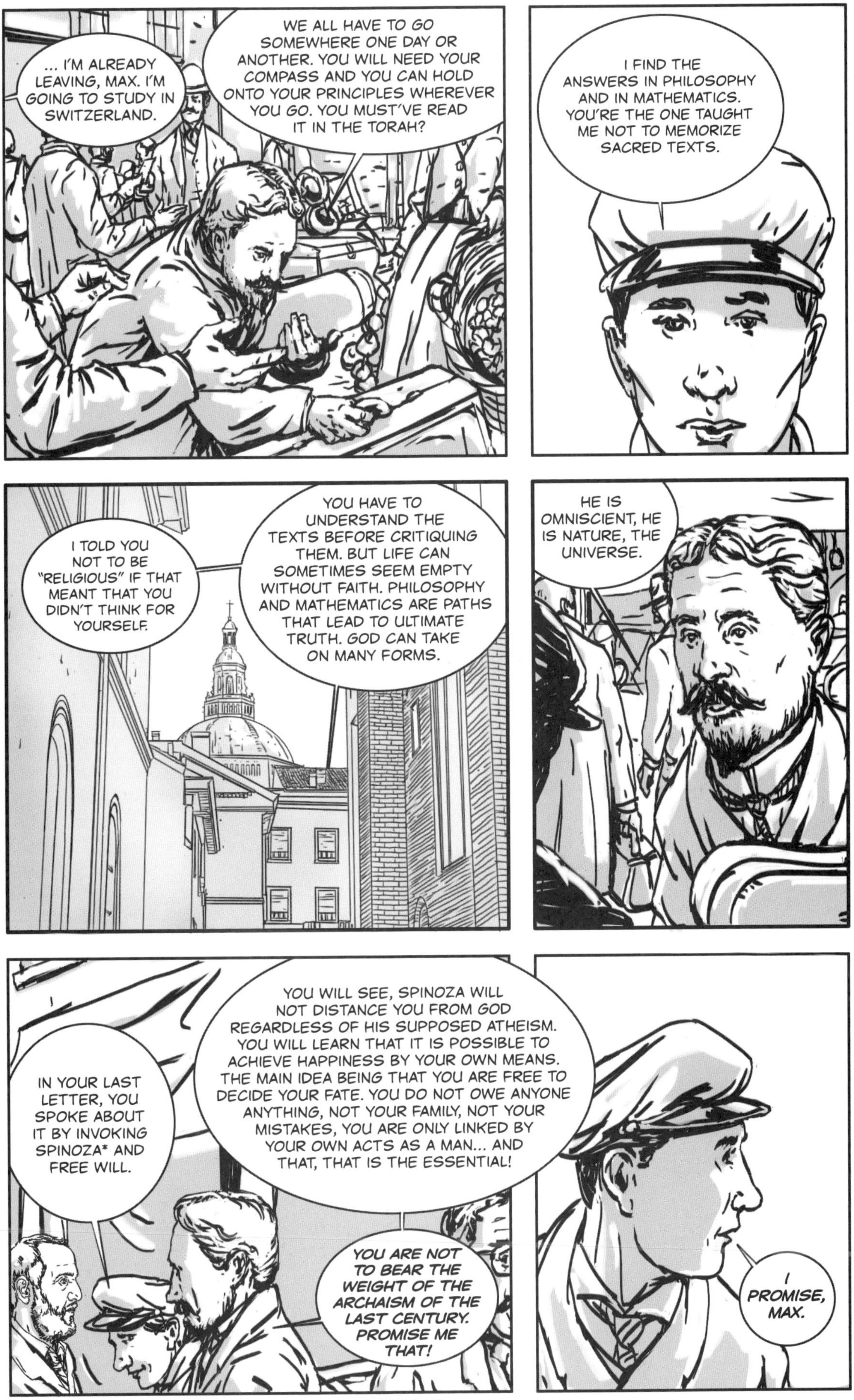

... I'M ALREADY LEAVING, MAX. I'M GOING TO STUDY IN SWITZERLAND.
WE ALL HAVE TO GO SOMEWHERE ONE DAY OR ANOTHER. YOU WILL NEED YOUR COMPASS AND YOU CAN HOLD ONTO YOUR PRINCIPLES WHEREVER YOU GO. YOU MUST'VE READ IT IN THE TORAH?
I FIND THE ANSWERS IN PHILOSOPHY AND IN MATHEMATICS. YOU'RE THE ONE TAUGHT ME NOT TO MEMORIZE SACRED TEXTS.
I TOLD YOU NOT TO BE "RELIGIOUS" IF THAT MEANT THAT YOU DIDN'T THINK FOR YOURSELF.
YOU HAVE TO UNDERSTAND THE TEXTS BEFORE CRITIQUING THEM. BUT LIFE CAN SOMETIMES SEEM EMPTY WITHOUT FAITH. PHILOSOPHY AND MATHEMATICS ARE PATHS THAT LEAD TO ULTIMATE TRUTH. GOD CAN TAKE ON MANY FORMS.
HE IS OMNISCIENT, HE IS NATURE, THE UNIVERSE.
IN YOUR LAST LETTER, YOU SPOKE ABOUT IT BY INVOKING SPINOZA* AND FREE WILL.
YOU WILL SEE, SPINOZA WILL NOT DISTANCE YOU FROM GOD REGARDLESS OF HIS SUPPOSED ATHEISM. YOU WILL LEARN THAT IT IS POSSIBLE TO ACHIEVE HAPPINESS BY YOUR OWN MEANS. THE MAIN IDEA BEING THAT YOU ARE FREE TO DECIDE YOUR FATE. YOU DO NOT OWE ANYONE ANYTHING, NOT YOUR FAMILY, NOT YOUR MISTAKES, YOU ARE ONLY LINKED BY YOUR OWN ACTS AS A MAN... AND THAT, THAT IS THE ESSENTIAL!
YOU ARE NOT TO BEAR THE WEIGHT OF THE ARCHAISM OF THE LAST CENTURY. PROMISE ME THAT!
I PROMISE, MAX.

* JEWISH PHILOSOPHER FROM HOLLAND IN THE 17TH CENTURY, ONE OF THE FIRST TO CRITICIZE THE DOGMAS OF THE MAJOR RELIGIONS.

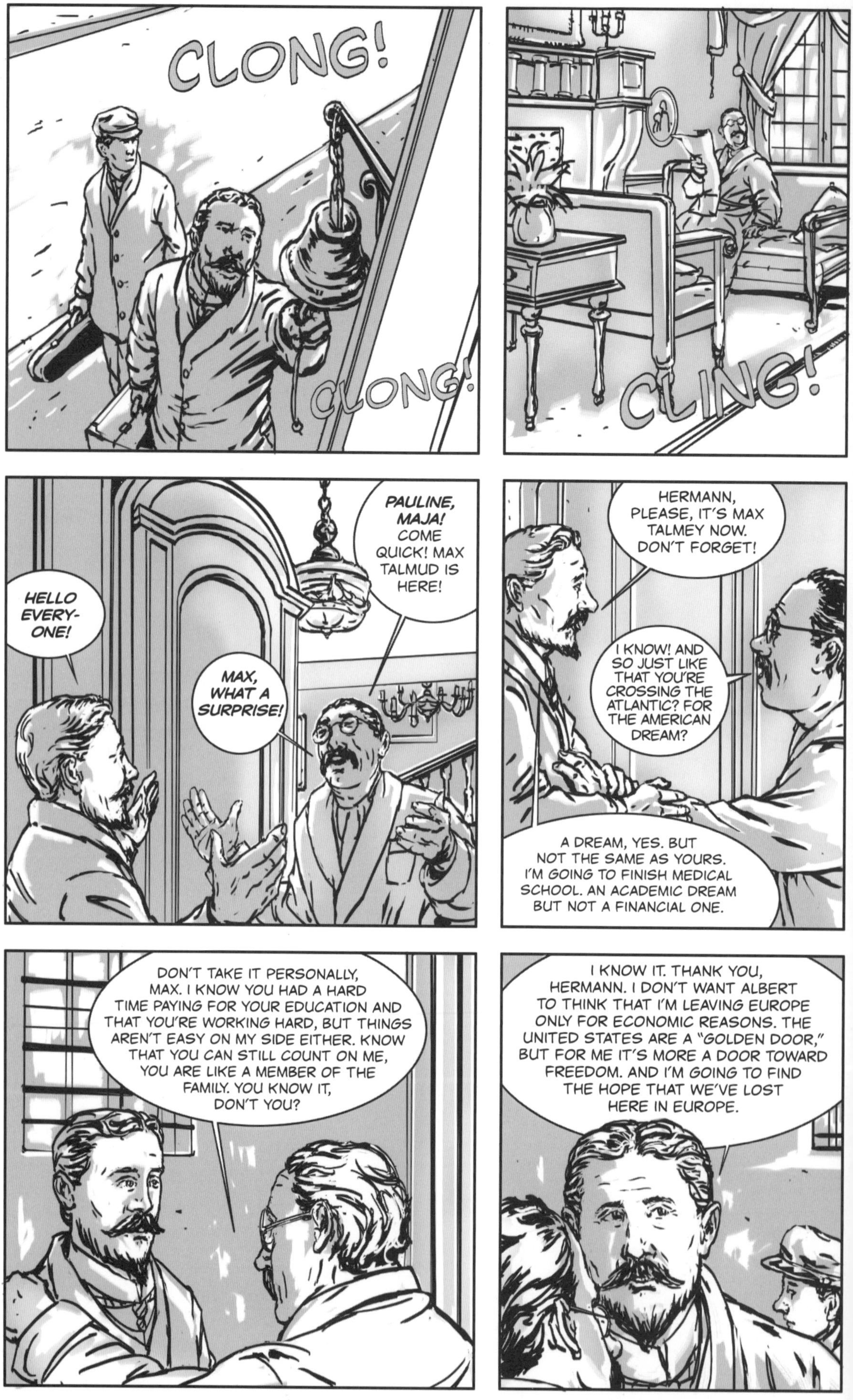
CLONG!
CLONG!
CLING!
HELLO EVERY-ONE!
PAULINE, MAJA! COME QUICK! MAX TALMUD IS HERE!
MAX, WHAT A SURPRISE!
HERMANN, PLEASE, IT'S MAX TALMEY NOW. DON'T FORGET!
I KNOW! AND SO JUST LIKE THAT YOU'RE CROSSING THE ATLANTIC? FOR THE AMERICAN DREAM?
A DREAM, YES. BUT NOT THE SAME AS YOURS. I'M GOING TO FINISH MEDICAL SCHOOL. AN ACADEMIC DREAM BUT NOT A FINANCIAL ONE.
DON'T TAKE IT PERSONALLY, MAX. I KNOW YOU HAD A HARD TIME PAYING FOR YOUR EDUCATION AND THAT YOU'RE WORKING HARD, BUT THINGS AREN'T EASY ON MY SIDE EITHER. KNOW THAT YOU CAN STILL COUNT ON ME, YOU ARE LIKE A MEMBER OF THE FAMILY. YOU KNOW IT, DON'T YOU?
I KNOW IT. THANK YOU, HERMANN. I DON'T WANT ALBERT TO THINK THAT I'M LEAVING EUROPE ONLY FOR ECONOMIC REASONS. THE UNITED STATES ARE A "GOLDEN DOOR," BUT FOR ME IT'S MORE A DOOR TOWARD FREEDOM. AND I'M GOING TO FIND THE HOPE THAT WE'VE LOST HERE IN EUROPE.

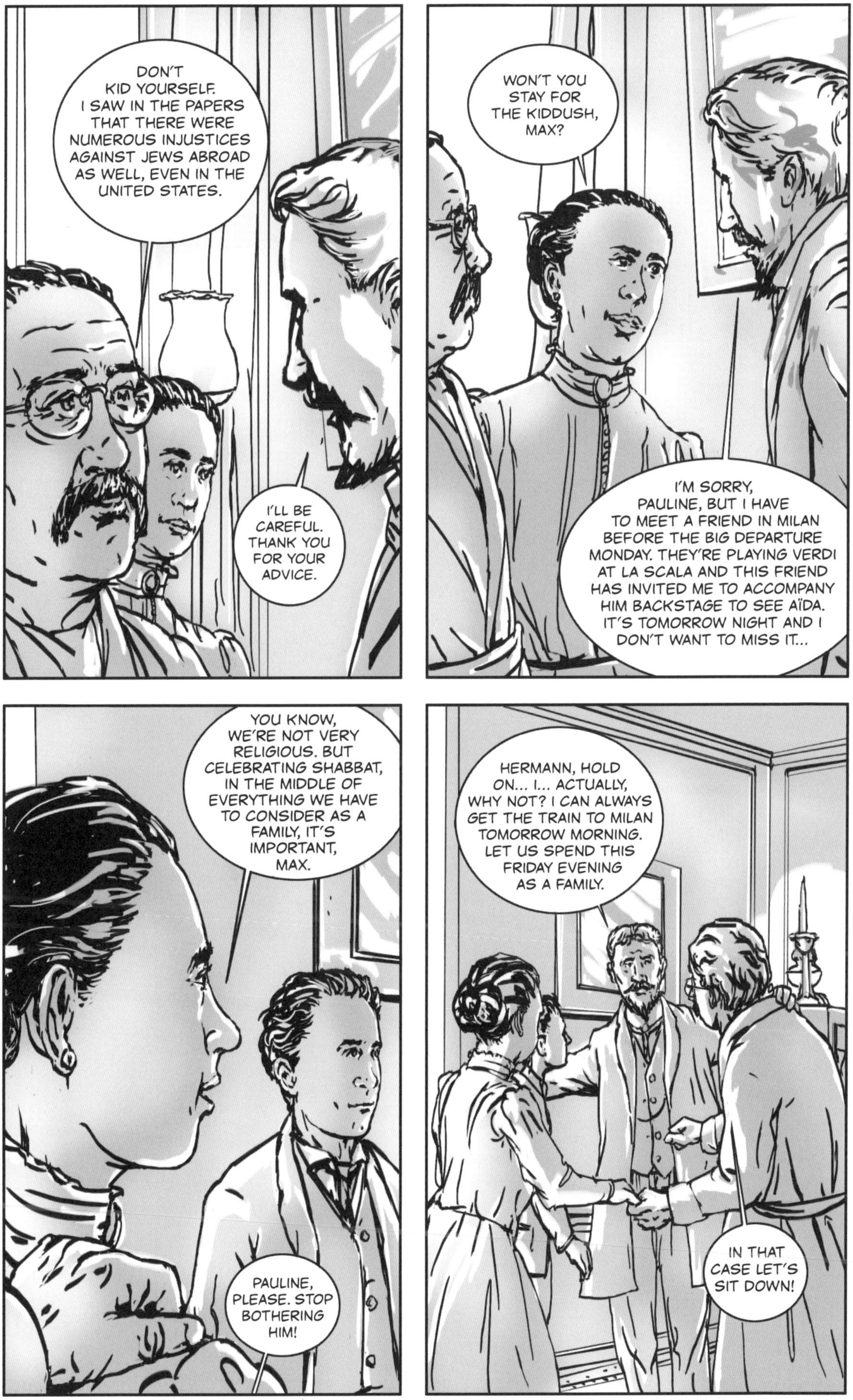
DON'T KID YOURSELF. I SAW IN THE PAPERS THAT THERE WERE NUMEROUS INJUSTICES AGAINST JEWS ABROAD AS WELL, EVEN IN THE UNITED STATES.
I'LL BE CAREFUL. THANK YOU FOR YOUR ADVICE.
WON'T YOU STAY FOR THE KIDDUSH, MAX?
I'M SORRY, PAULINE, BUT I HAVE TO MEET A FRIEND IN MILAN BEFORE THE BIG DEPARTURE MONDAY. THEY'RE PLAYING VERDI AT LA SCALA AND THIS FRIEND HAS INVITED ME TO ACCOMPANY HIM BACKSTAGE TO SEE AÏDA. IT'S TOMORROW NIGHT AND I DON'T WANT TO MISS IT...
YOU KNOW, WE'RE NOT VERY RELIGIOUS. BUT CELEBRATING SHABBAT, IN THE MIDDLE OF EVERYTHING WE HAVE TO CONSIDER AS A FAMILY, IT'S IMPORTANT, MAX.
PAULINE, PLEASE. STOP BOTHERING HIM!
HERMANN, HOLD ON... I... ACTUALLY, WHY NOT? I CAN ALWAYS GET THE TRAIN TO MILAN TOMORROW MORNING. LET US SPEND THIS FRIDAY EVENING AS A FAMILY.
IN THAT CASE LET'S SIT DOWN!

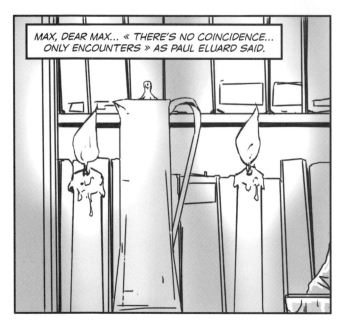

MAX, DEAR MAX... « THERE'S NO COINCIDENCE... ONLY ENCOUNTERS » AS PAUL ELUARD SAID.

I KNOW NOTHING CAN REPLACE THE FRIENDSHIP THAT BOUND US THOSE YEARS. ALL THOSE CONVERSATIONS, ALL THOSE MOMENTS.

MAJA, WHERE ARE YOU? COME SEE WHO'S STAYING FOR DINNER.

OUNETANA TOKEF KEDOUCHAT HAYOM*...

I WILL ALWAYS REMEMBER THE DAY YOU GAVE ME THAT INTRODUCTION TO EUCLIDEAN GEOMETRY BOOK... A WONDERFUL THING! I WAS ONLY 11 YEARS OLD AND IT OPENED MY EYES TO A WORLD FULL OF HOPE AND IMAGINATION.

*KIDDUSH PRAYER, IN HEBREW

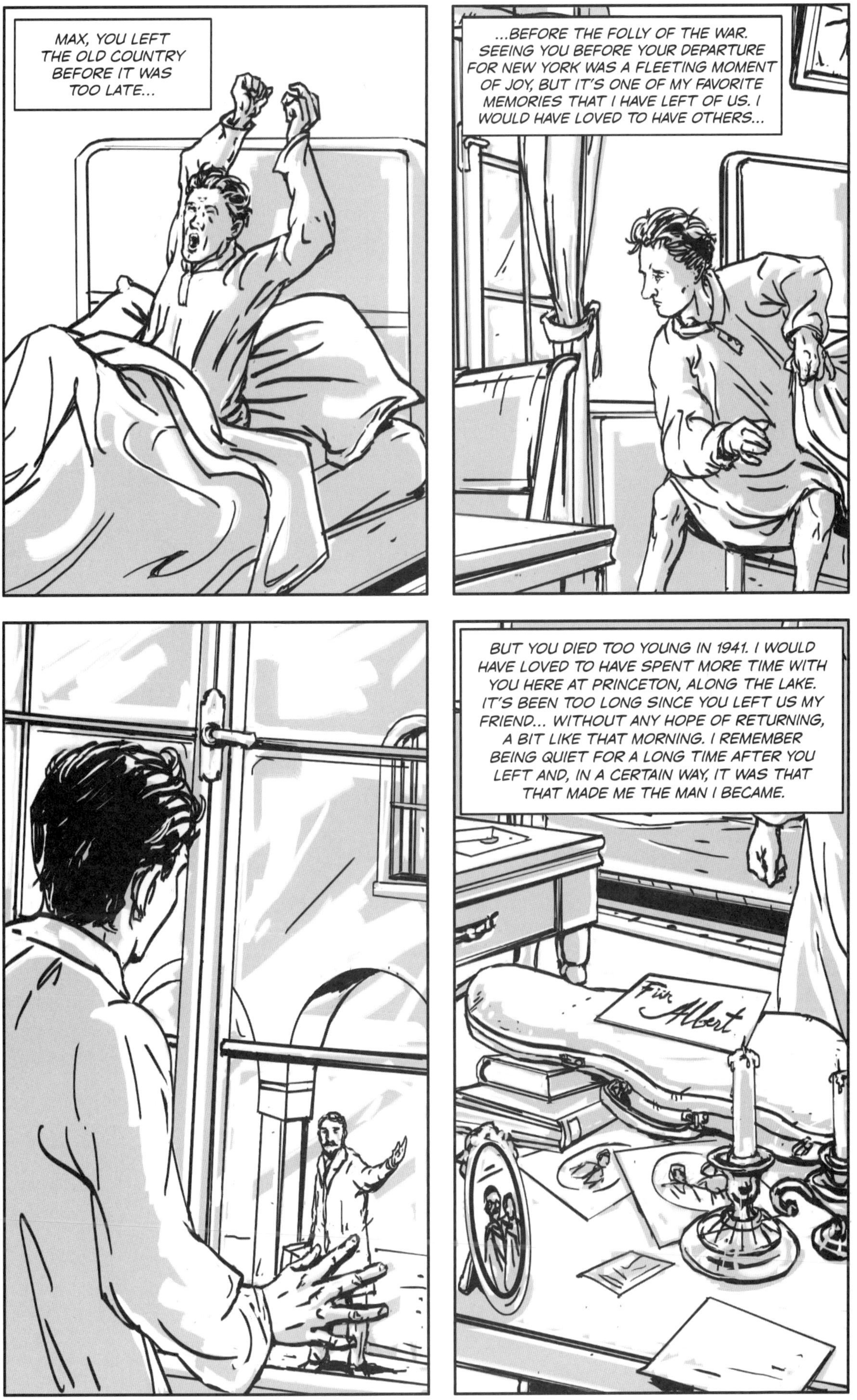
MAX, YOU LEFT THE OLD COUNTRY BEFORE IT WAS TOO LATE...
...BEFORE THE FOLLY OF THE WAR. SEEING YOU BEFORE YOUR DEPARTURE FOR NEW YORK WAS A FLEETING MOMENT OF JOY, BUT IT'S ONE OF MY FAVORITE MEMORIES THAT I HAVE LEFT OF US. I WOULD HAVE LOVED TO HAVE OTHERS...
BUT YOU DIED TOO YOUNG IN 1941. I WOULD HAVE LOVED TO HAVE SPENT MORE TIME WITH YOU HERE AT PRINCETON, ALONG THE LAKE. IT'S BEEN TOO LONG SINCE YOU LEFT US MY FRIEND... WITHOUT ANY HOPE OF RETURNING, A BIT LIKE THAT MORNING. I REMEMBER BEING QUIET FOR A LONG TIME AFTER YOU LEFT AND, IN A CERTAIN WAY, IT WAS THAT THAT MADE ME THE MAN I BECAME.
Für Albert

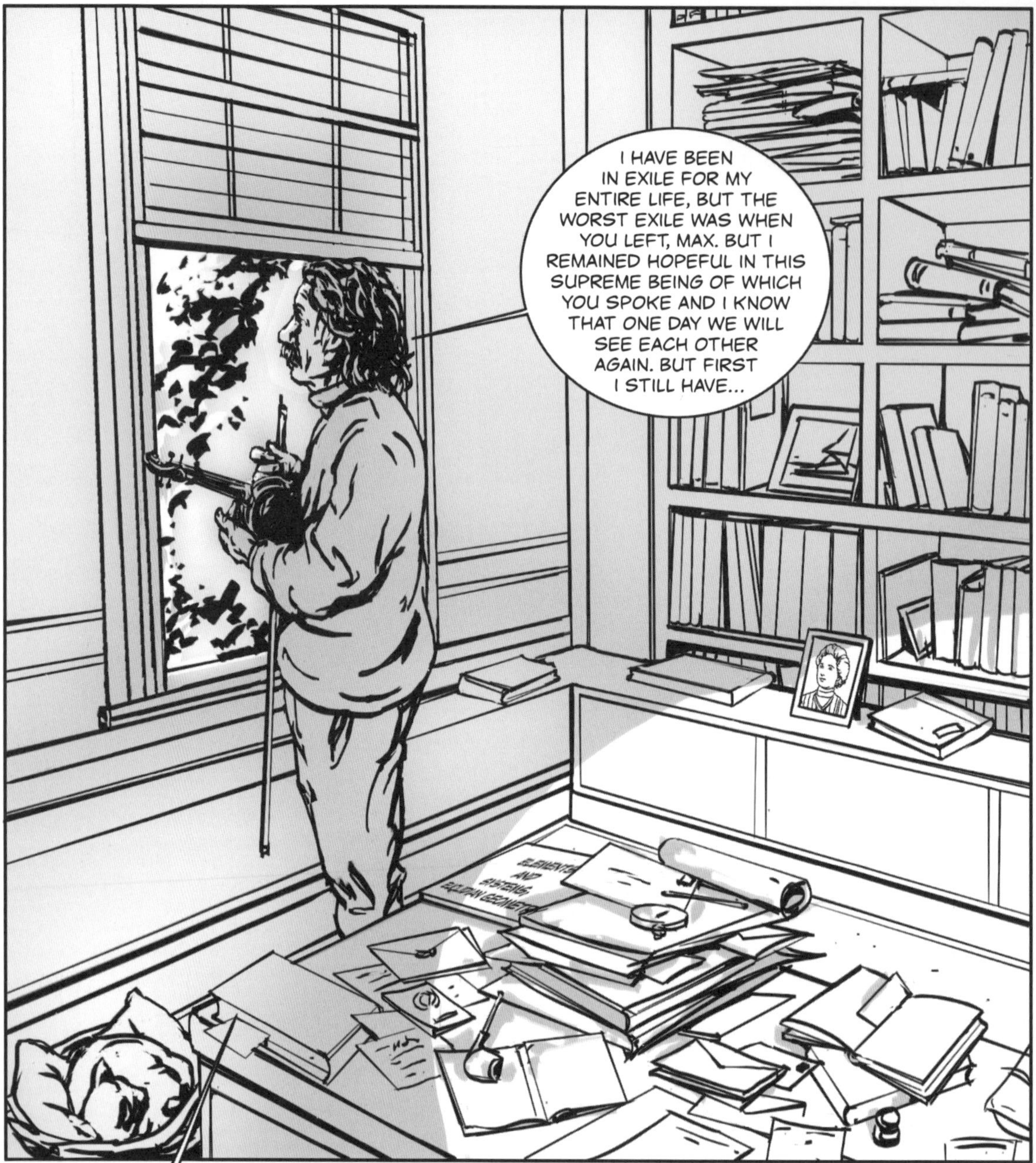
I HAVE BEEN IN EXILE FOR MY ENTIRE LIFE, BUT THE WORST EXILE WAS WHEN YOU LEFT, MAX. BUT I REMAINED HOPEFUL IN THIS SUPREME BEING OF WHICH YOU SPOKE AND I KNOW THAT ONE DAY WE WILL SEE EACH OTHER AGAIN. BUT FIRST I STILL HAVE...

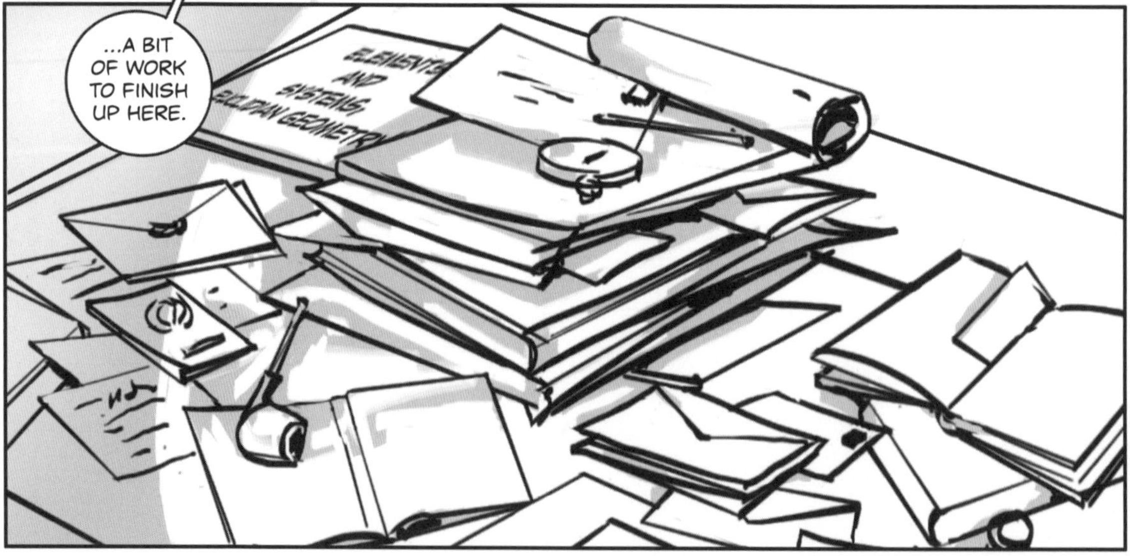
...A BIT OF WORK TO FINISH UP HERE.
ELEMENTS AND SYSTEMS: EUCLIDIAN GEOMETRY

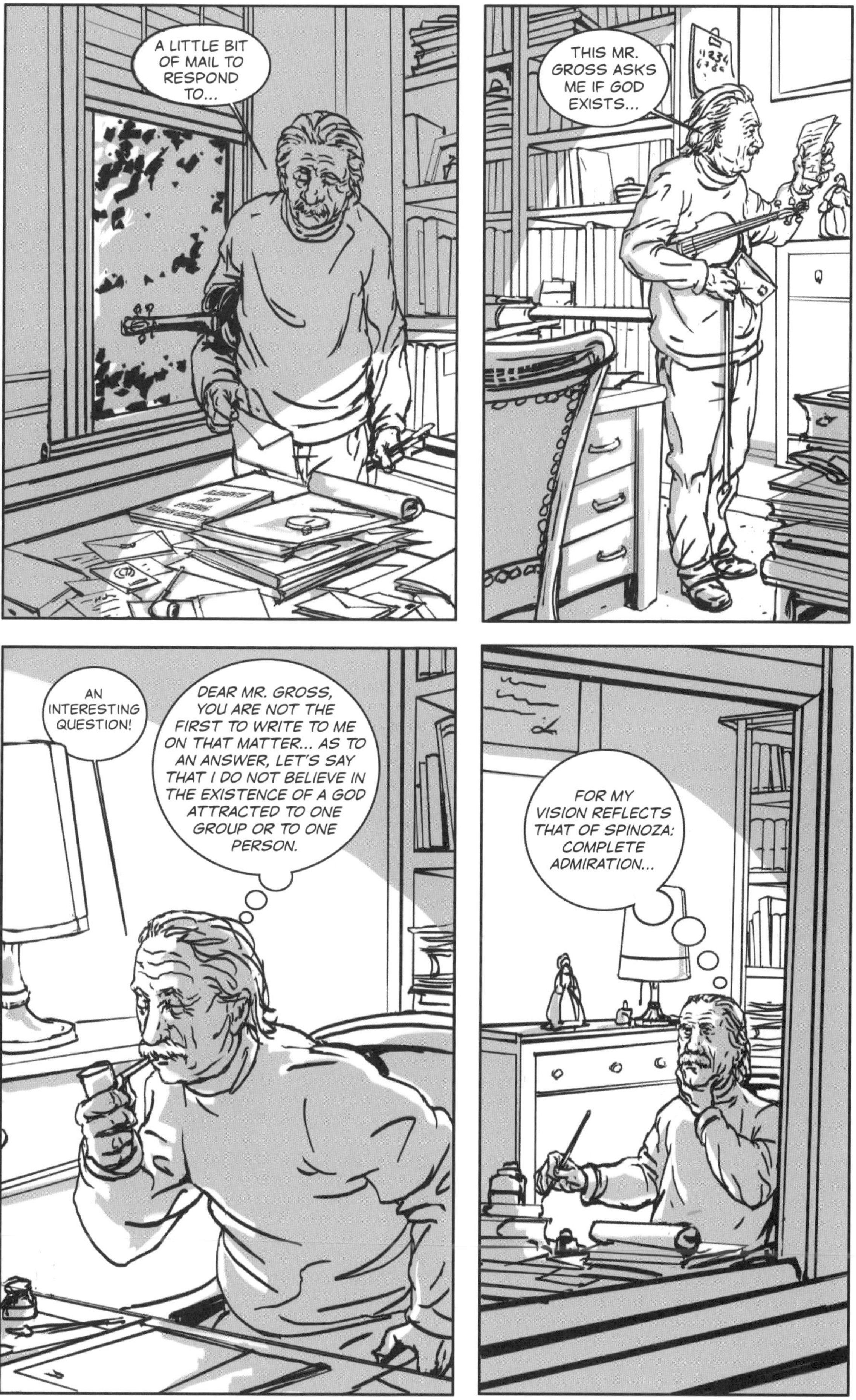
A LITTLE BIT OF MAIL TO RESPOND TO...
THIS MR. GROSS ASKS ME IF GOD EXISTS...
AN INTERESTING QUESTION!
DEAR MR. GROSS, YOU ARE NOT THE FIRST TO WRITE TO ME ON THAT MATTER... AS TO AN ANSWER, LET'S SAY THAT I DO NOT BELIEVE IN THE EXISTENCE OF A GOD ATTRACTED TO ONE GROUP OR TO ONE PERSON.
FOR MY VISION REFLECTS THAT OF SPINOZA: COMPLETE ADMIRATION...

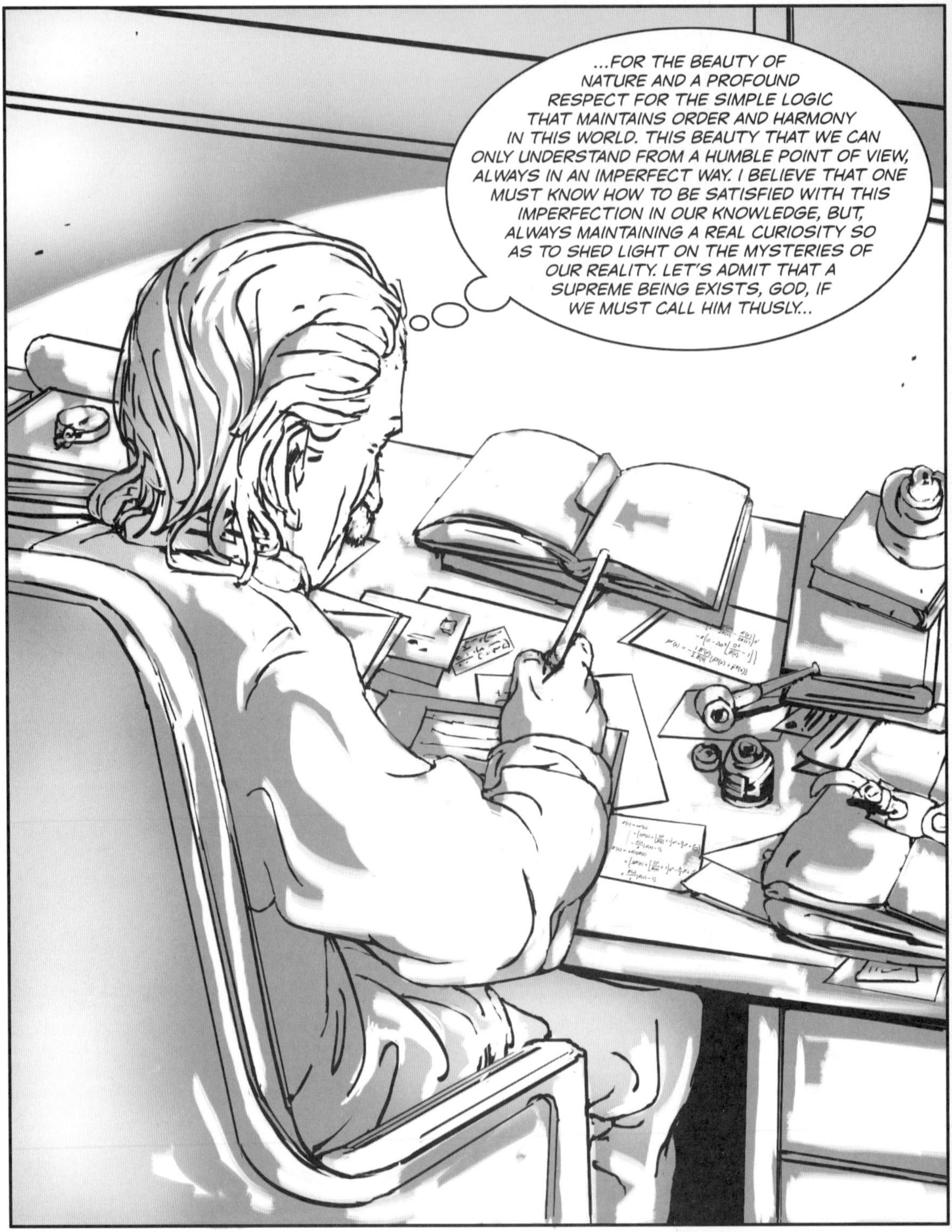
...FOR THE BEAUTY OF NATURE AND A PROFOUND RESPECT FOR THE SIMPLE LOGIC THAT MAINTAINS ORDER AND HARMONY IN THIS WORLD. THIS BEAUTY THAT WE CAN ONLY UNDERSTAND FROM A HUMBLE POINT OF VIEW, ALWAYS IN AN IMPERFECT WAY. I BELIEVE THAT ONE MUST KNOW HOW TO BE SATISFIED WITH THIS IMPERFECTION IN OUR KNOWLEDGE, BUT, ALWAYS MAINTAINING A REAL CURIOSITY SO AS TO SHED LIGHT ON THE MYSTERIES OF OUR REALITY. LET'S ADMIT THAT A SUPREME BEING EXISTS, GOD, IF WE MUST CALL HIM THUSLY...

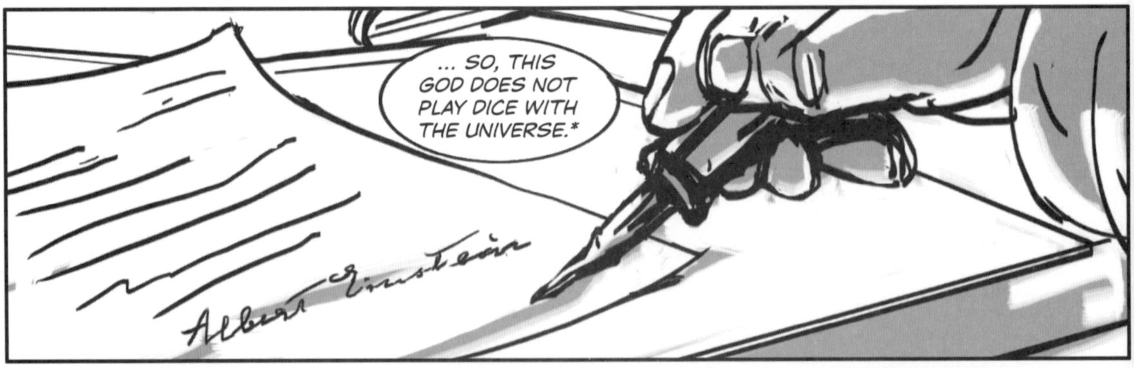
... SO, THIS GOD DOES NOT PLAY DICE WITH THE UNIVERSE.*
Albert Einstein

* FOR HIS WHOLE LIFE EINSTEIN REJECTED THE NOTION OF LUCK THAT WAS AT THE HEART OF QUANTUM MECHANICS INCLUDING THE WORK OF HEINSENBERG AND BORN AND POPULARIZED BY THE IMAGE OF SHRODINGER'S CAT.

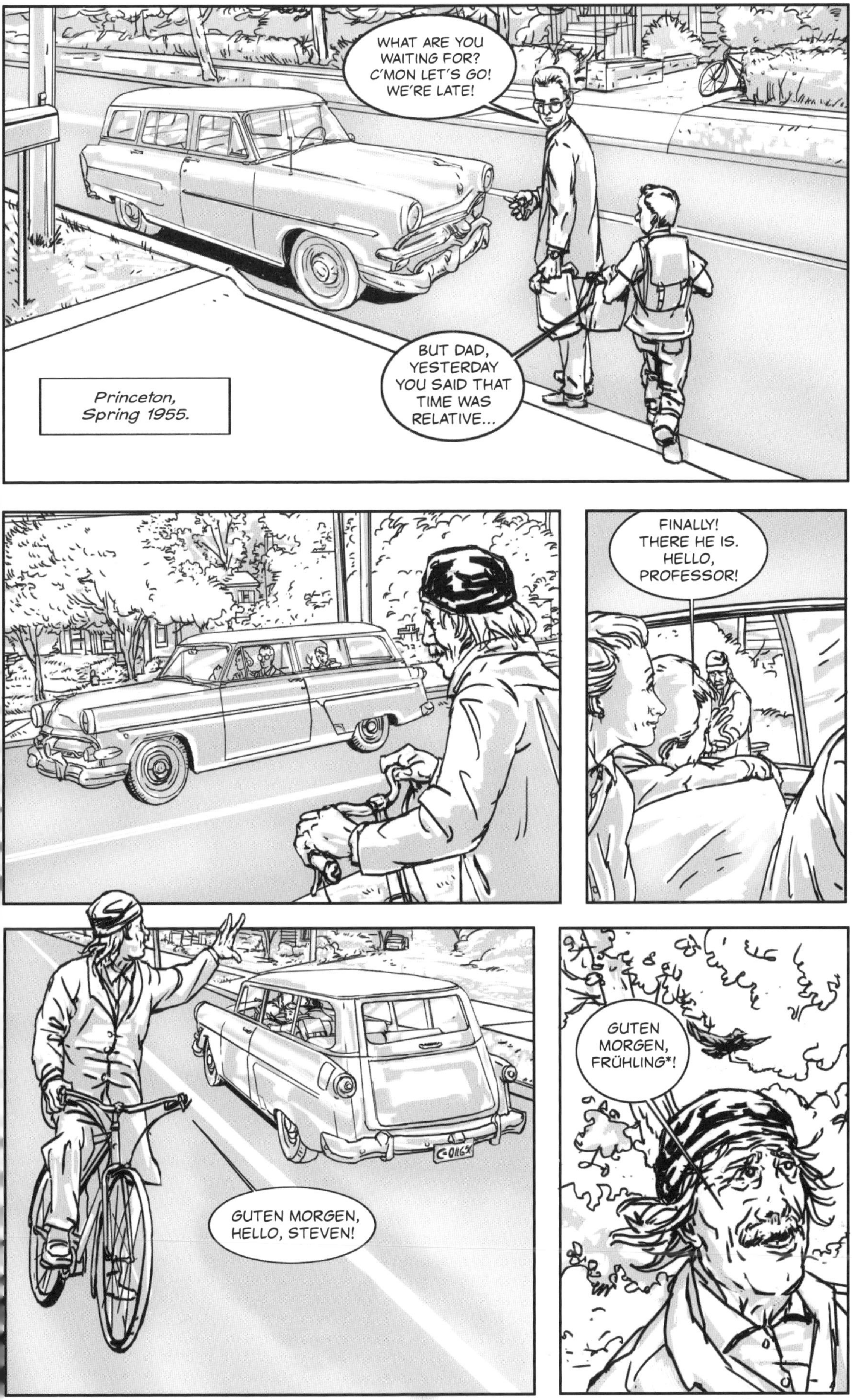
Princeton, Spring 1955.
WHAT ARE YOU WAITING FOR? C'MON LET'S GO! WE'RE LATE!
BUT DAD, YESTERDAY YOU SAID THAT TIME WAS RELATIVE...
FINALLY! THERE HE IS. HELLO, PROFESSOR!
GUTEN MORGEN, HELLO, STEVEN!
GUTEN MORGEN, FRÜHLING*!

*HELLO, SPRING!

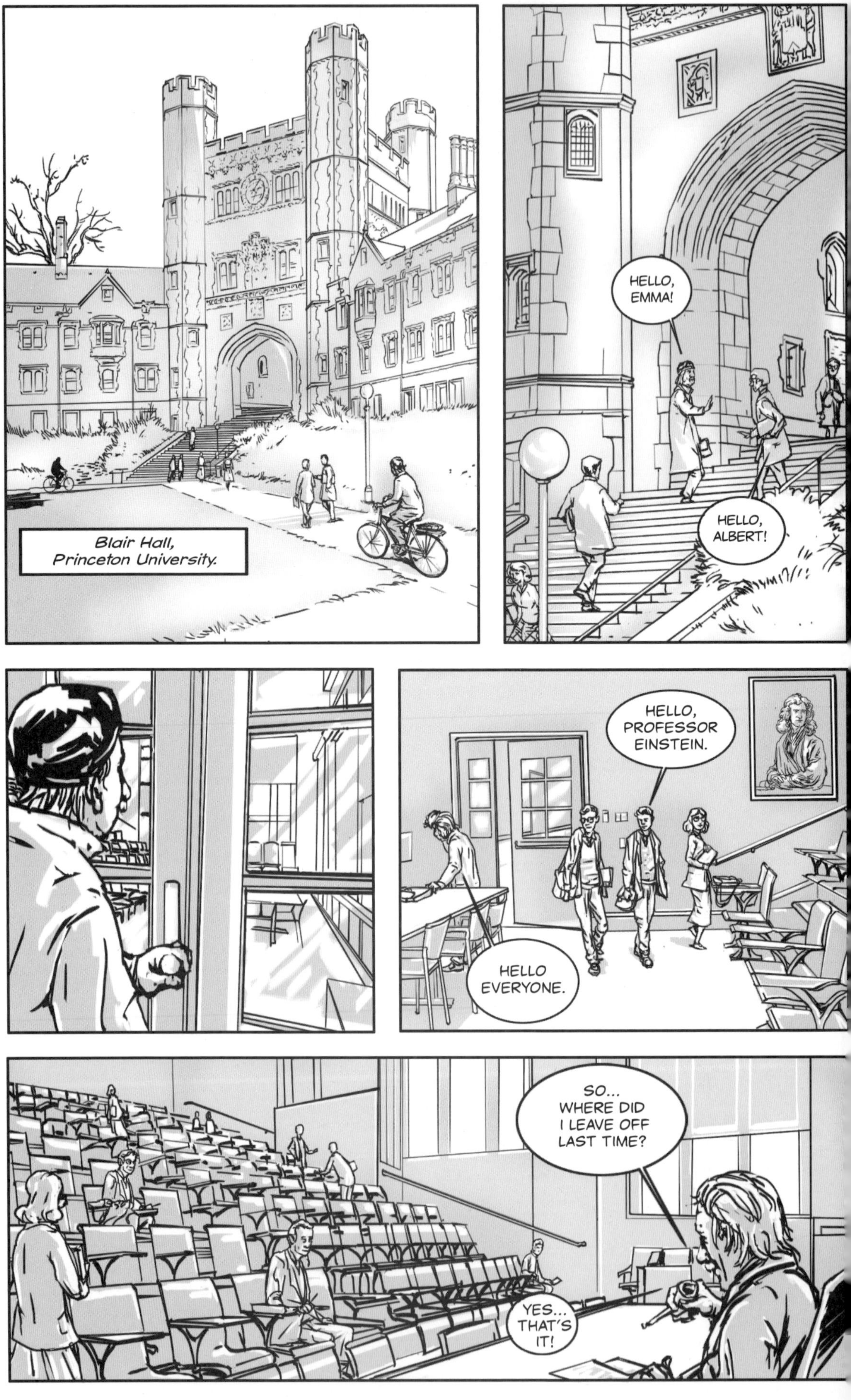
Blair Hall, Princeton University.
HELLO, EMMA!
HELLO, ALBERT!
HELLO, PROFESSOR EINSTEIN.
HELLO EVERYONE.
SO... WHERE DID I LEAVE OFF LAST TIME?
YES... THAT'S IT!

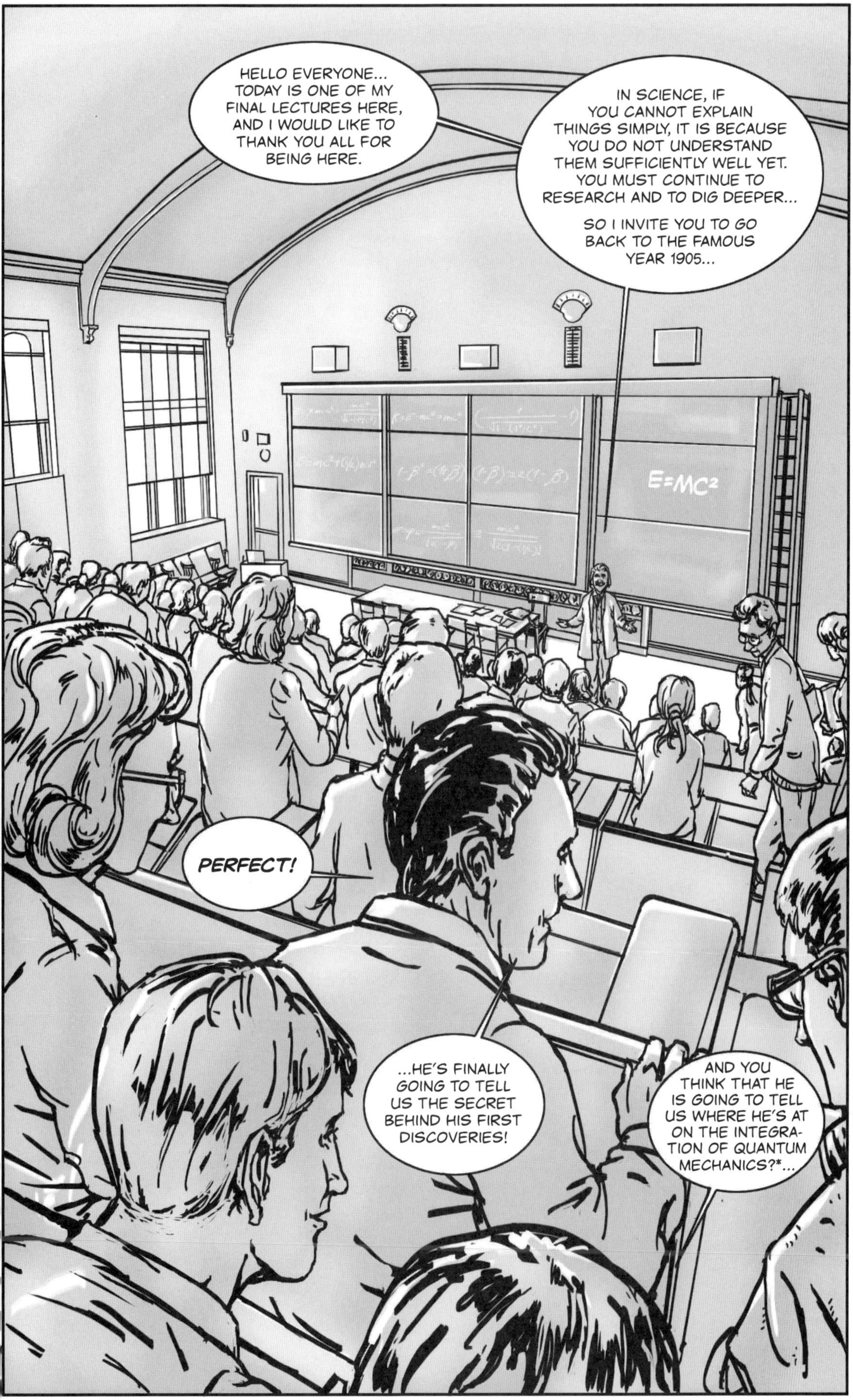
HELLO EVERYONE... TODAY IS ONE OF MY FINAL LECTURES HERE, AND I WOULD LIKE TO THANK YOU ALL FOR BEING HERE.
IN SCIENCE, IF YOU CANNOT EXPLAIN THINGS SIMPLY, IT IS BECAUSE YOU DO NOT UNDERSTAND THEM SUFFICIENTLY WELL YET. YOU MUST CONTINUE TO RESEARCH AND TO DIG DEEPER...
SO I INVITE YOU TO GO BACK TO THE FAMOUS YEAR 1905...
E=MC²
PERFECT!
...HE'S FINALLY GOING TO TELL US THE SECRET BEHIND HIS FIRST DISCOVERIES!
AND YOU THINK THAT HE IS GOING TO TELL US WHERE HE'S AT ON THE INTEGRATION OF QUANTUM MECHANICS?*...

*SINCE THE 20S, EINSTEIN TRIED TO EXPLAIN IN ONE THEORY THE BEHAVIOR OF THE PLANETS, RULED BY RELATIVITY, AND THAT OF ATOMS, RULED BY QUANTUM MECHANICS.

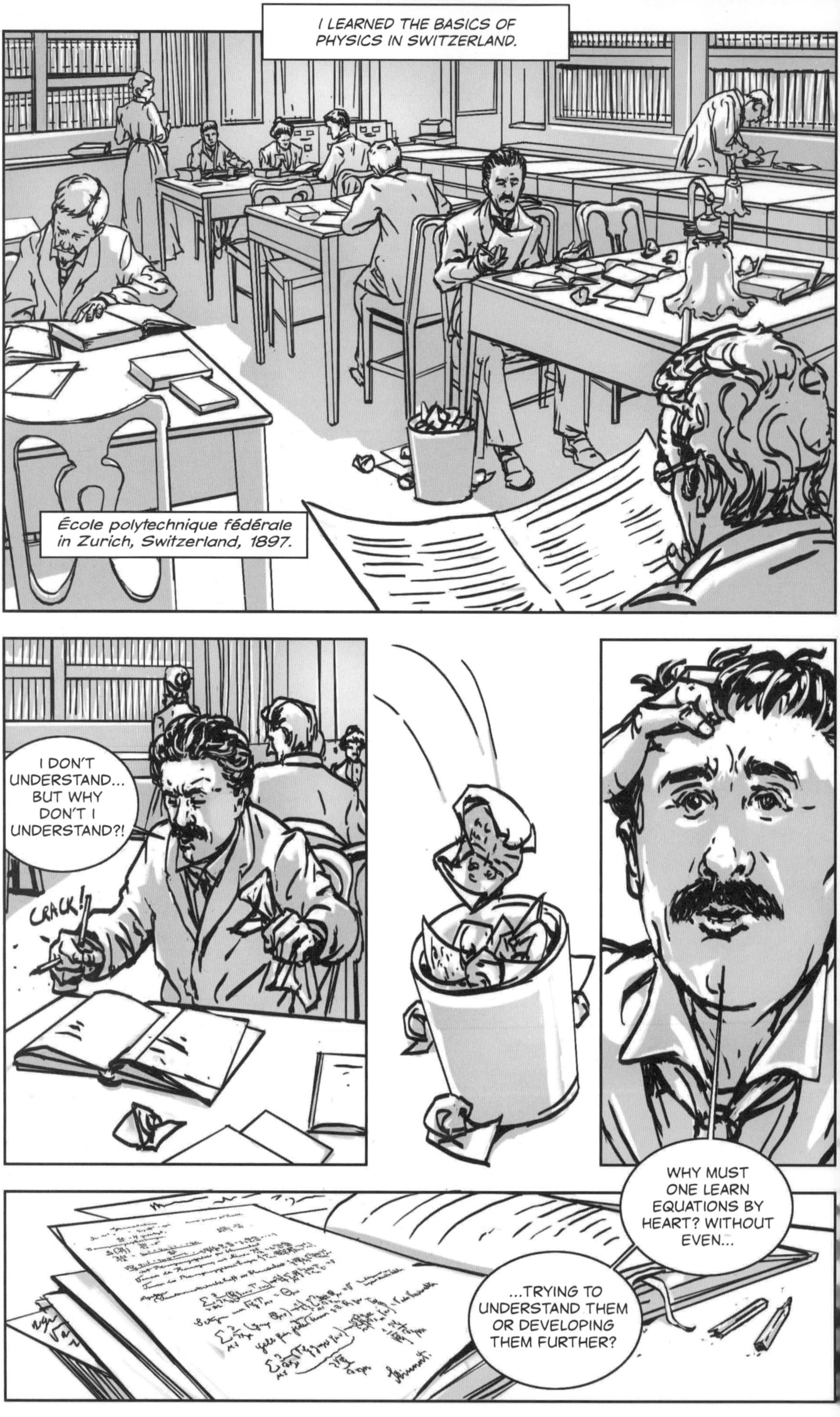
I LEARNED THE BASICS OF PHYSICS IN SWITZERLAND.
École polytechnique fédérale in Zurich, Switzerland, 1897.
I DON'T UNDERSTAND... BUT WHY DON'T I UNDERSTAND?!
CRACK!
WHY MUST ONE LEARN EQUATIONS BY HEART? WITHOUT EVEN...
...TRYING TO UNDERSTAND THEM OR DEVELOPING THEM FURTHER?

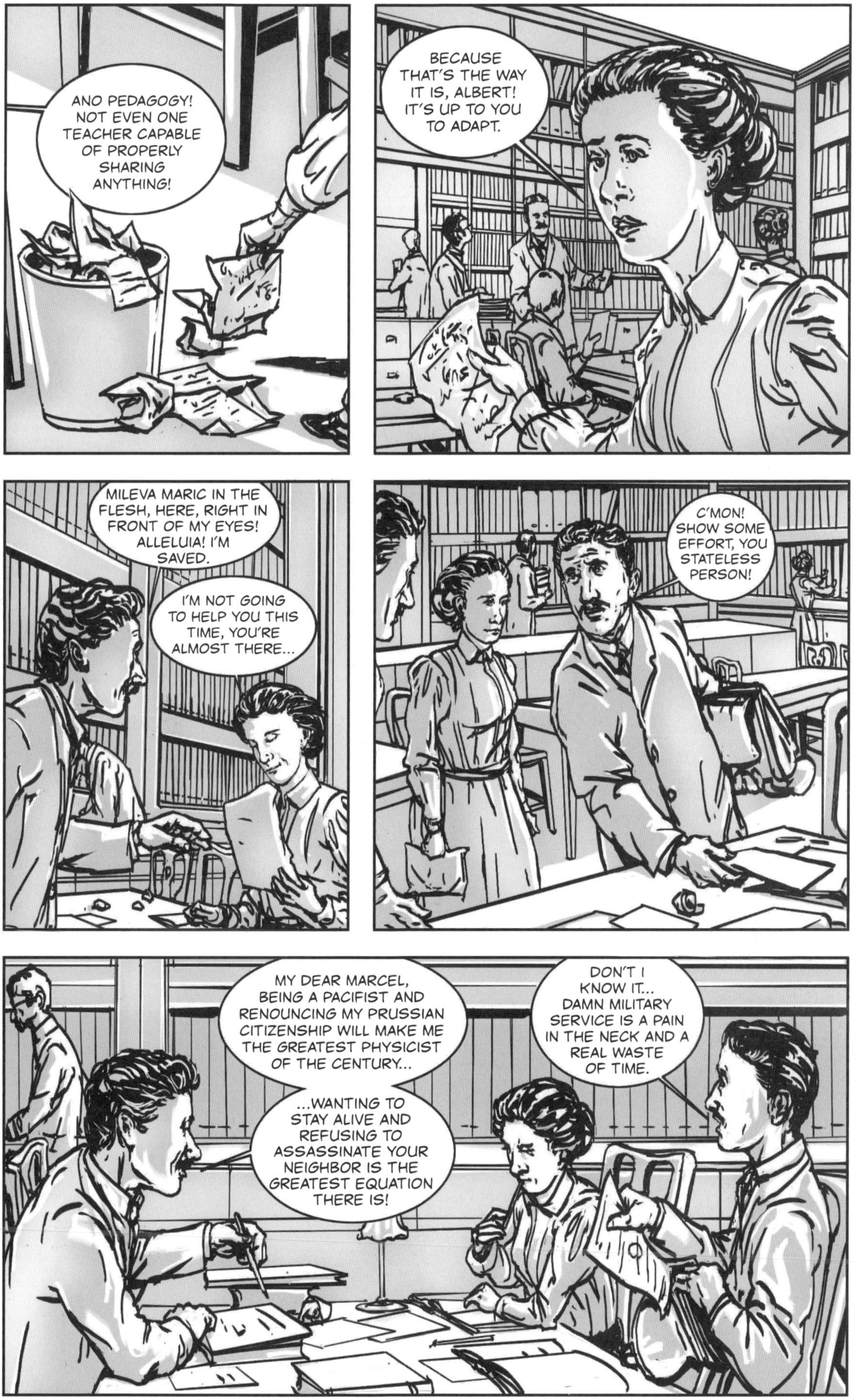

ANO PEDAGOGY! NOT EVEN ONE TEACHER CAPABLE OF PROPERLY SHARING ANYTHING!
BECAUSE THAT'S THE WAY IT IS, ALBERT! IT'S UP TO YOU TO ADAPT.
MILEVA MARIC IN THE FLESH, HERE, RIGHT IN FRONT OF MY EYES! ALLELUIA! I'M SAVED.
I'M NOT GOING TO HELP YOU THIS TIME, YOU'RE ALMOST THERE...
C'MON! SHOW SOME EFFORT, YOU STATELESS PERSON!
MY DEAR MARCEL, BEING A PACIFIST AND RENOUNCING MY PRUSSIAN CITIZENSHIP WILL MAKE ME THE GREATEST PHYSICIST OF THE CENTURY...
...WANTING TO STAY ALIVE AND REFUSING TO ASSASSINATE YOUR NEIGHBOR IS THE GREATEST EQUATION THERE IS!
DON'T I KNOW IT... DAMN MILITARY SERVICE IS A PAIN IN THE NECK AND A REAL WASTE OF TIME.

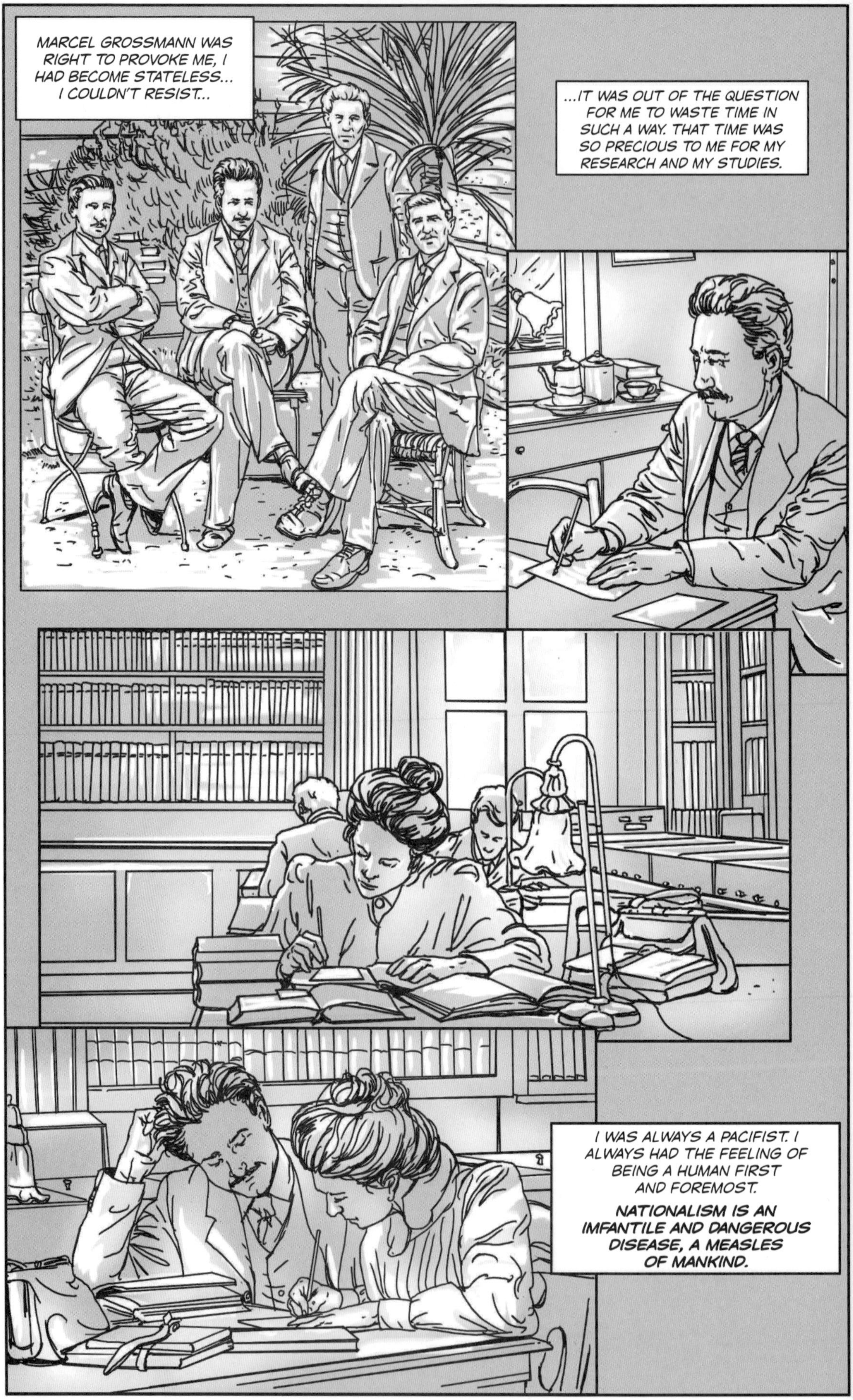
MARCEL GROSSMANN WAS RIGHT TO PROVOKE ME, I HAD BECOME STATELESS... I COULDN'T RESIST...
...IT WAS OUT OF THE QUESTION FOR ME TO WASTE TIME IN SUCH A WAY. THAT TIME WAS SO PRECIOUS TO ME FOR MY RESEARCH AND MY STUDIES.
I WAS ALWAYS A PACIFIST. I ALWAYS HAD THE FEELING OF BEING A HUMAN FIRST AND FOREMOST.
NATIONALISM IS AN IMFANTILE AND DANGEROUS DISEASE, A MEASLES OF MANKIND.

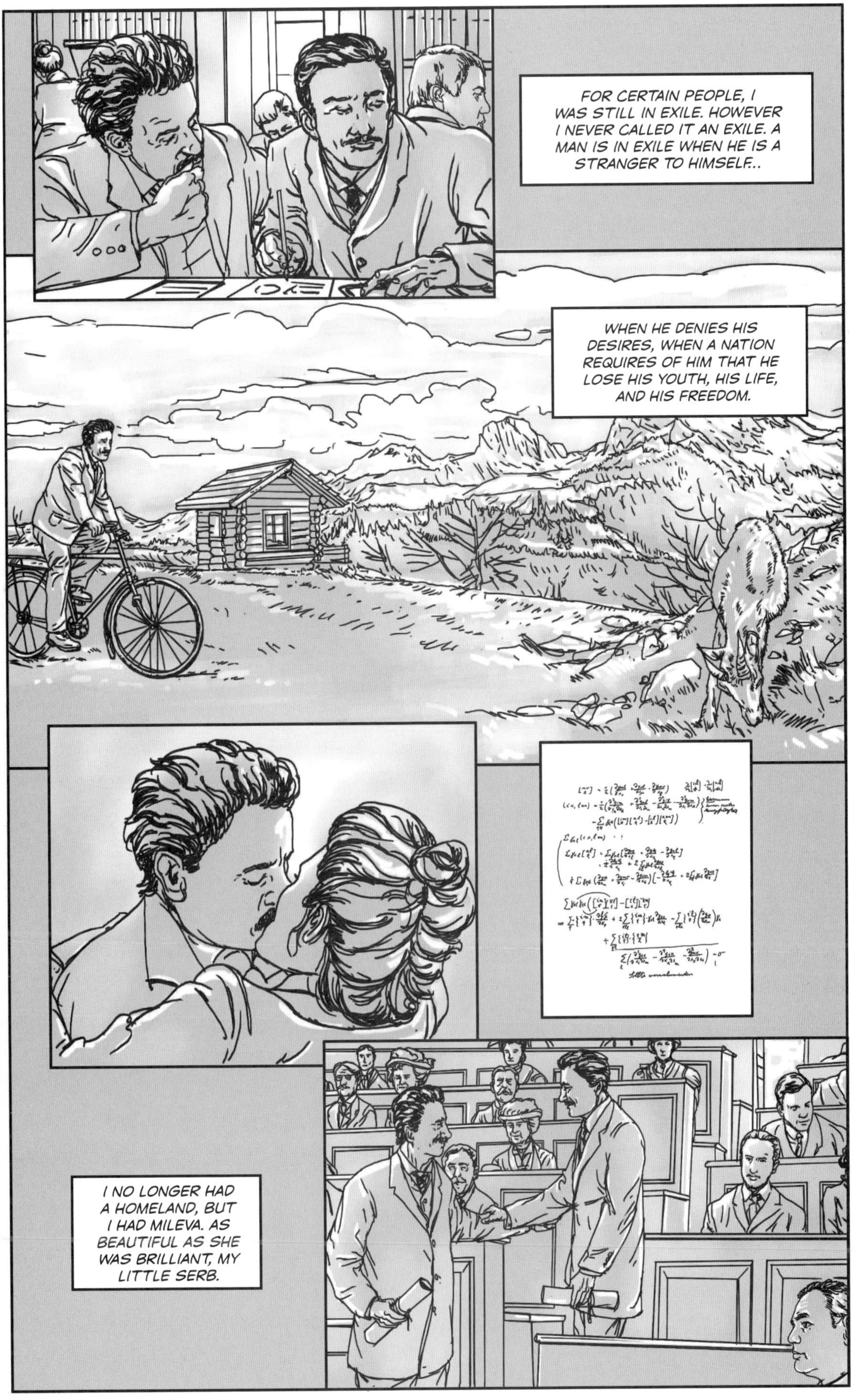
FOR CERTAIN PEOPLE, I WAS STILL IN EXILE. HOWEVER I NEVER CALLED IT AN EXILE. A MAN IS IN EXILE WHEN HE IS A STRANGER TO HIMSELF...
WHEN HE DENIES HIS DESIRES, WHEN A NATION REQUIRES OF HIM THAT HE LOSE HIS YOUTH, HIS LIFE, AND HIS FREEDOM.
I NO LONGER HAD A HOMELAND, BUT I HAD MILEVA. AS BEAUTIFUL AS SHE WAS BRILLIANT, MY LITTLE SERB.

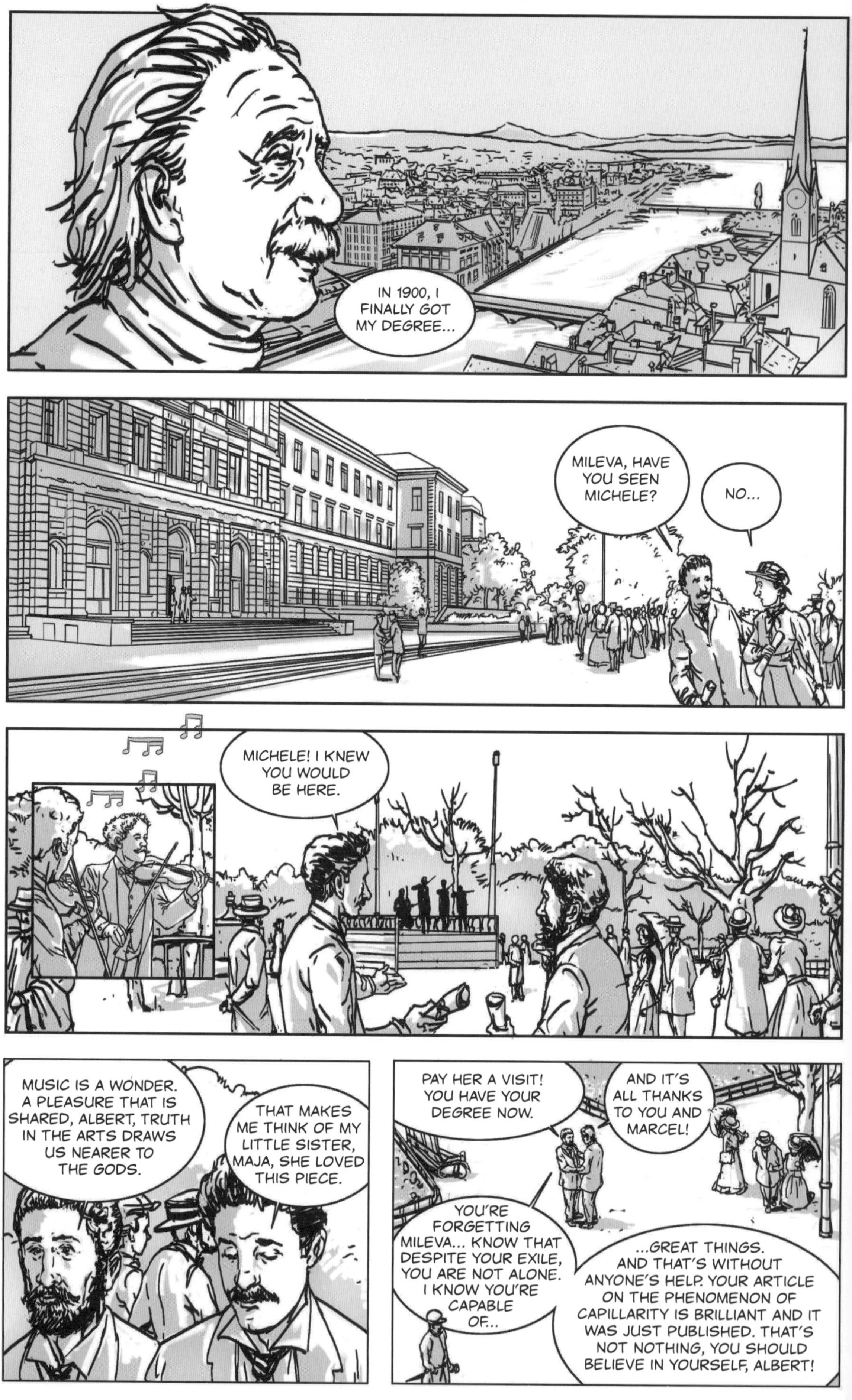
IN 1900, I FINALLY GOT MY DEGREE...
MILEVA, HAVE YOU SEEN MICHELE?
NO...
MICHELE! I KNEW YOU WOULD BE HERE.
MUSIC IS A WONDER. A PLEASURE THAT IS SHARED, ALBERT, TRUTH IN THE ARTS DRAWS US NEARER TO THE GODS.
THAT MAKES ME THINK OF MY LITTLE SISTER, MAJA, SHE LOVED THIS PIECE.
PAY HER A VISIT! YOU HAVE YOUR DEGREE NOW.
AND IT'S ALL THANKS TO YOU AND MARCEL!
YOU'RE FORGETTING MILEVA... KNOW THAT DESPITE YOUR EXILE, YOU ARE NOT ALONE. I KNOW YOU'RE CAPABLE OF...
...GREAT THINGS. AND THAT'S WITHOUT ANYONE'S HELP. YOUR ARTICLE ON THE PHENOMENON OF CAPILLARITY IS BRILLIANT AND IT WAS JUST PUBLISHED. THAT'S NOT NOTHING, YOU SHOULD BELIEVE IN YOURSELF, ALBERT!

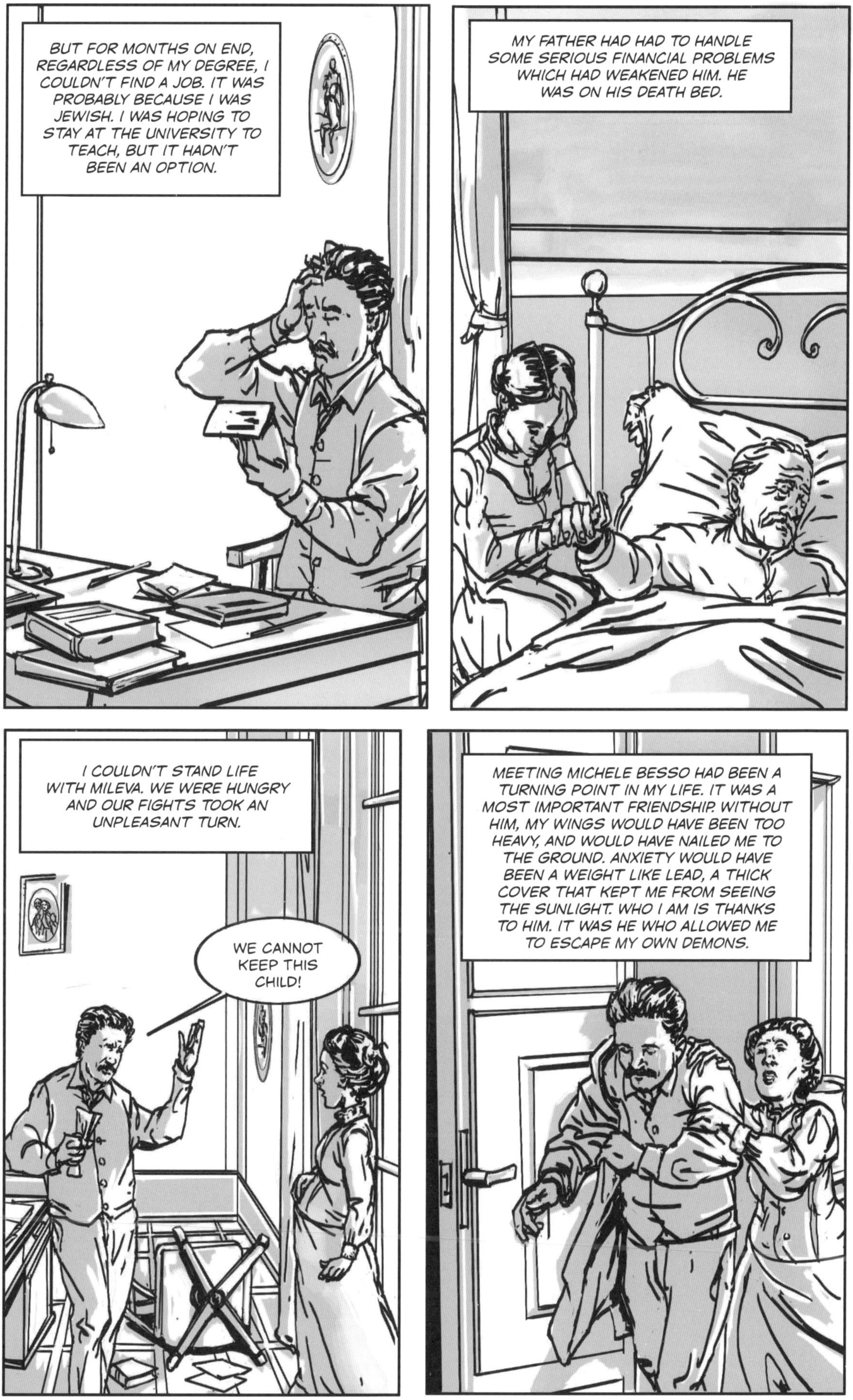
BUT FOR MONTHS ON END, REGARDLESS OF MY DEGREE, I COULDN'T FIND A JOB. IT WAS PROBABLY BECAUSE I WAS JEWISH. I WAS HOPING TO STAY AT THE UNIVERSITY TO TEACH, BUT IT HADN'T BEEN AN OPTION.
MY FATHER HAD HAD TO HANDLE SOME SERIOUS FINANCIAL PROBLEMS WHICH HAD WEAKENED HIM. HE WAS ON HIS DEATH BED.
I COULDN'T STAND LIFE WITH MILEVA. WE WERE HUNGRY AND OUR FIGHTS TOOK AN UNPLEASANT TURN.
WE CANNOT KEEP THIS CHILD!
MEETING MICHELE BESSO HAD BEEN A TURNING POINT IN MY LIFE. IT WAS A MOST IMPORTANT FRIENDSHIP. WITHOUT HIM, MY WINGS WOULD HAVE BEEN TOO HEAVY, AND WOULD HAVE NAILED ME TO THE GROUND. ANXIETY WOULD HAVE BEEN A WEIGHT LIKE LEAD, A THICK COVER THAT KEPT ME FROM SEEING THE SUNLIGHT. WHO I AM IS THANKS TO HIM. IT WAS HE WHO ALLOWED ME TO ESCAPE MY OWN DEMONS.

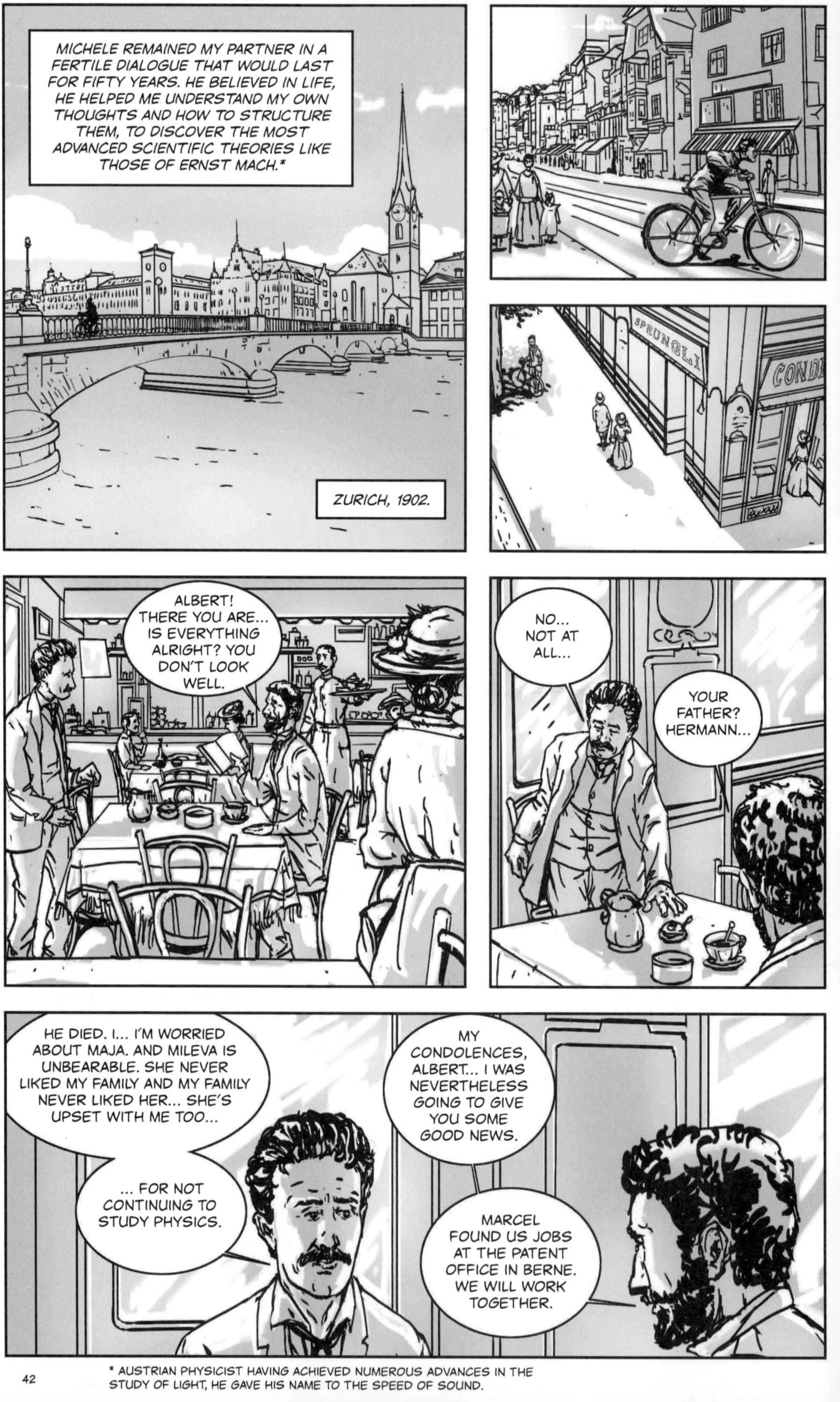
MICHELE REMAINED MY PARTNER IN A FERTILE DIALOGUE THAT WOULD LAST FOR FIFTY YEARS. HE BELIEVED IN LIFE, HE HELPED ME UNDERSTAND MY OWN THOUGHTS AND HOW TO STRUCTURE THEM, TO DISCOVER THE MOST ADVANCED SCIENTIFIC THEORIES LIKE THOSE OF ERNST MACH.*
ZURICH, 1902.
SPRUNGLI
ALBERT! THERE YOU ARE... IS EVERYTHING ALRIGHT? YOU DON'T LOOK WELL.
NO... NOT AT ALL...
YOUR FATHER? HERMANN...
HE DIED. I... I'M WORRIED ABOUT MAJA. AND MILEVA IS UNBEARABLE. SHE NEVER LIKED MY FAMILY AND MY FAMILY NEVER LIKED HER... SHE'S UPSET WITH ME TOO...
... FOR NOT CONTINUING TO STUDY PHYSICS.
MY CONDOLENCES, ALBERT... I WAS NEVERTHELESS GOING TO GIVE YOU SOME GOOD NEWS.
MARCEL FOUND US JOBS AT THE PATENT OFFICE IN BERNE. WE WILL WORK TOGETHER.

* AUSTRIAN PHYSICIST HAVING ACHIEVED NUMEROUS ADVANCES IN THE STUDY OF LIGHT, HE GAVE HIS NAME TO THE SPEED OF SOUND.

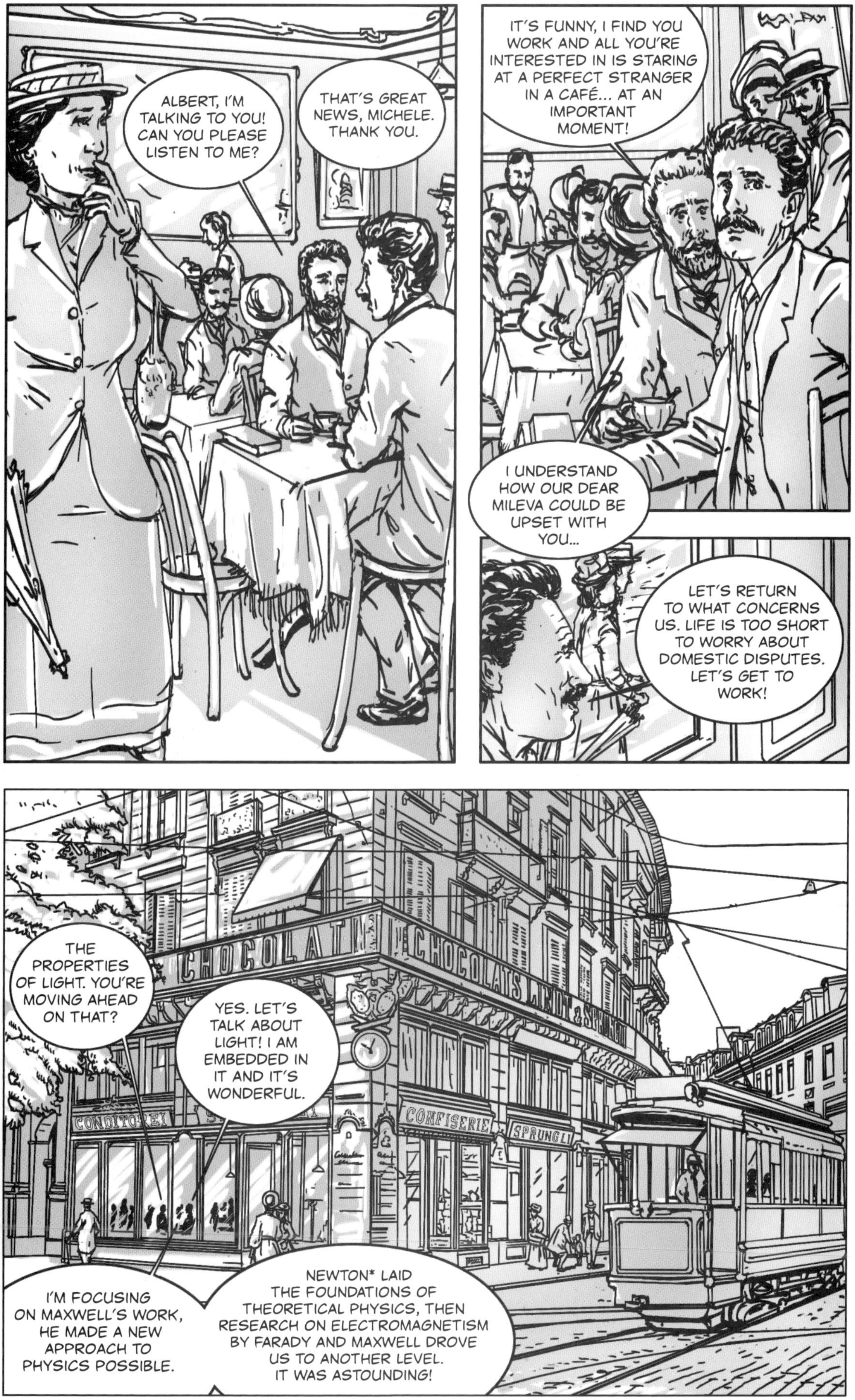
ALBERT, I'M TALKING TO YOU! CAN YOU PLEASE LISTEN TO ME?
THAT'S GREAT NEWS, MICHELE. THANK YOU.
IT'S FUNNY, I FIND YOU WORK AND ALL YOU'RE INTERESTED IN IS STARING AT A PERFECT STRANGER IN A CAFÉ... AT AN IMPORTANT MOMENT!
I UNDERSTAND HOW OUR DEAR MILEVA COULD BE UPSET WITH YOU...
LET'S RETURN TO WHAT CONCERNS US. LIFE IS TOO SHORT TO WORRY ABOUT DOMESTIC DISPUTES. LET'S GET TO WORK!
CHOCOLAT
CHOCOLATS LINDT & SPRÜNGLI
CONDITOREI
CONFISERIE
SPRUNGLI
THE PROPERTIES OF LIGHT. YOU'RE MOVING AHEAD ON THAT?
YES. LET'S TALK ABOUT LIGHT! I AM EMBEDDED IN IT AND IT'S WONDERFUL.
I'M FOCUSING ON MAXWELL'S WORK, HE MADE A NEW APPROACH TO PHYSICS POSSIBLE.
NEWTON* LAID THE FOUNDATIONS OF THEORETICAL PHYSICS, THEN RESEARCH ON ELECTROMAGNETISM BY FARADY AND MAXWELL DROVE US TO ANOTHER LEVEL. IT WAS ASTOUNDING!

* ENGLISH 18TH CENTURY SCHOLAR WHO LAID THE FOUNDATION FOR CLASSICAL PHYSICS WITH HIS LAW OF UNIVERSAL GRAVITATION, A FORCE THAT ATTRACTS ALL BODIES AMONG THEMSELVES ACCORDING TO THEIR MASS.

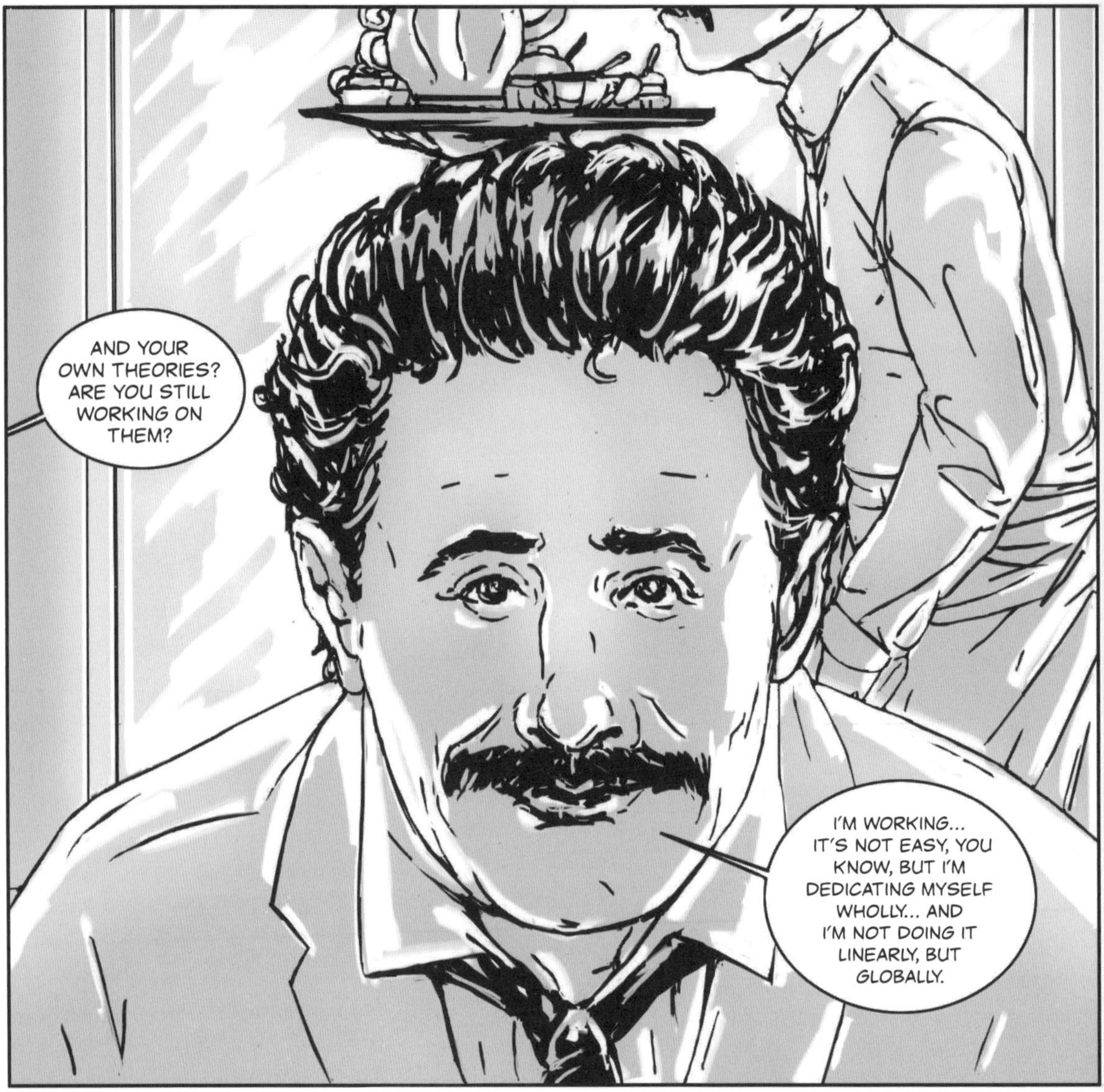
AND YOUR OWN THEORIES? ARE YOU STILL WORKING ON THEM?
I'M WORKING... IT'S NOT EASY, YOU KNOW, BUT I'M DEDICATING MYSELF WHOLLY... AND I'M NOT DOING IT LINEARLY, BUT GLOBALLY.

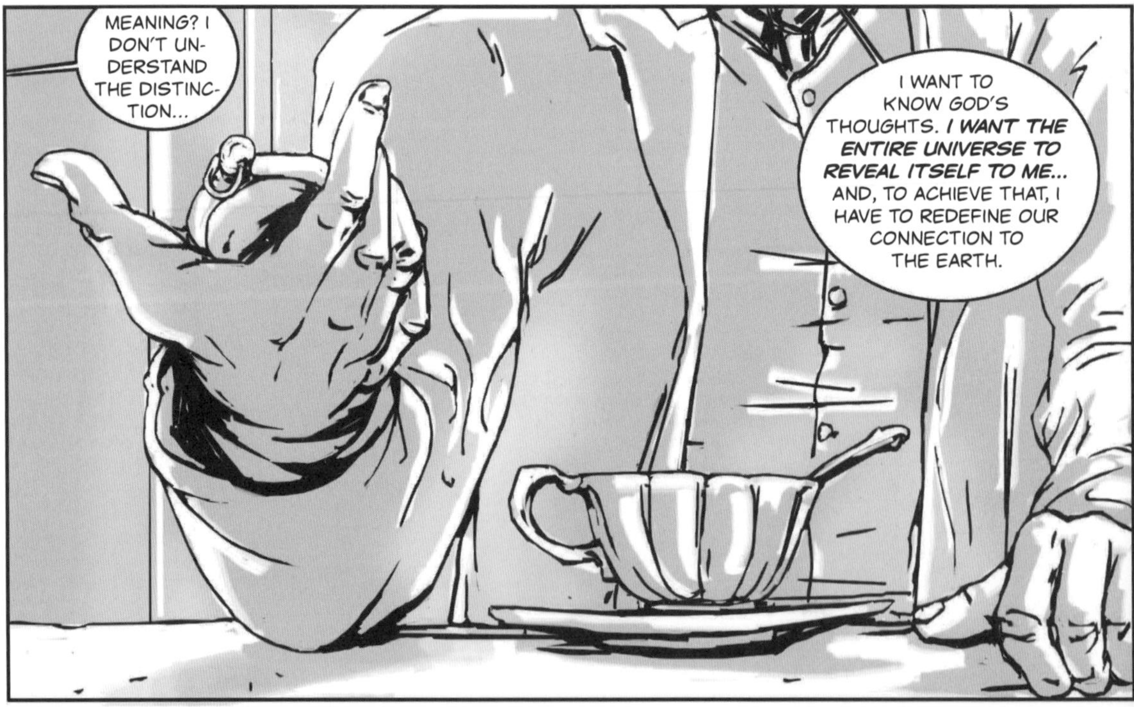
MEANING? I DON'T UNDERSTAND THE DISTINCTION...
I WANT TO KNOW GOD'S THOUGHTS. ***I WANT THE ENTIRE UNIVERSE TO REVEAL ITSELF TO ME...*** AND, TO ACHIEVE THAT, I HAVE TO REDEFINE OUR CONNECTION TO THE EARTH.

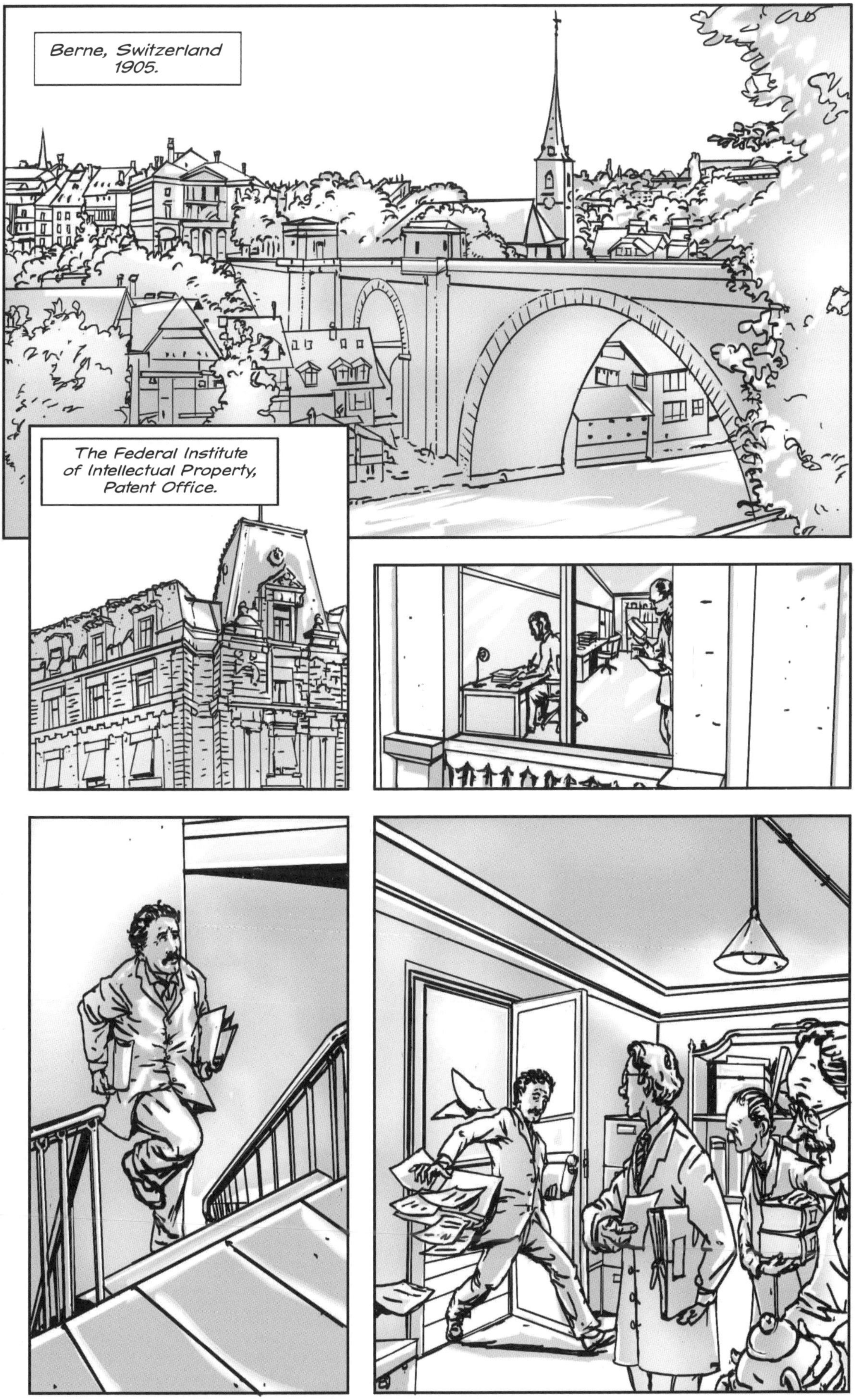
Berne, Switzerland
1905.
The Federal Institute
of Intellectual Property,
Patent Office.

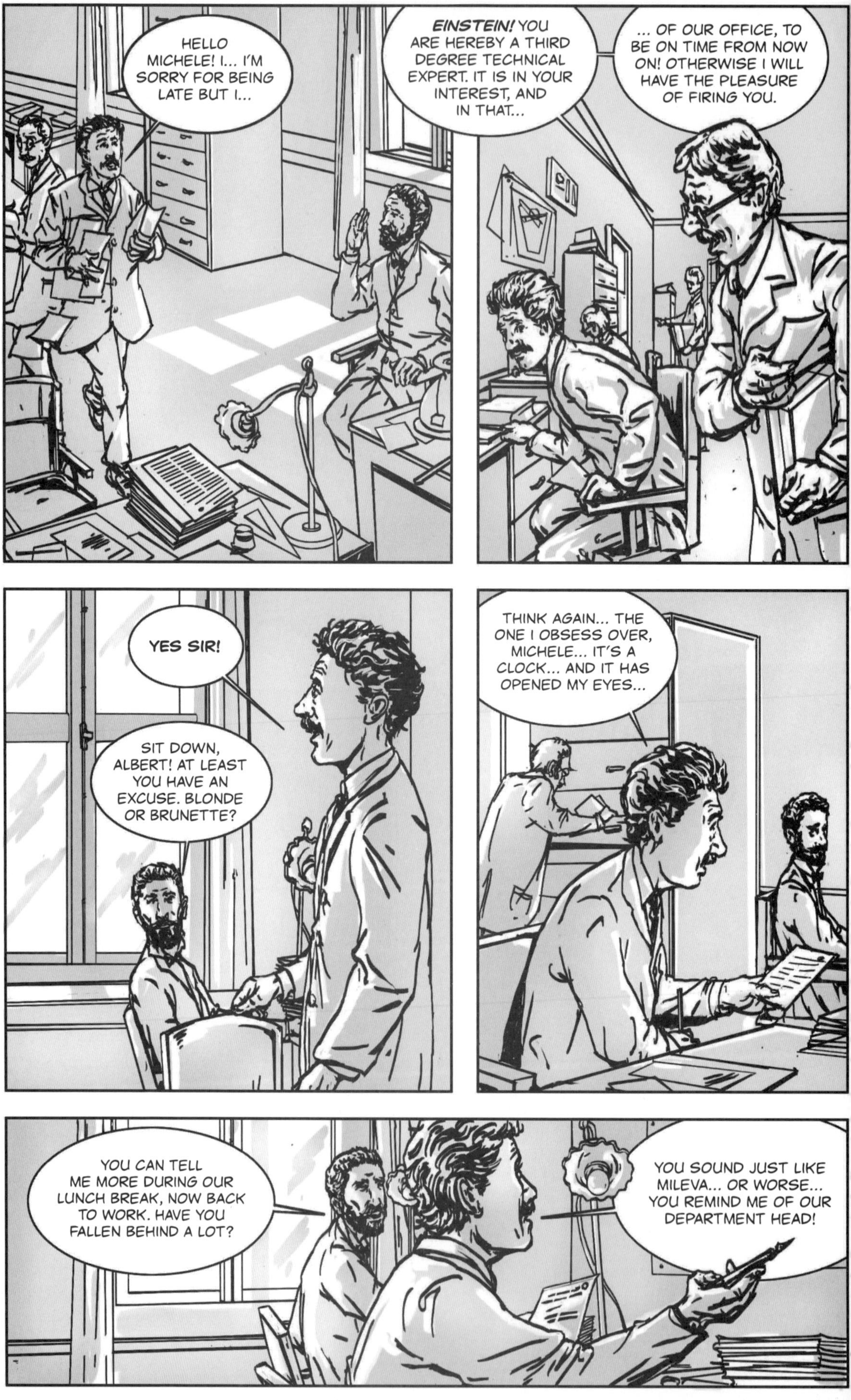
HELLO MICHELE! I... I'M SORRY FOR BEING LATE BUT I...
EINSTEIN! YOU ARE HEREBY A THIRD DEGREE TECHNICAL EXPERT. IT IS IN YOUR INTEREST, AND IN THAT...
... OF OUR OFFICE, TO BE ON TIME FROM NOW ON! OTHERWISE I WILL HAVE THE PLEASURE OF FIRING YOU.
YES SIR!
SIT DOWN, ALBERT! AT LEAST YOU HAVE AN EXCUSE. BLONDE OR BRUNETTE?
THINK AGAIN... THE ONE I OBSESS OVER, MICHELE... IT'S A CLOCK... AND IT HAS OPENED MY EYES...
YOU CAN TELL ME MORE DURING OUR LUNCH BREAK, NOW BACK TO WORK. HAVE YOU FALLEN BEHIND A LOT?
YOU SOUND JUST LIKE MILEVA... OR WORSE... YOU REMIND ME OF OUR DEPARTMENT HEAD!

I HAD JUST TURNED 26 YEARS OLD... AFTER OUR MARRIAGE IN 1903, MILEVA GAVE BIRTH TO OUR FIRST SON, HANS-ALBERT... BUT WE FOUGHT OFTEN.

MY WORK AT THE PATENT OFFICE ALLOWED ME TO ESCAPE FROM THAT TENSION.

DAY AFTER DAY, I WAS SUPPOSED TO APPROVE PATENTS IN ELECTROMAGNETISM THAT WERE DROPPED OFF AT THE INSTITUTE. THIS ALLOWED ME TO ACQUIRE A SENSE FOR SUMMARY AND TO ORGANIZE MY THOUGHTS.

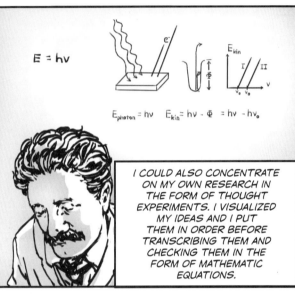

$E = h\nu$

$$E_{photon} = h\nu \qquad E_{kin} = h\nu - \Phi = h\nu - h\nu_0$$

I COULD ALSO CONCENTRATE ON MY OWN RESEARCH IN THE FORM OF THOUGHT EXPERIMENTS. I VISUALIZED MY IDEAS AND I PUT THEM IN ORDER BEFORE TRANSCRIBING THEM AND CHECKING THEM IN THE FORM OF MATHEMATIC EQUATIONS.

IT IS AT THIS POINT IN TIME THAT THE CONFEDERATION HAD ASKED PHYSICISTS TO WORK ON THE SYNCHRONIZATION OF CLOCKS SO THAT ALL THE STATIONS COULD BE ON THE SAME PAGE REGARDING TRAIN SCHEDULES.

REFLECTING ON THIS QUESTION WAS A NECESSARY EXPERIENCE FOR ME TO DEVELOP MY FIRST THEORIES. THEY WERE GOING TO ANNOUNCE THE THEORY OF SPECIAL RELATIVITY. QUESTIONING THE REAL AND SHAKING UP OUR RELATIONSHIP BETWEEN TIME AND SPACE, THAT WAS MY GOAL AND MY KNOWLEDGE OF ELECTROMAGNETISM* WAS GOING TO BE A GREAT HELP.

* BRANCH OF PHYSICS STUDYING THE INTERACTIONS BETWEEN ELECTRICALLY CHARGED PARTICLES. OF PARTICULAR INTEREST ARE DIFFERENT WAVES, INCLUDING THOSE THAT CONSTITUTE LIGHT.

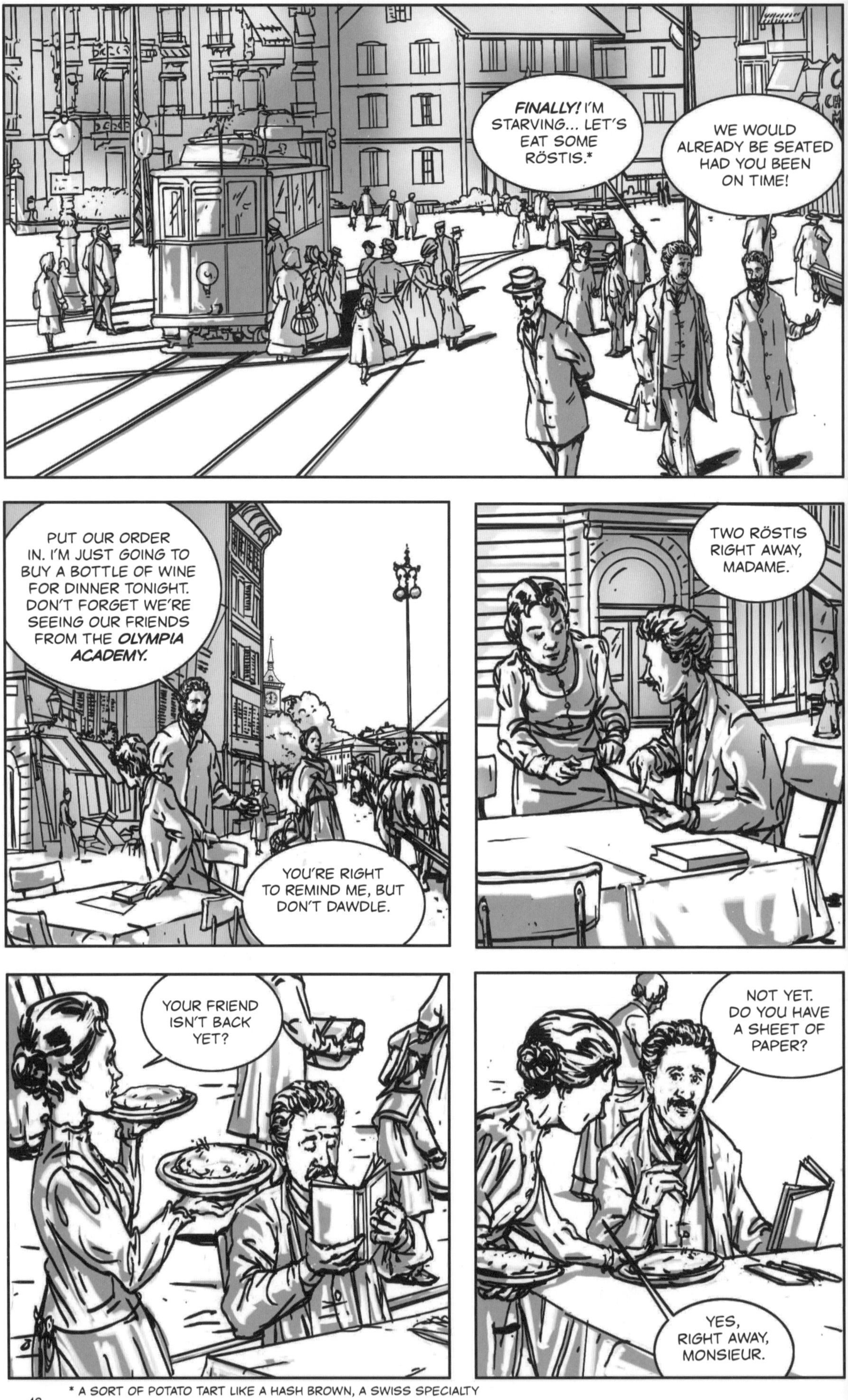
FINALLY! I'M STARVING... LET'S EAT SOME RÖSTIS.*
WE WOULD ALREADY BE SEATED HAD YOU BEEN ON TIME!
PUT OUR ORDER IN. I'M JUST GOING TO BUY A BOTTLE OF WINE FOR DINNER TONIGHT. DON'T FORGET WE'RE SEEING OUR FRIENDS FROM THE OLYMPIA ACADEMY.
YOU'RE RIGHT TO REMIND ME, BUT DON'T DAWDLE.
TWO RÖSTIS RIGHT AWAY, MADAME.
YOUR FRIEND ISN'T BACK YET?
NOT YET. DO YOU HAVE A SHEET OF PAPER?
YES, RIGHT AWAY, MONSIEUR.

* A SORT OF POTATO TART LIKE A HASH BROWN, A SWISS SPECIALTY

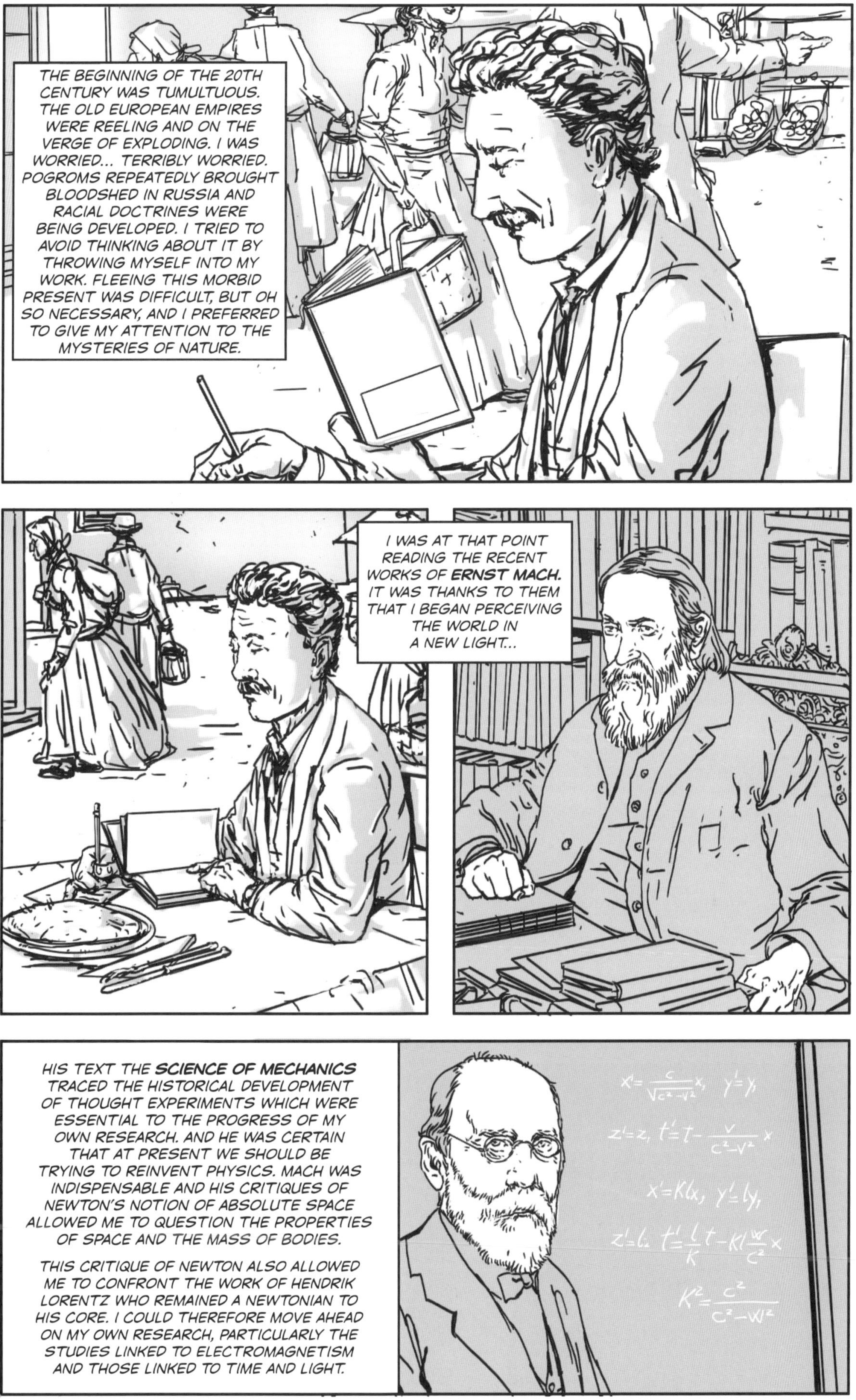
THE BEGINNING OF THE 20TH CENTURY WAS TUMULTUOUS. THE OLD EUROPEAN EMPIRES WERE REELING AND ON THE VERGE OF EXPLODING. I WAS WORRIED... TERRIBLY WORRIED. POGROMS REPEATEDLY BROUGHT BLOODSHED IN RUSSIA AND RACIAL DOCTRINES WERE BEING DEVELOPED. I TRIED TO AVOID THINKING ABOUT IT BY THROWING MYSELF INTO MY WORK. FLEEING THIS MORBID PRESENT WAS DIFFICULT, BUT OH SO NECESSARY, AND I PREFERRED TO GIVE MY ATTENTION TO THE MYSTERIES OF NATURE.
I WAS AT THAT POINT READING THE RECENT WORKS OF **ERNST MACH.** IT WAS THANKS TO THEM THAT I BEGAN PERCEIVING THE WORLD IN A NEW LIGHT...
HIS TEXT THE **SCIENCE OF MECHANICS** TRACED THE HISTORICAL DEVELOPMENT OF THOUGHT EXPERIMENTS WHICH WERE ESSENTIAL TO THE PROGRESS OF MY OWN RESEARCH. AND HE WAS CERTAIN THAT AT PRESENT WE SHOULD BE TRYING TO REINVENT PHYSICS. MACH WAS INDISPENSABLE AND HIS CRITIQUES OF NEWTON'S NOTION OF ABSOLUTE SPACE ALLOWED ME TO QUESTION THE PROPERTIES OF SPACE AND THE MASS OF BODIES.
THIS CRITIQUE OF NEWTON ALSO ALLOWED ME TO CONFRONT THE WORK OF HENDRIK LORENTZ WHO REMAINED A NEWTONIAN TO HIS CORE. I COULD THEREFORE MOVE AHEAD ON MY OWN RESEARCH, PARTICULARLY THE STUDIES LINKED TO ELECTROMAGNETISM AND THOSE LINKED TO TIME AND LIGHT.

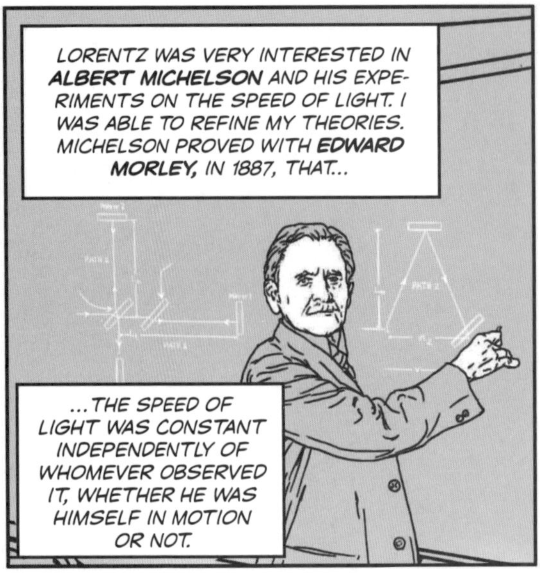
LORENTZ WAS VERY INTERESTED IN **ALBERT MICHELSON** AND HIS EXPERIMENTS ON THE SPEED OF LIGHT. I WAS ABLE TO REFINE MY THEORIES. MICHELSON PROVED WITH **EDWARD MORLEY,** IN 1887, THAT...
...THE SPEED OF LIGHT WAS CONSTANT INDEPENDENTLY OF WHOMEVER OBSERVED IT, WHETHER HE WAS HIMSELF IN MOTION OR NOT.

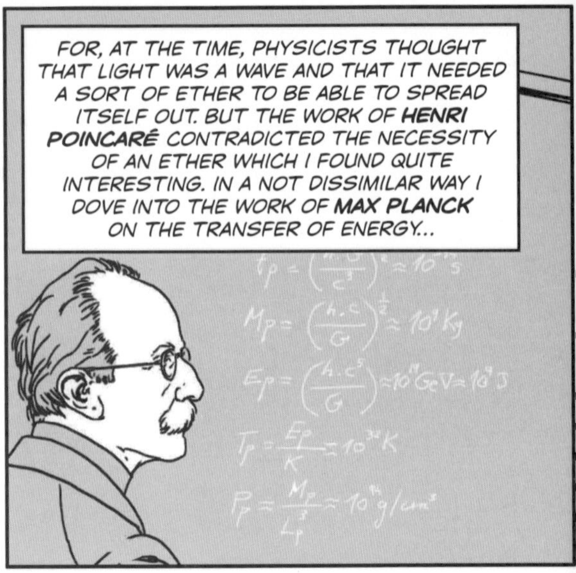
FOR, AT THE TIME, PHYSICISTS THOUGHT THAT LIGHT WAS A WAVE AND THAT IT NEEDED A SORT OF ETHER TO BE ABLE TO SPREAD ITSELF OUT. BUT THE WORK OF **HENRI POINCARÉ** CONTRADICTED THE NECESSITY OF AN ETHER WHICH I FOUND QUITE INTERESTING. IN A NOT DISSIMILAR WAY I DOVE INTO THE WORK OF **MAX PLANCK** ON THE TRANSFER OF ENERGY...

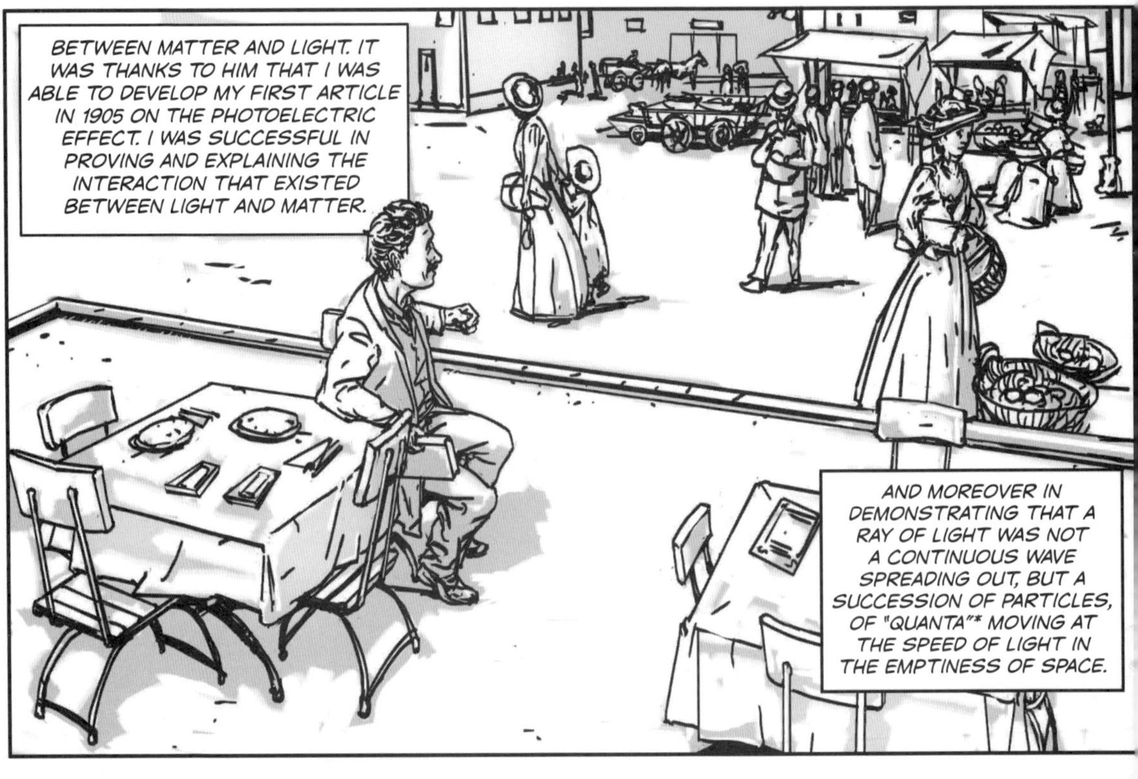
BETWEEN MATTER AND LIGHT. IT WAS THANKS TO HIM THAT I WAS ABLE TO DEVELOP MY FIRST ARTICLE IN 1905 ON THE PHOTOELECTRIC EFFECT. I WAS SUCCESSFUL IN PROVING AND EXPLAINING THE INTERACTION THAT EXISTED BETWEEN LIGHT AND MATTER.
AND MOREOVER IN DEMONSTRATING THAT A RAY OF LIGHT WAS NOT A CONTINUOUS WAVE SPREADING OUT, BUT A SUCCESSION OF PARTICLES, OF "QUANTA"* MOVING AT THE SPEED OF LIGHT IN THE EMPTINESS OF SPACE.

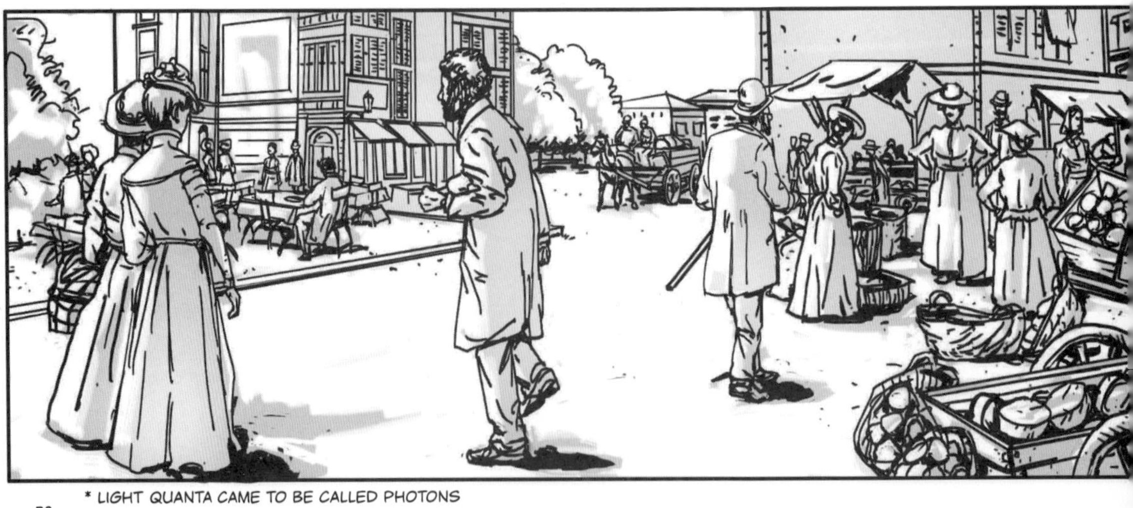

* LIGHT QUANTA CAME TO BE CALLED PHOTONS

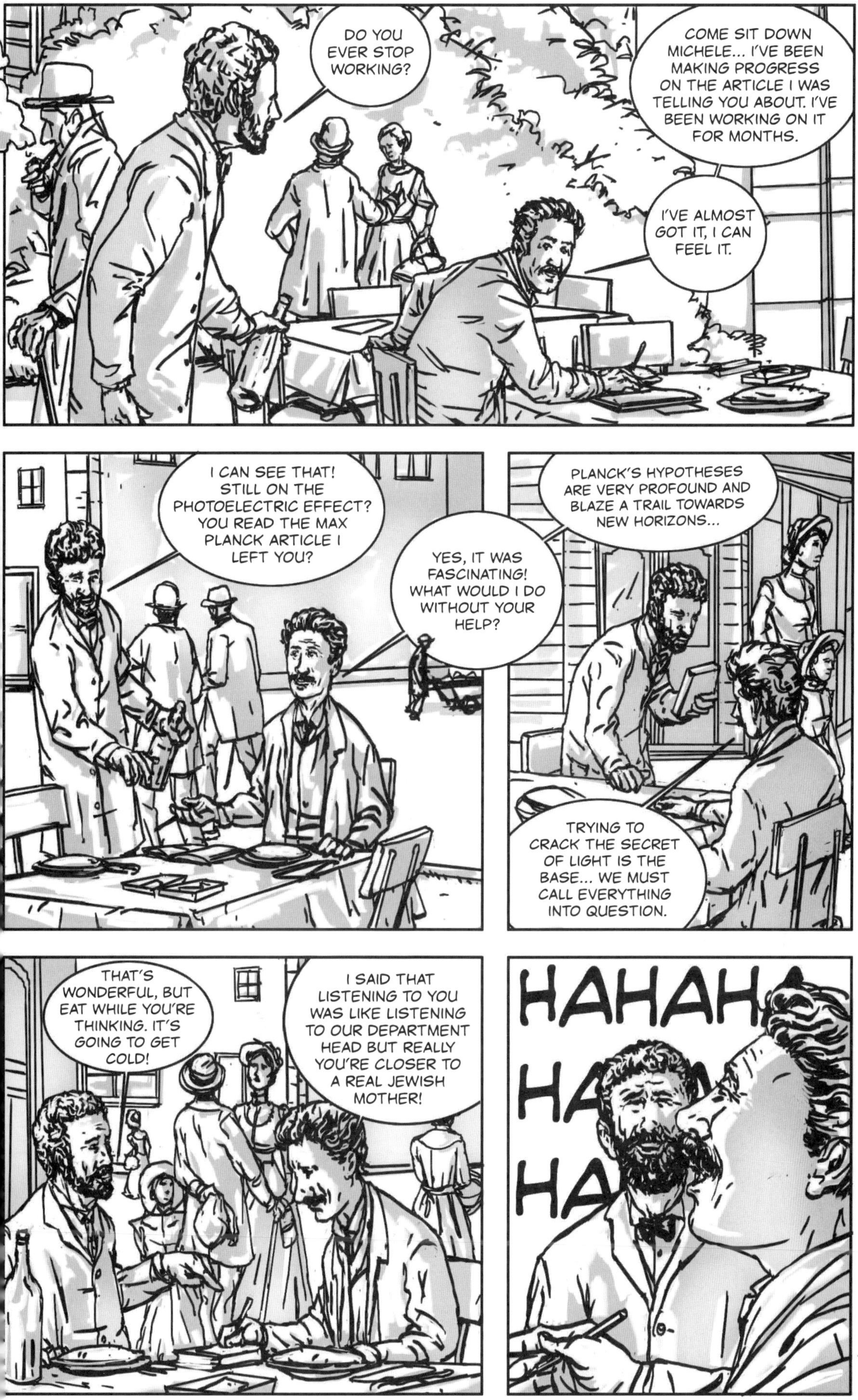
DO YOU EVER STOP WORKING?
COME SIT DOWN MICHELE... I'VE BEEN MAKING PROGRESS ON THE ARTICLE I WAS TELLING YOU ABOUT. I'VE BEEN WORKING ON IT FOR MONTHS.
I'VE ALMOST GOT IT, I CAN FEEL IT.
I CAN SEE THAT! STILL ON THE PHOTOELECTRIC EFFECT? YOU READ THE MAX PLANCK ARTICLE I LEFT YOU?
YES, IT WAS FASCINATING! WHAT WOULD I DO WITHOUT YOUR HELP?
PLANCK'S HYPOTHESES ARE VERY PROFOUND AND BLAZE A TRAIL TOWARDS NEW HORIZONS...
TRYING TO CRACK THE SECRET OF LIGHT IS THE BASE... WE MUST CALL EVERYTHING INTO QUESTION.
THAT'S WONDERFUL, BUT EAT WHILE YOU'RE THINKING. IT'S GOING TO GET COLD!
I SAID THAT LISTENING TO YOU WAS LIKE LISTENING TO OUR DEPARTMENT HEAD BUT REALLY YOU'RE CLOSER TO A REAL JEWISH MOTHER!

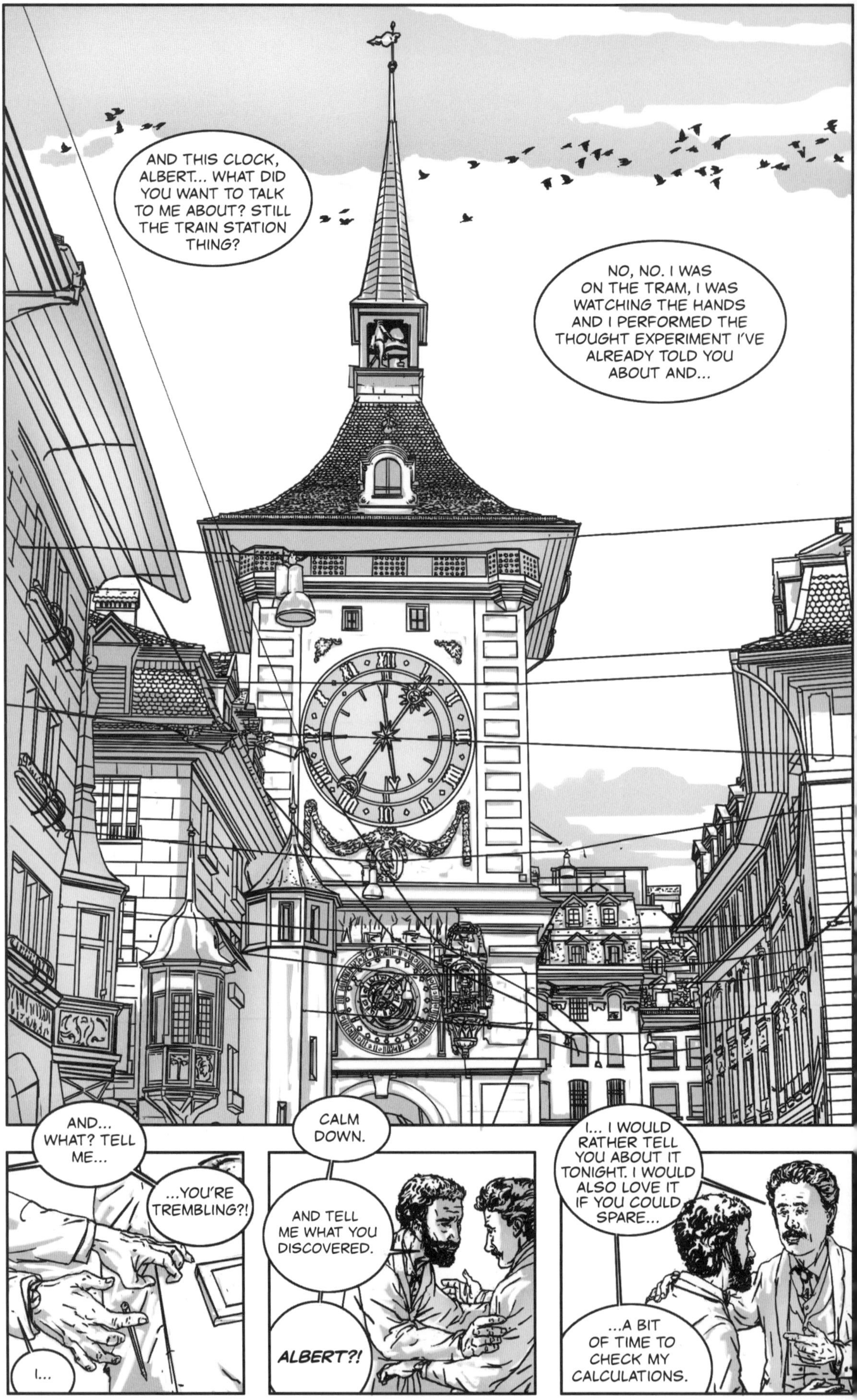
AND THIS CLOCK, ALBERT... WHAT DID YOU WANT TO TALK TO ME ABOUT? STILL THE TRAIN STATION THING?
NO, NO. I WAS ON THE TRAM, I WAS WATCHING THE HANDS AND I PERFORMED THE THOUGHT EXPERIMENT I'VE ALREADY TOLD YOU ABOUT AND...
AND... WHAT? TELL ME...
...YOU'RE TREMBLING?!
I...
CALM DOWN.
AND TELL ME WHAT YOU DISCOVERED.
ALBERT?!
I... I WOULD RATHER TELL YOU ABOUT IT TONIGHT. I WOULD ALSO LOVE IT IF YOU COULD SPARE...
...A BIT OF TIME TO CHECK MY CALCULATIONS.

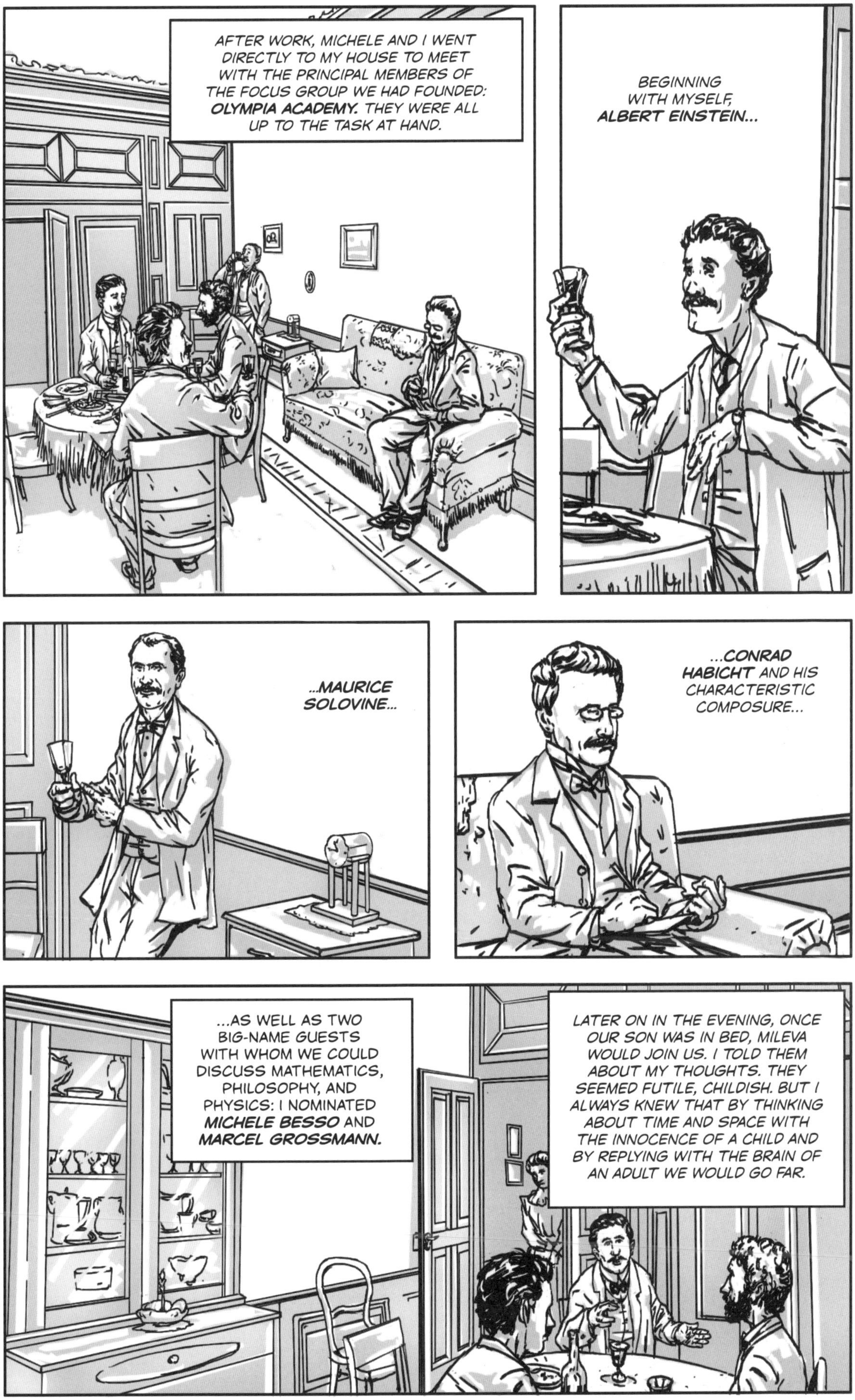
AFTER WORK, MICHELE AND I WENT DIRECTLY TO MY HOUSE TO MEET WITH THE PRINCIPAL MEMBERS OF THE FOCUS GROUP WE HAD FOUNDED: **OLYMPIA ACADEMY.** THEY WERE ALL UP TO THE TASK AT HAND.
BEGINNING WITH MYSELF, **ALBERT EINSTEIN...**
...MAURICE SOLOVINE...
...CONRAD HABICHT AND HIS CHARACTERISTIC COMPOSURE...
...AS WELL AS TWO BIG-NAME GUESTS WITH WHOM WE COULD DISCUSS MATHEMATICS, PHILOSOPHY, AND PHYSICS: I NOMINATED **MICHELE BESSO** AND **MARCEL GROSSMANN.**
LATER ON IN THE EVENING, ONCE OUR SON WAS IN BED, MILEVA WOULD JOIN US. I TOLD THEM ABOUT MY THOUGHTS. THEY SEEMED FUTILE, CHILDISH. BUT I ALWAYS KNEW THAT BY THINKING ABOUT TIME AND SPACE WITH THE INNOCENCE OF A CHILD AND BY REPLYING WITH THE BRAIN OF AN ADULT WE WOULD GO FAR.

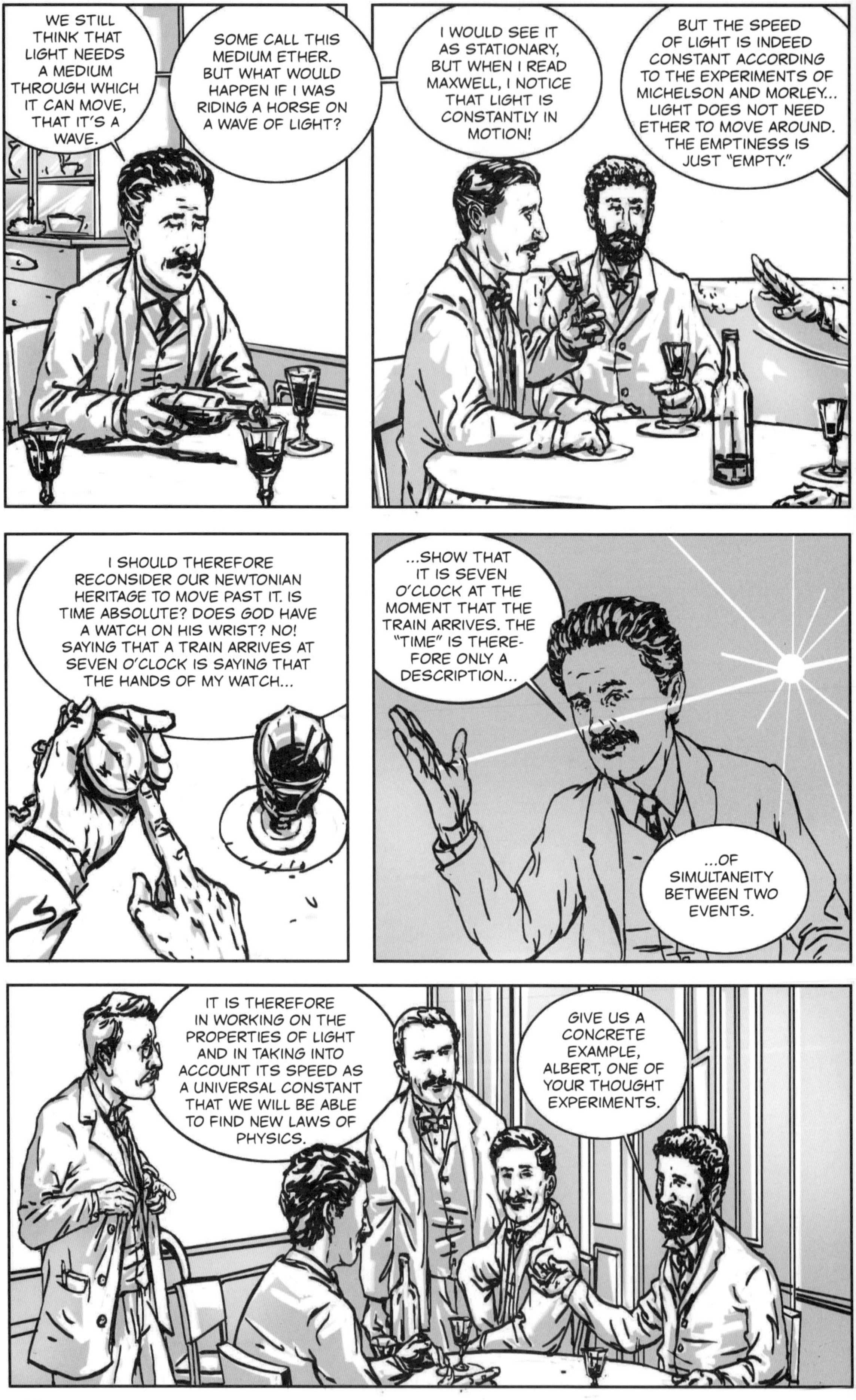
WE STILL THINK THAT LIGHT NEEDS A MEDIUM THROUGH WHICH IT CAN MOVE, THAT IT'S A WAVE.
SOME CALL THIS MEDIUM ETHER. BUT WHAT WOULD HAPPEN IF I WAS RIDING A HORSE ON A WAVE OF LIGHT?
I WOULD SEE IT AS STATIONARY, BUT WHEN I READ MAXWELL, I NOTICE THAT LIGHT IS CONSTANTLY IN MOTION!
BUT THE SPEED OF LIGHT IS INDEED CONSTANT ACCORDING TO THE EXPERIMENTS OF MICHELSON AND MORLEY... LIGHT DOES NOT NEED ETHER TO MOVE AROUND. THE EMPTINESS IS JUST "EMPTY."
I SHOULD THEREFORE RECONSIDER OUR NEWTONIAN HERITAGE TO MOVE PAST IT. IS TIME ABSOLUTE? DOES GOD HAVE A WATCH ON HIS WRIST? NO! SAYING THAT A TRAIN ARRIVES AT SEVEN O'CLOCK IS SAYING THAT THE HANDS OF MY WATCH...
...SHOW THAT IT IS SEVEN O'CLOCK AT THE MOMENT THAT THE TRAIN ARRIVES. THE "TIME" IS THEREFORE ONLY A DESCRIPTION...
...OF SIMULTANEITY BETWEEN TWO EVENTS.
IT IS THEREFORE IN WORKING ON THE PROPERTIES OF LIGHT AND IN TAKING INTO ACCOUNT ITS SPEED AS A UNIVERSAL CONSTANT THAT WE WILL BE ABLE TO FIND NEW LAWS OF PHYSICS.
GIVE US A CONCRETE EXAMPLE, ALBERT, ONE OF YOUR THOUGHT EXPERIMENTS.

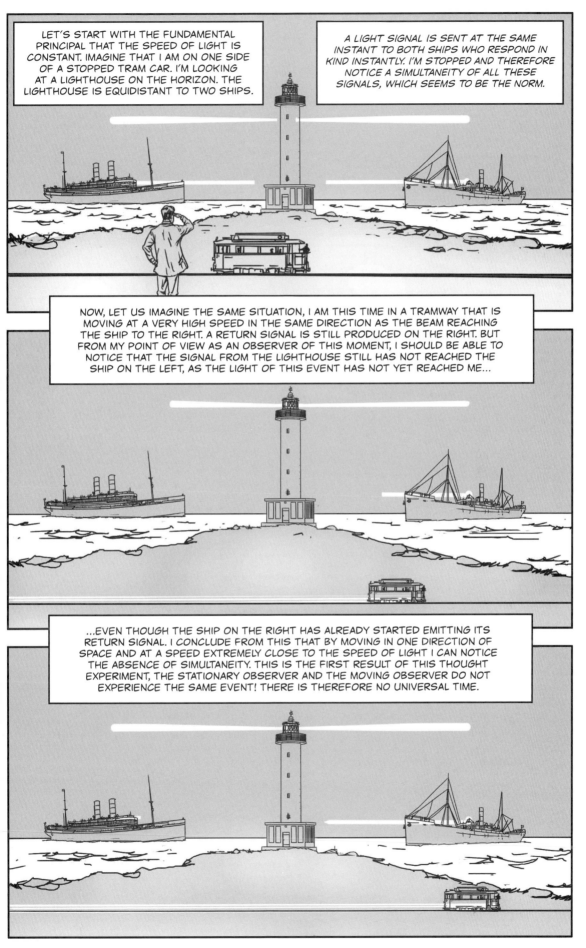

LET'S START WITH THE FUNDAMENTAL PRINCIPAL THAT THE SPEED OF LIGHT IS CONSTANT. IMAGINE THAT I AM ON ONE SIDE OF A STOPPED TRAM CAR. I'M LOOKING AT A LIGHTHOUSE ON THE HORIZON. THE LIGHTHOUSE IS EQUIDISTANT TO TWO SHIPS.

A LIGHT SIGNAL IS SENT AT THE SAME INSTANT TO BOTH SHIPS WHO RESPOND IN KIND INSTANTLY. I'M STOPPED AND THEREFORE NOTICE A SIMULTANEITY OF ALL THESE SIGNALS, WHICH SEEMS TO BE THE NORM.

NOW, LET US IMAGINE THE SAME SITUATION, I AM THIS TIME IN A TRAMWAY THAT IS MOVING AT A VERY HIGH SPEED IN THE SAME DIRECTION AS THE BEAM REACHING THE SHIP TO THE RIGHT. A RETURN SIGNAL IS STILL PRODUCED ON THE RIGHT. BUT FROM MY POINT OF VIEW AS AN OBSERVER OF THIS MOMENT, I SHOULD BE ABLE TO NOTICE THAT THE SIGNAL FROM THE LIGHTHOUSE STILL HAS NOT REACHED THE SHIP ON THE LEFT, AS THE LIGHT OF THIS EVENT HAS NOT YET REACHED ME...

...EVEN THOUGH THE SHIP ON THE RIGHT HAS ALREADY STARTED EMITTING ITS RETURN SIGNAL. I CONCLUDE FROM THIS THAT BY MOVING IN ONE DIRECTION OF SPACE AND AT A SPEED EXTREMELY CLOSE TO THE SPEED OF LIGHT I CAN NOTICE THE ABSENCE OF SIMULTANEITY. THIS IS THE FIRST RESULT OF THIS THOUGHT EXPERIMENT, THE STATIONARY OBSERVER AND THE MOVING OBSERVER DO NOT EXPERIENCE THE SAME EVENT! THERE IS THEREFORE NO UNIVERSAL TIME.

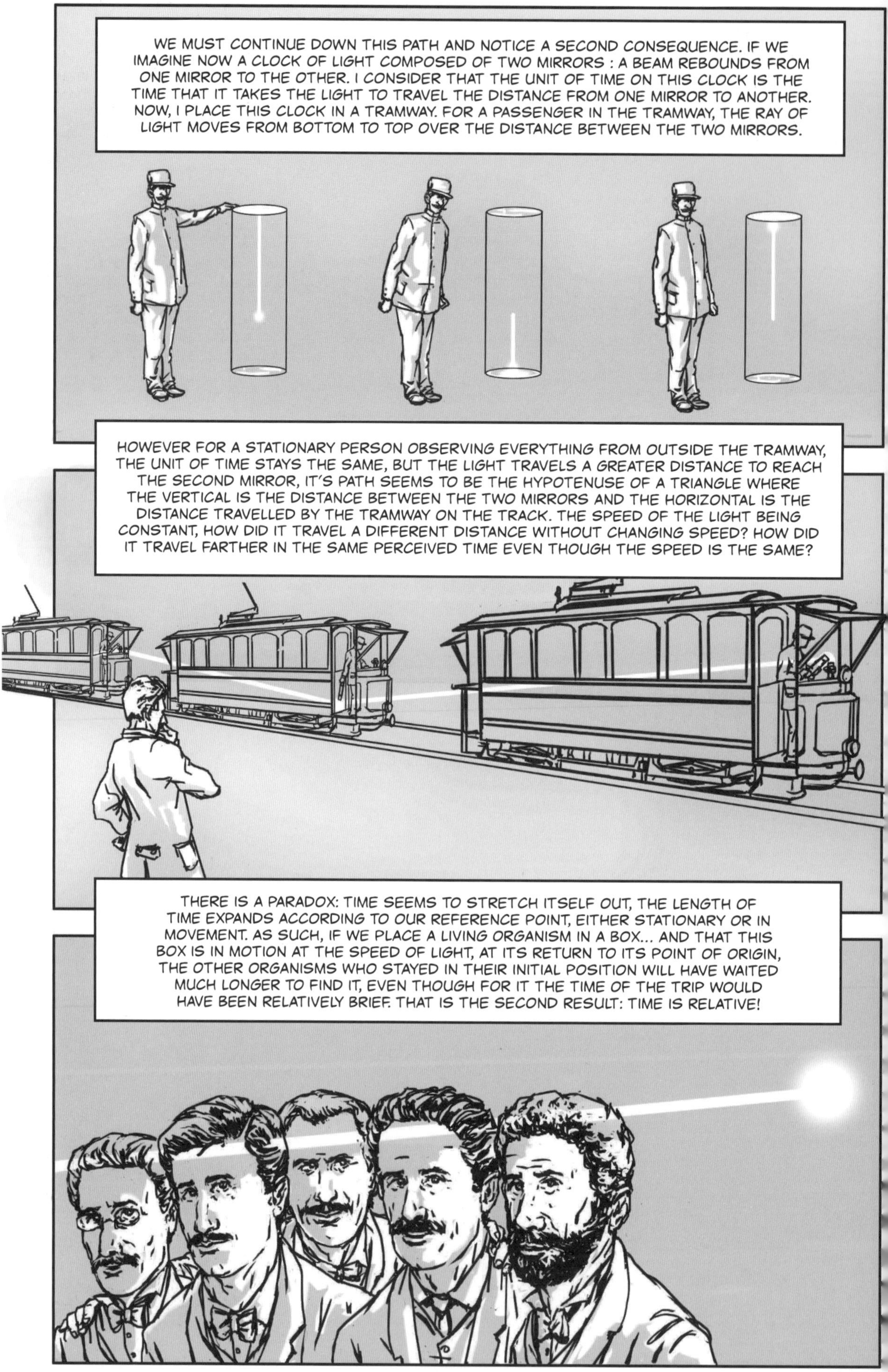
WE MUST CONTINUE DOWN THIS PATH AND NOTICE A SECOND CONSEQUENCE. IF WE IMAGINE NOW A CLOCK OF LIGHT COMPOSED OF TWO MIRRORS : A BEAM REBOUNDS FROM ONE MIRROR TO THE OTHER. I CONSIDER THAT THE UNIT OF TIME ON THIS CLOCK IS THE TIME THAT IT TAKES THE LIGHT TO TRAVEL THE DISTANCE FROM ONE MIRROR TO ANOTHER. NOW, I PLACE THIS CLOCK IN A TRAMWAY. FOR A PASSENGER IN THE TRAMWAY, THE RAY OF LIGHT MOVES FROM BOTTOM TO TOP OVER THE DISTANCE BETWEEN THE TWO MIRRORS.
HOWEVER FOR A STATIONARY PERSON OBSERVING EVERYTHING FROM OUTSIDE THE TRAMWAY, THE UNIT OF TIME STAYS THE SAME, BUT THE LIGHT TRAVELS A GREATER DISTANCE TO REACH THE SECOND MIRROR, IT'S PATH SEEMS TO BE THE HYPOTENUSE OF A TRIANGLE WHERE THE VERTICAL IS THE DISTANCE BETWEEN THE TWO MIRRORS AND THE HORIZONTAL IS THE DISTANCE TRAVELLED BY THE TRAMWAY ON THE TRACK. THE SPEED OF THE LIGHT BEING CONSTANT, HOW DID IT TRAVEL A DIFFERENT DISTANCE WITHOUT CHANGING SPEED? HOW DID IT TRAVEL FARTHER IN THE SAME PERCEIVED TIME EVEN THOUGH THE SPEED IS THE SAME?
THERE IS A PARADOX: TIME SEEMS TO STRETCH ITSELF OUT, THE LENGTH OF TIME EXPANDS ACCORDING TO OUR REFERENCE POINT, EITHER STATIONARY OR IN MOVEMENT. AS SUCH, IF WE PLACE A LIVING ORGANISM IN A BOX... AND THAT THIS BOX IS IN MOTION AT THE SPEED OF LIGHT, AT ITS RETURN TO ITS POINT OF ORIGIN, THE OTHER ORGANISMS WHO STAYED IN THEIR INITIAL POSITION WILL HAVE WAITED MUCH LONGER TO FIND IT, EVEN THOUGH FOR IT THE TIME OF THE TRIP WOULD HAVE BEEN RELATIVELY BRIEF. THAT IS THE SECOND RESULT: TIME IS RELATIVE!

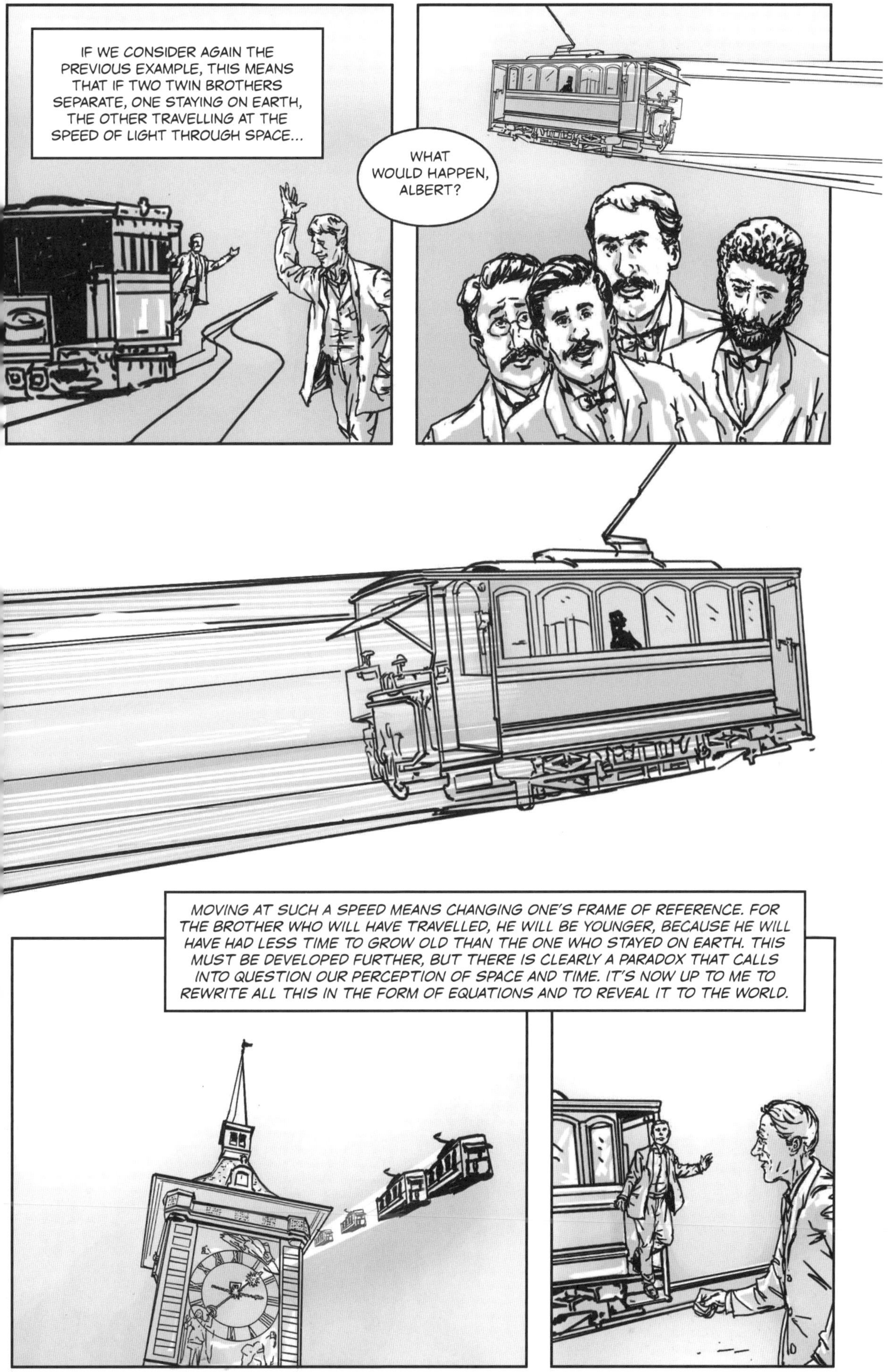
IF WE CONSIDER AGAIN THE PREVIOUS EXAMPLE, THIS MEANS THAT IF TWO TWIN BROTHERS SEPARATE, ONE STAYING ON EARTH, THE OTHER TRAVELLING AT THE SPEED OF LIGHT THROUGH SPACE...
WHAT WOULD HAPPEN, ALBERT?
MOVING AT SUCH A SPEED MEANS CHANGING ONE'S FRAME OF REFERENCE. FOR THE BROTHER WHO WILL HAVE TRAVELLED, HE WILL BE YOUNGER, BECAUSE HE WILL HAVE HAD LESS TIME TO GROW OLD THAN THE ONE WHO STAYED ON EARTH. THIS MUST BE DEVELOPED FURTHER, BUT THERE IS CLEARLY A PARADOX THAT CALLS INTO QUESTION OUR PERCEPTION OF SPACE AND TIME. IT'S NOW UP TO ME TO REWRITE ALL THIS IN THE FORM OF EQUATIONS AND TO REVEAL IT TO THE WORLD.

WE WERE ALL A BIT STUNNED... AFTER DINNER, WE WENT OUT IN THE STREETS OF BERN TO TAKE FULL ADVANTAGE OF THE NIGHT.

THANKS TO THE CIRCLE OF THE OLYMPIA ACADEMY AND TO MICHELE BESSO, I COULD MAKE PROGRESS AND STRUCTURE MY THINKING. EVERYONE, WITHOUT EXCEPTION, CONTRIBUTED TO THIS FERTILE DIALOGUE...

...I NEVER COULD HAVE HOPED FOR BETTER COMPANIONS OR A BETTER AUDIENCE TO WHOM I COULD EXPRESS MY IDEAS AND WHO COULD SEE THOSE IDEAS EMERGE. THEY GAVE A PRECISE FRAMEWORK TO MY THEORIES.

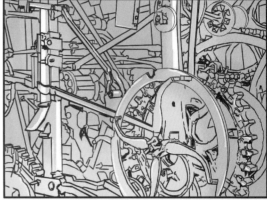

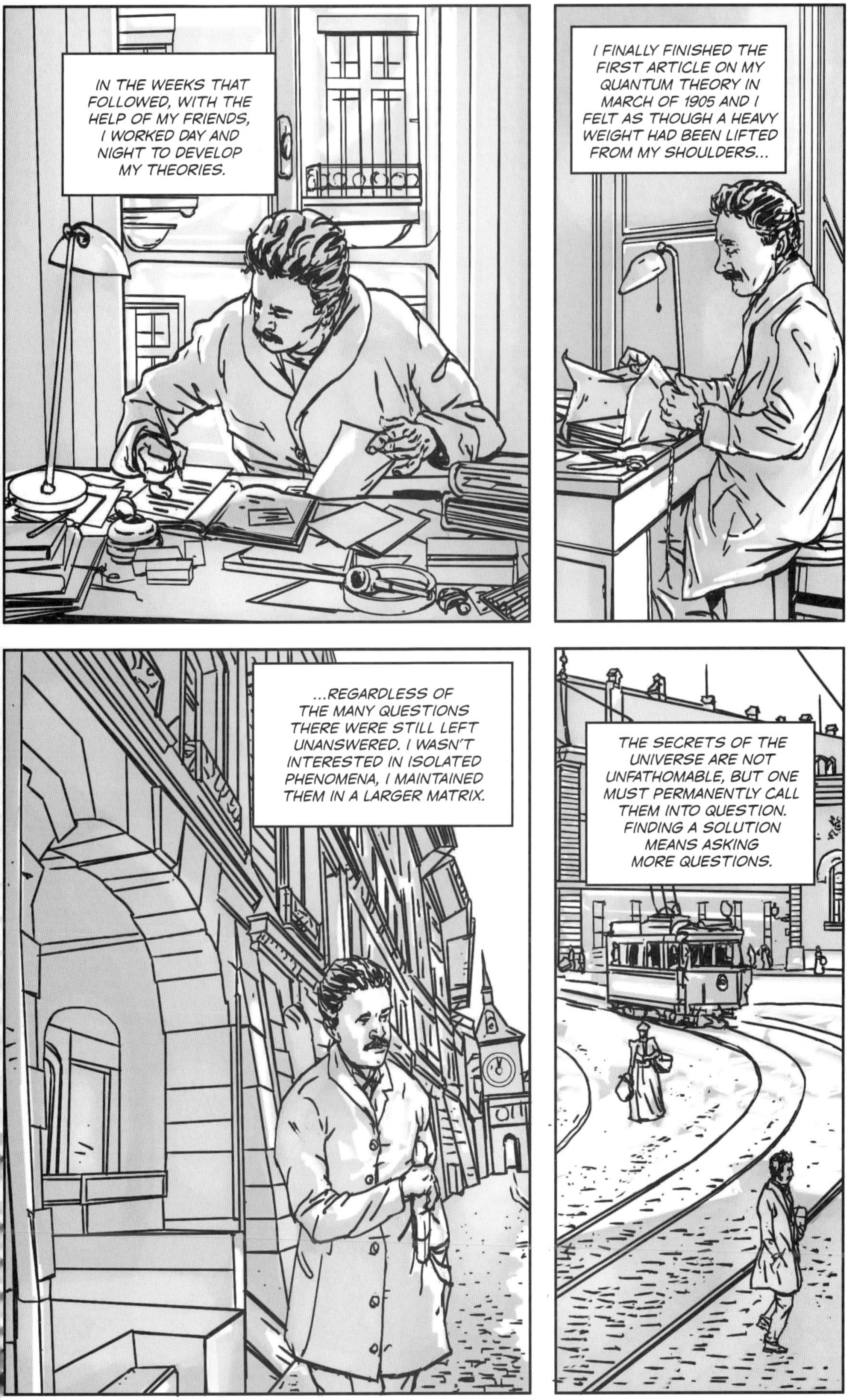
IN THE WEEKS THAT FOLLOWED, WITH THE HELP OF MY FRIENDS, I WORKED DAY AND NIGHT TO DEVELOP MY THEORIES.
I FINALLY FINISHED THE FIRST ARTICLE ON MY QUANTUM THEORY IN MARCH OF 1905 AND I FELT AS THOUGH A HEAVY WEIGHT HAD BEEN LIFTED FROM MY SHOULDERS...
...REGARDLESS OF THE MANY QUESTIONS THERE WERE STILL LEFT UNANSWERED. I WASN'T INTERESTED IN ISOLATED PHENOMENA, I MAINTAINED THEM IN A LARGER MATRIX.
THE SECRETS OF THE UNIVERSE ARE NOT UNFATHOMABLE, BUT ONE MUST PERMANENTLY CALL THEM INTO QUESTION. FINDING A SOLUTION MEANS ASKING MORE QUESTIONS.

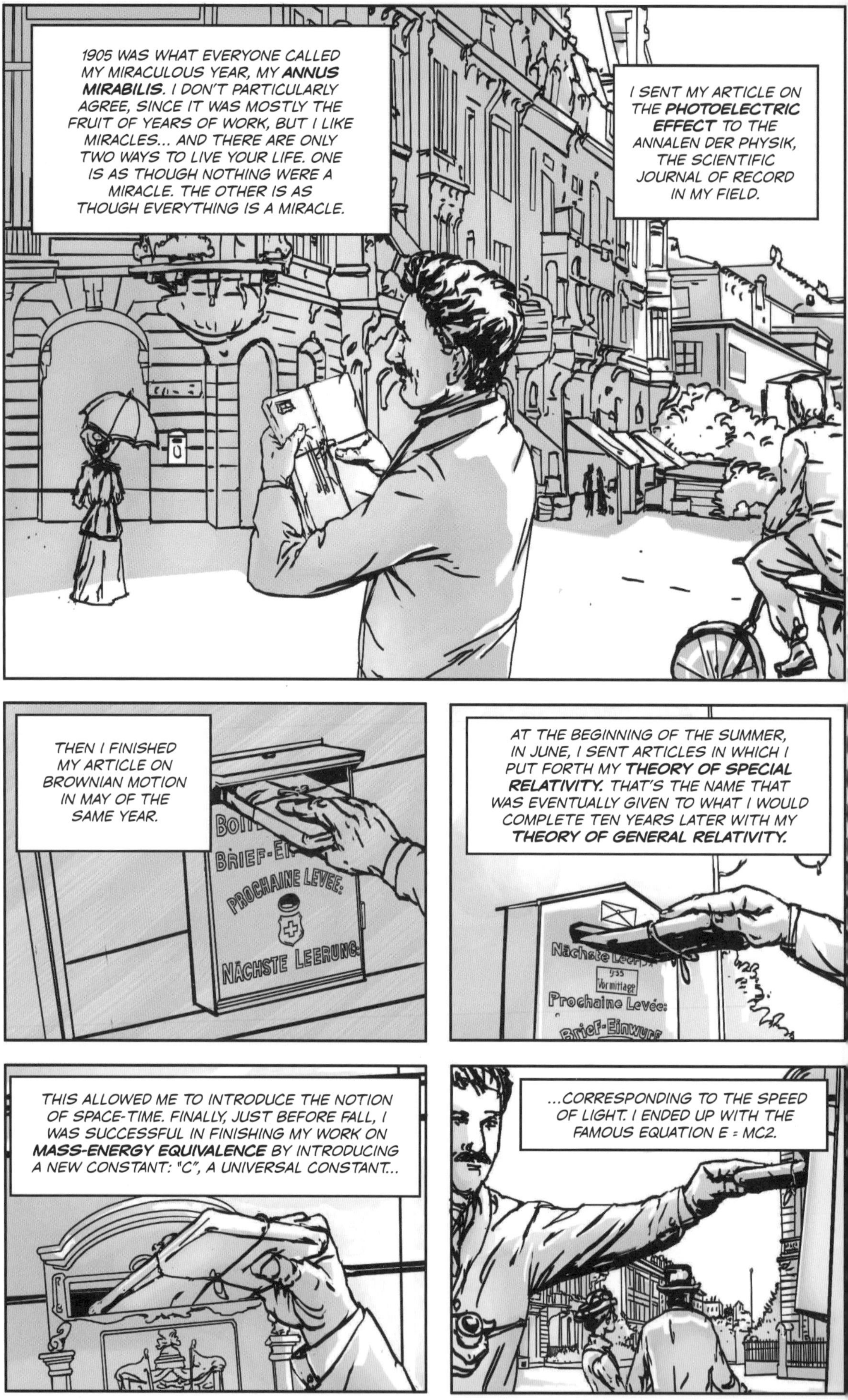
1905 WAS WHAT EVERYONE CALLED MY MIRACULOUS YEAR, MY **ANNUS MIRABILIS**. I DON'T PARTICULARLY AGREE, SINCE IT WAS MOSTLY THE FRUIT OF YEARS OF WORK, BUT I LIKE MIRACLES... AND THERE ARE ONLY TWO WAYS TO LIVE YOUR LIFE. ONE IS AS THOUGH NOTHING WERE A MIRACLE. THE OTHER IS AS THOUGH EVERYTHING IS A MIRACLE.
I SENT MY ARTICLE ON THE **PHOTOELECTRIC EFFECT** TO THE ANNALEN DER PHYSIK, THE SCIENTIFIC JOURNAL OF RECORD IN MY FIELD.
THEN I FINISHED MY ARTICLE ON BROWNIAN MOTION IN MAY OF THE SAME YEAR.
PROCHAINE LEVEE:
NÄCHSTE LEERUNG:
AT THE BEGINNING OF THE SUMMER, IN JUNE, I SENT ARTICLES IN WHICH I PUT FORTH MY **THEORY OF SPECIAL RELATIVITY.** THAT'S THE NAME THAT WAS EVENTUALLY GIVEN TO WHAT I WOULD COMPLETE TEN YEARS LATER WITH MY **THEORY OF GENERAL RELATIVITY.**
Vormittags
Prochaine Levée:
Brief-Einwurf
THIS ALLOWED ME TO INTRODUCE THE NOTION OF SPACE-TIME. FINALLY, JUST BEFORE FALL, I WAS SUCCESSFUL IN FINISHING MY WORK ON **MASS-ENERGY EQUIVALENCE** BY INTRODUCING A NEW CONSTANT: "C", A UNIVERSAL CONSTANT...
...CORRESPONDING TO THE SPEED OF LIGHT. I ENDED UP WITH THE FAMOUS EQUATION E = MC2.

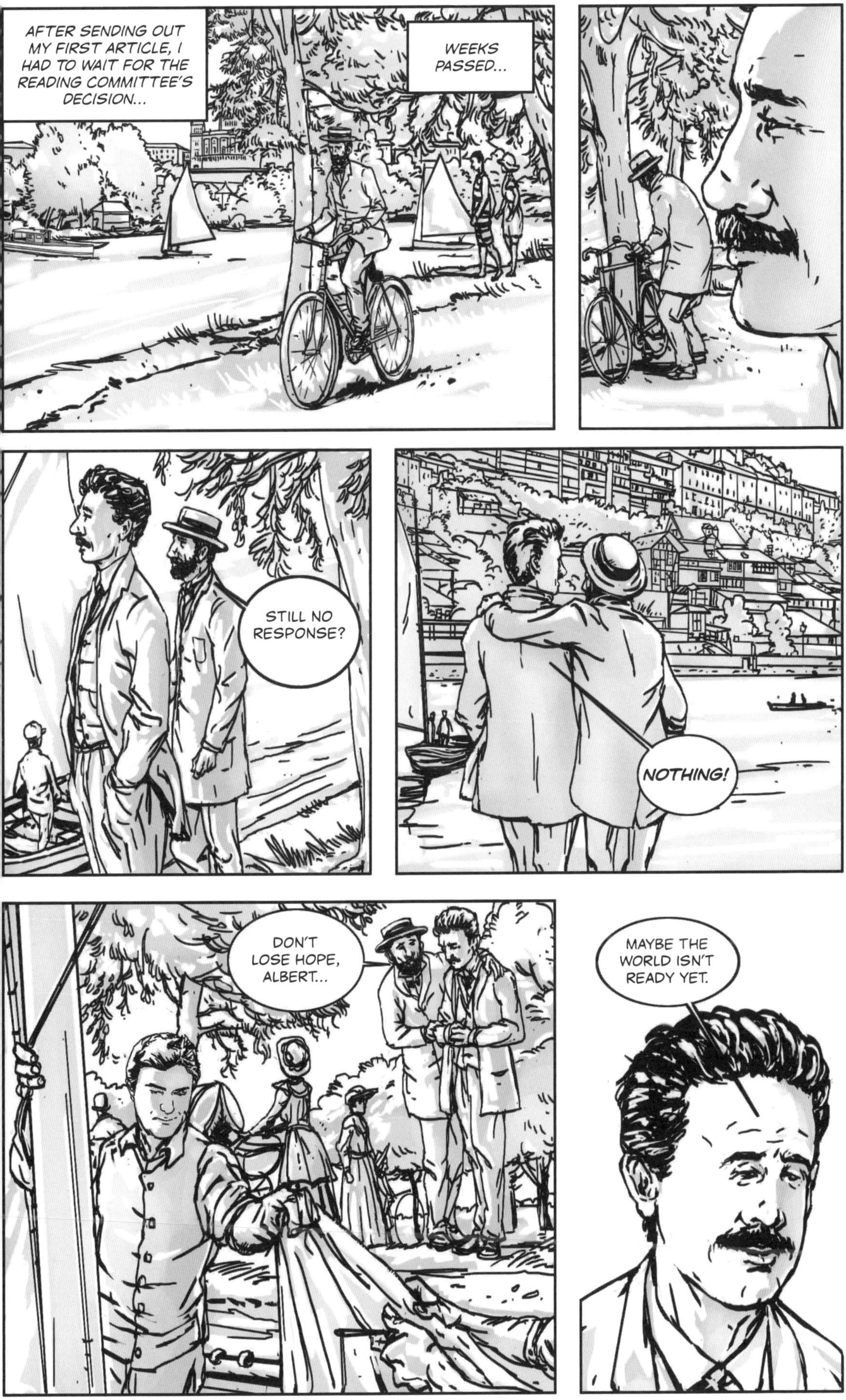
AFTER SENDING OUT MY FIRST ARTICLE, I HAD TO WAIT FOR THE READING COMMITTEE'S DECISION...
WEEKS PASSED...
STILL NO RESPONSE?
NOTHING!
DON'T LOSE HOPE, ALBERT...
MAYBE THE WORLD ISN'T READY YET.

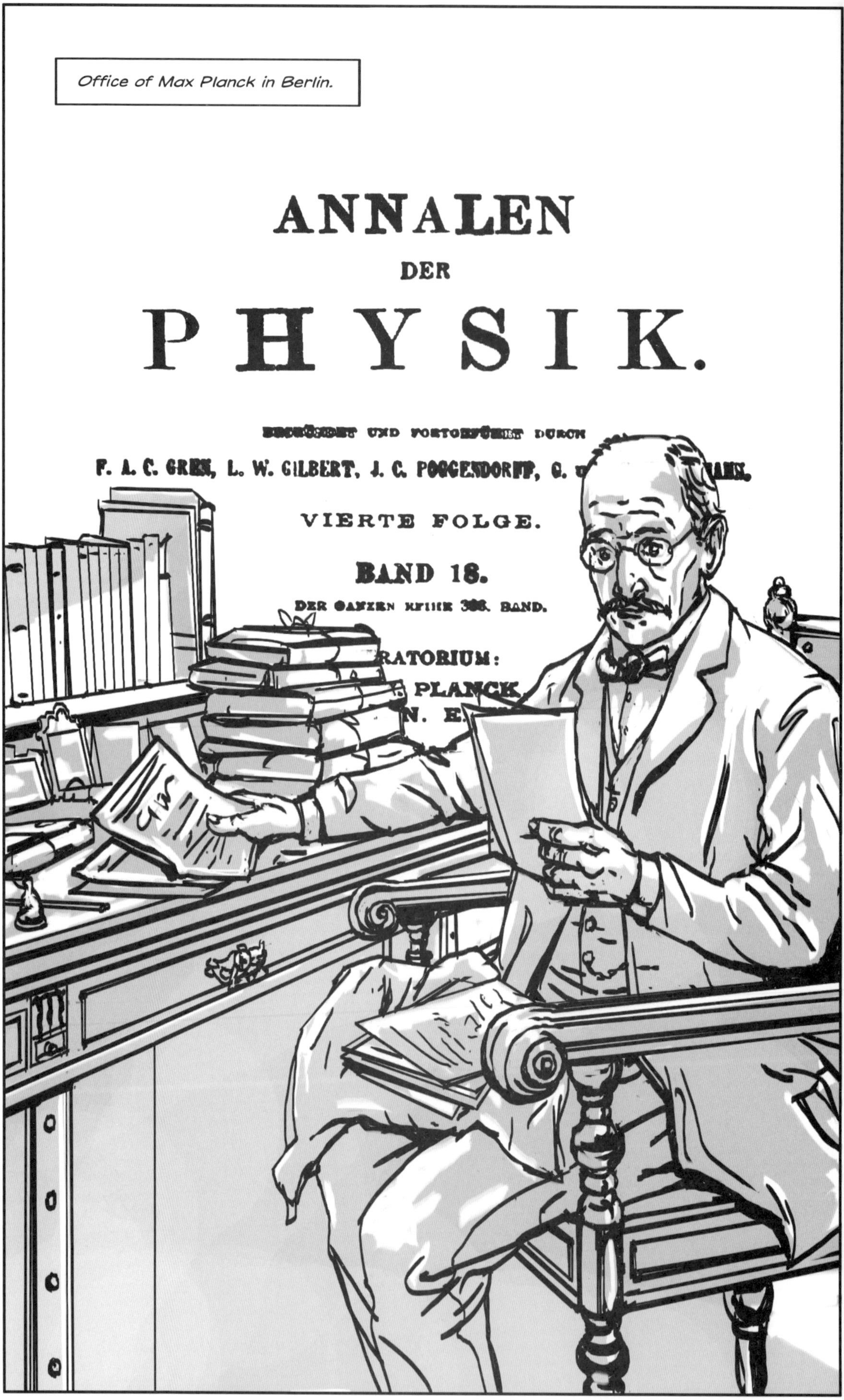
Office of Max Planck in Berlin.
ANNALEN
DER
PHYSIK.
VIERTE FOLGE.
BAND 18.

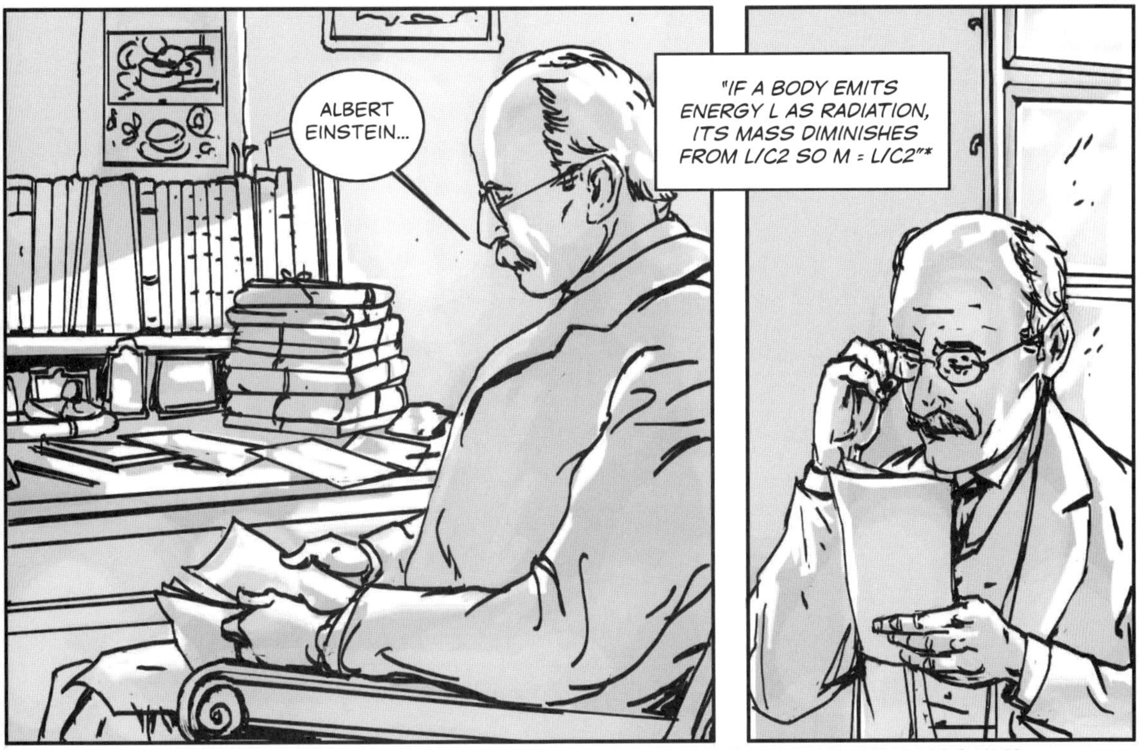
ALBERT EINSTEIN...
"IF A BODY EMITS ENERGY L AS RADIATION, ITS MASS DIMINISHES FROM L/C2 SO M = L/C2"*

*IT WAS NOT UNTIL 1923 AND THE APPEARANCE OF THE ENGLISH TRANSLATION THAT THE NOTATION E = MC2 IS ESTABLISHED.

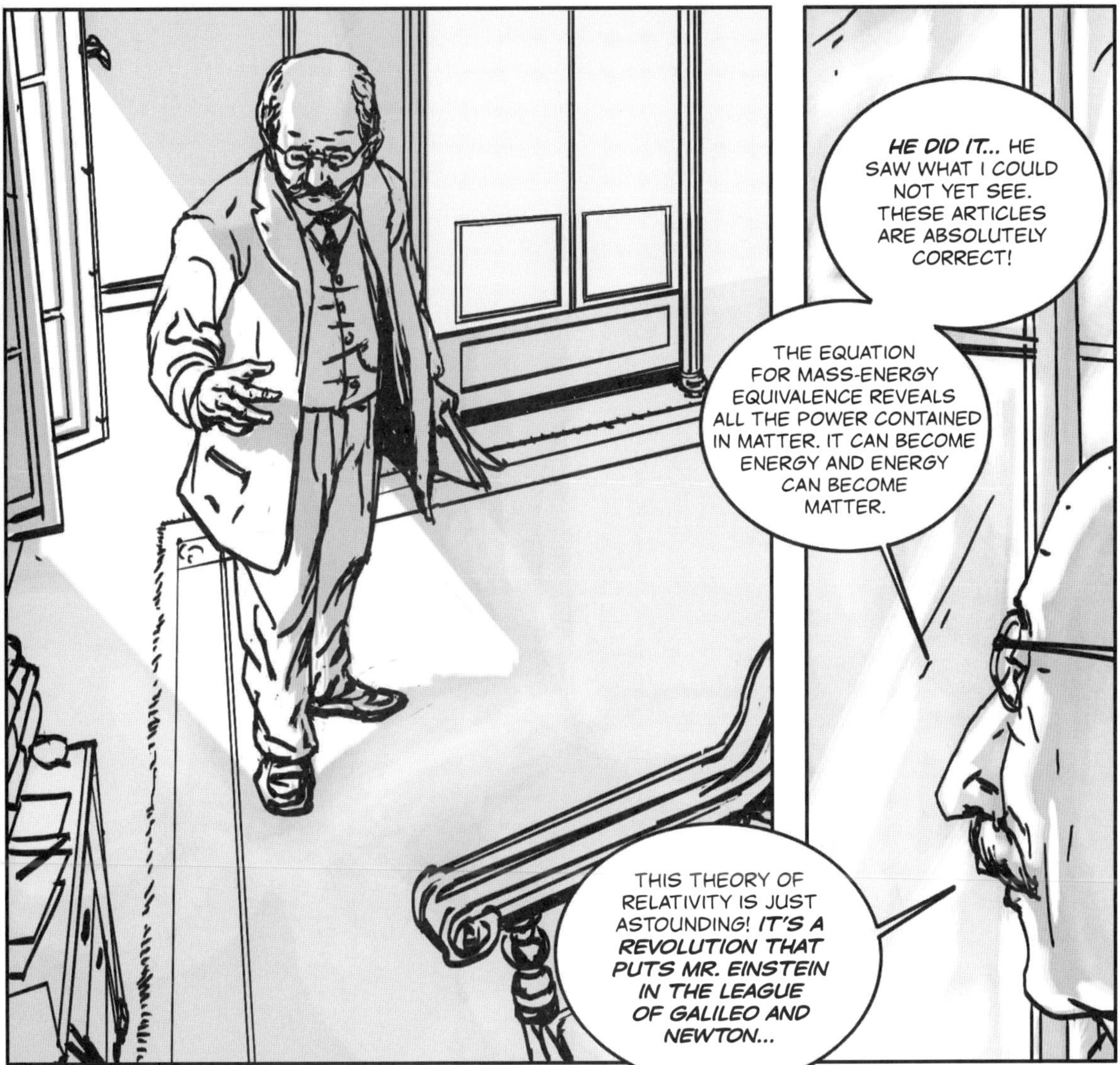
HE DID IT... HE SAW WHAT I COULD NOT YET SEE. THESE ARTICLES ARE ABSOLUTELY CORRECT!
THE EQUATION FOR MASS-ENERGY EQUIVALENCE REVEALS ALL THE POWER CONTAINED IN MATTER. IT CAN BECOME ENERGY AND ENERGY CAN BECOME MATTER.
THIS THEORY OF RELATIVITY IS JUST ASTOUNDING! IT'S A REVOLUTION THAT PUTS MR. EINSTEIN IN THE LEAGUE OF GALILEO AND NEWTON...

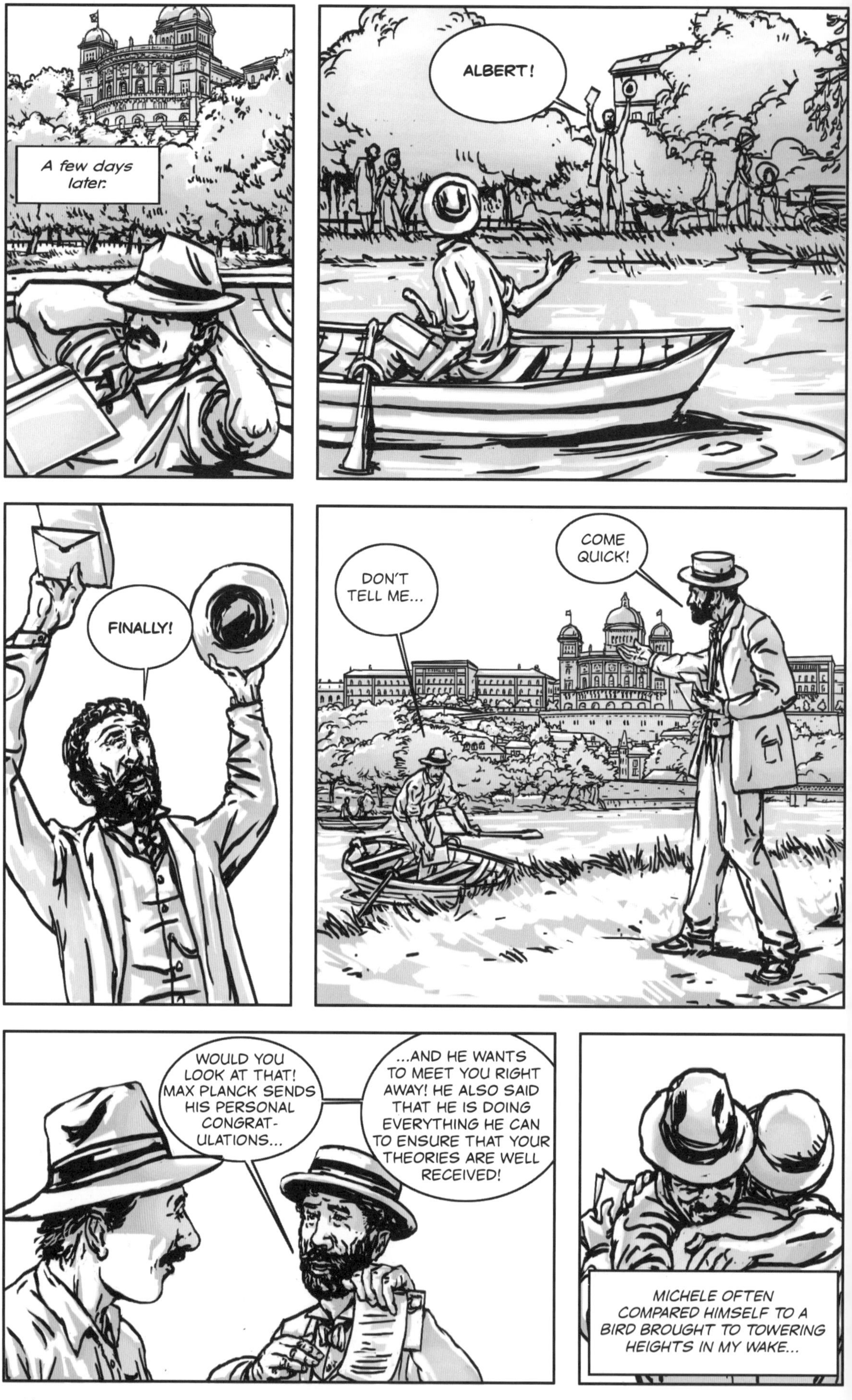
A few days later.
ALBERT!
FINALLY!
DON'T TELL ME...
COME QUICK!
WOULD YOU LOOK AT THAT! MAX PLANCK SENDS HIS PERSONAL CONGRAT-ULATIONS...
...AND HE WANTS TO MEET YOU RIGHT AWAY! HE ALSO SAID THAT HE IS DOING EVERYTHING HE CAN TO ENSURE THAT YOUR THEORIES ARE WELL RECEIVED!
MICHELE OFTEN COMPARED HIMSELF TO A BIRD BROUGHT TO TOWERING HEIGHTS IN MY WAKE...

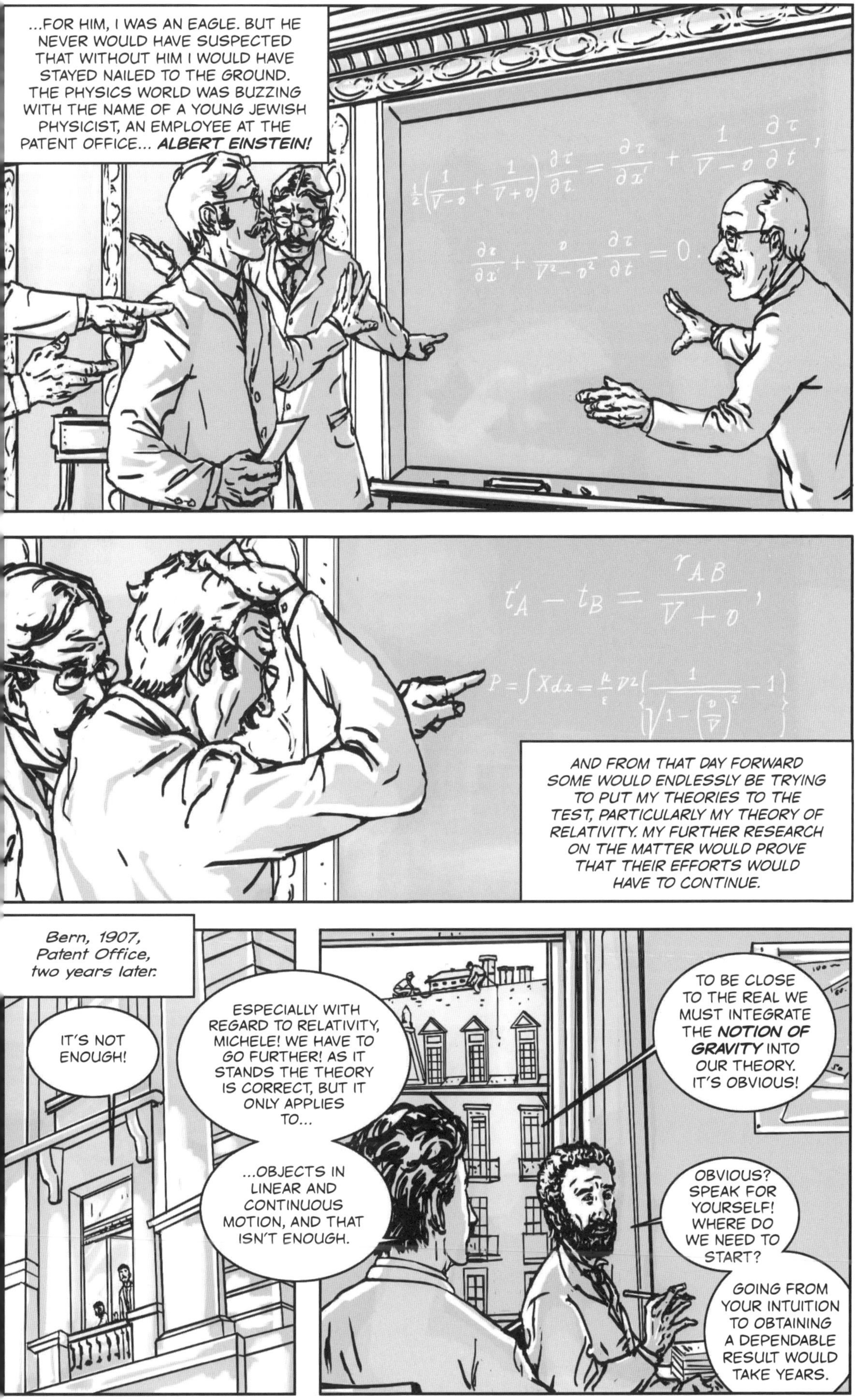
...FOR HIM, I WAS AN EAGLE. BUT HE NEVER WOULD HAVE SUSPECTED THAT WITHOUT HIM I WOULD HAVE STAYED NAILED TO THE GROUND. THE PHYSICS WORLD WAS BUZZING WITH THE NAME OF A YOUNG JEWISH PHYSICIST, AN EMPLOYEE AT THE PATENT OFFICE... ALBERT EINSTEIN!
AND FROM THAT DAY FORWARD SOME WOULD ENDLESSLY BE TRYING TO PUT MY THEORIES TO THE TEST, PARTICULARLY MY THEORY OF RELATIVITY. MY FURTHER RESEARCH ON THE MATTER WOULD PROVE THAT THEIR EFFORTS WOULD HAVE TO CONTINUE.
Bern, 1907, Patent Office, two years later.
IT'S NOT ENOUGH!
ESPECIALLY WITH REGARD TO RELATIVITY, MICHELE! WE HAVE TO GO FURTHER! AS IT STANDS THE THEORY IS CORRECT, BUT IT ONLY APPLIES TO...
...OBJECTS IN LINEAR AND CONTINUOUS MOTION, AND THAT ISN'T ENOUGH.
TO BE CLOSE TO THE REAL WE MUST INTEGRATE THE NOTION OF GRAVITY INTO OUR THEORY. IT'S OBVIOUS!
OBVIOUS? SPEAK FOR YOURSELF! WHERE DO WE NEED TO START?
GOING FROM YOUR INTUITION TO OBTAINING A DEPENDABLE RESULT WOULD TAKE YEARS.

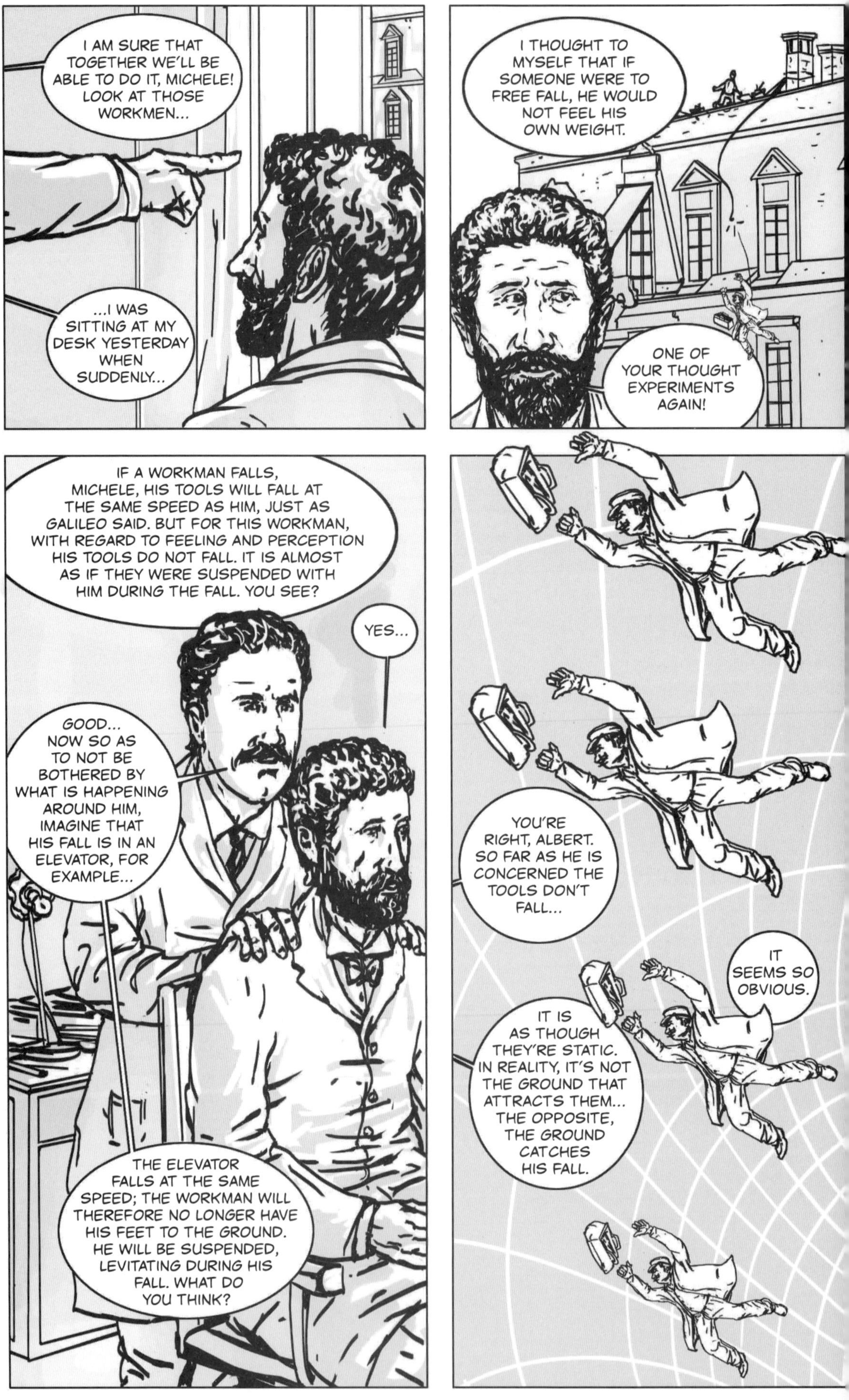
I AM SURE THAT TOGETHER WE'LL BE ABLE TO DO IT, MICHELE! LOOK AT THOSE WORKMEN...
...I WAS SITTING AT MY DESK YESTERDAY WHEN SUDDENLY...
I THOUGHT TO MYSELF THAT IF SOMEONE WERE TO FREE FALL, HE WOULD NOT FEEL HIS OWN WEIGHT.
ONE OF YOUR THOUGHT EXPERIMENTS AGAIN!
IF A WORKMAN FALLS, MICHELE, HIS TOOLS WILL FALL AT THE SAME SPEED AS HIM, JUST AS GALILEO SAID. BUT FOR THIS WORKMAN, WITH REGARD TO FEELING AND PERCEPTION HIS TOOLS DO NOT FALL. IT IS ALMOST AS IF THEY WERE SUSPENDED WITH HIM DURING THE FALL. YOU SEE?
YES...
GOOD... NOW SO AS TO NOT BE BOTHERED BY WHAT IS HAPPENING AROUND HIM, IMAGINE THAT HIS FALL IS IN AN ELEVATOR, FOR EXAMPLE...
THE ELEVATOR FALLS AT THE SAME SPEED; THE WORKMAN WILL THEREFORE NO LONGER HAVE HIS FEET TO THE GROUND. HE WILL BE SUSPENDED, LEVITATING DURING HIS FALL. WHAT DO YOU THINK?
YOU'RE RIGHT, ALBERT. SO FAR AS HE IS CONCERNED THE TOOLS DON'T FALL...
IT SEEMS SO OBVIOUS.
IT IS AS THOUGH THEY'RE STATIC. IN REALITY, IT'S NOT THE GROUND THAT ATTRACTS THEM... THE OPPOSITE, THE GROUND CATCHES HIS FALL.

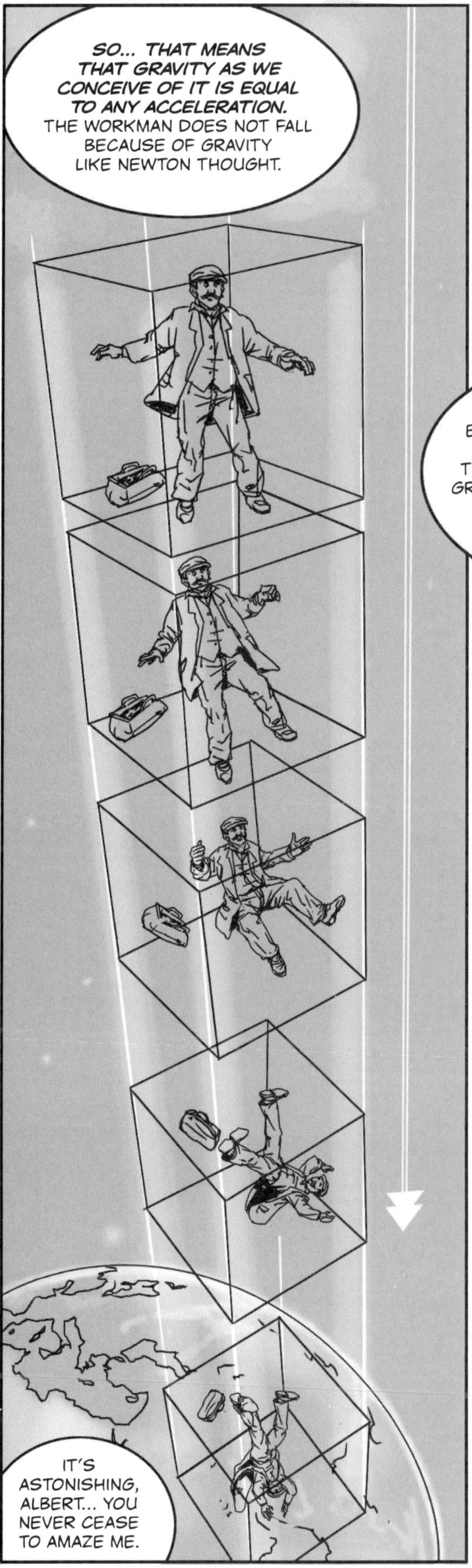
SO... THAT MEANS THAT GRAVITY AS WE CONCEIVE OF IT IS EQUAL TO ANY ACCELERATION. THE WORKMAN DOES NOT FALL BECAUSE OF GRAVITY LIKE NEWTON THOUGHT.
IT'S ASTONISHING, ALBERT... YOU NEVER CEASE TO AMAZE ME.
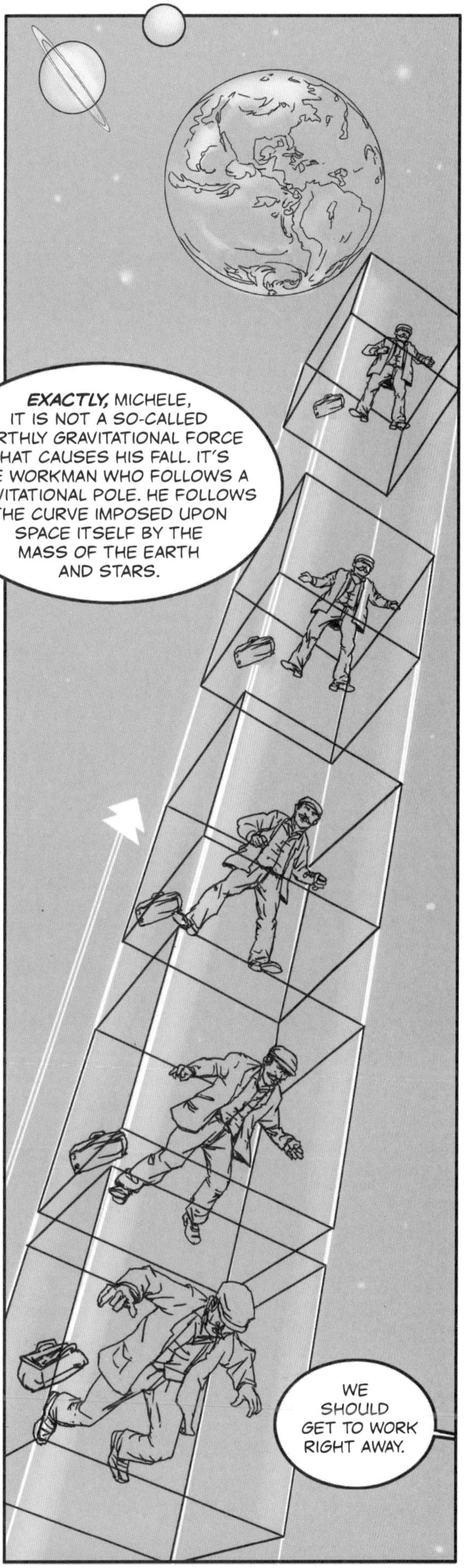
EXACTLY, MICHELE, IT IS NOT A SO-CALLED EARTHLY GRAVITATIONAL FORCE THAT CAUSES HIS FALL. IT'S THE WORKMAN WHO FOLLOWS A GRAVITATIONAL POLE. HE FOLLOWS THE CURVE IMPOSED UPON SPACE ITSELF BY THE MASS OF THE EARTH AND STARS.
WE SHOULD GET TO WORK RIGHT AWAY.

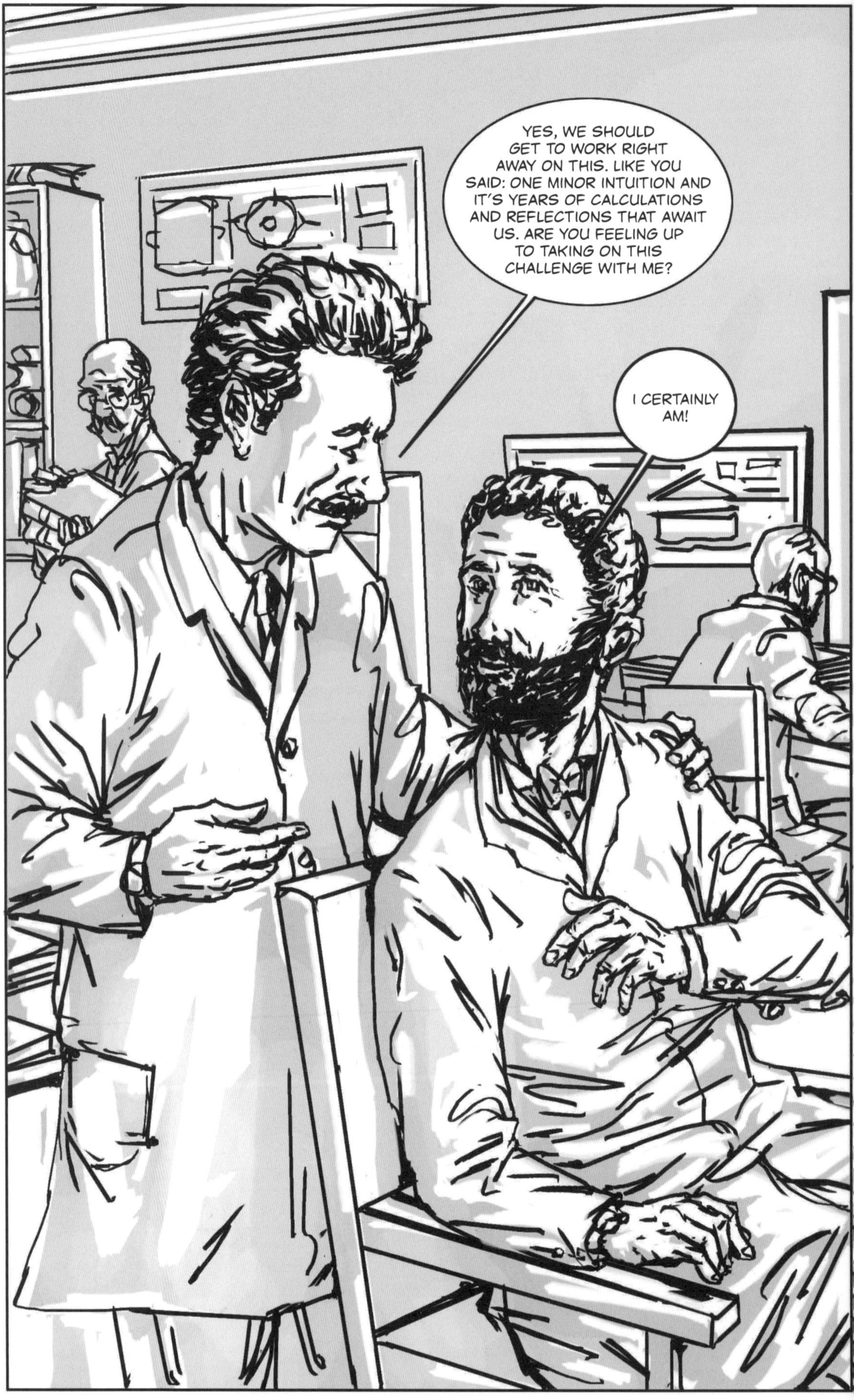
YES, WE SHOULD GET TO WORK RIGHT AWAY ON THIS. LIKE YOU SAID: ONE MINOR INTUITION AND IT'S YEARS OF CALCULATIONS AND REFLECTIONS THAT AWAIT US. ARE YOU FEELING UP TO TAKING ON THIS CHALLENGE WITH ME?
I CERTAINLY AM!

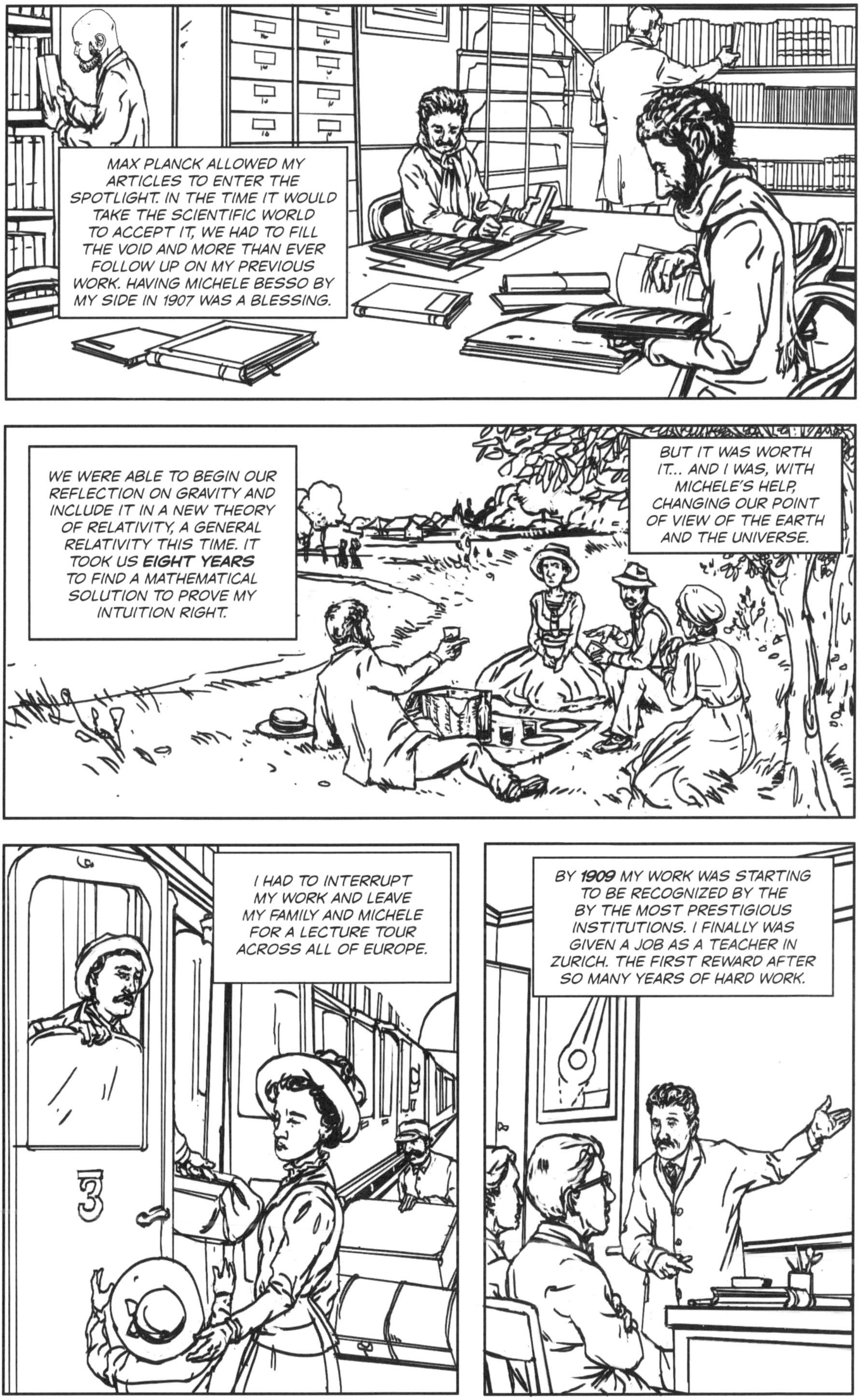

MAX PLANCK ALLOWED MY ARTICLES TO ENTER THE SPOTLIGHT. IN THE TIME IT WOULD TAKE THE SCIENTIFIC WORLD TO ACCEPT IT, WE HAD TO FILL THE VOID AND MORE THAN EVER FOLLOW UP ON MY PREVIOUS WORK. HAVING MICHELE BESSO BY MY SIDE IN 1907 WAS A BLESSING.
WE WERE ABLE TO BEGIN OUR REFLECTION ON GRAVITY AND INCLUDE IT IN A NEW THEORY OF RELATIVITY, A GENERAL RELATIVITY THIS TIME. IT TOOK US **EIGHT YEARS** TO FIND A MATHEMATICAL SOLUTION TO PROVE MY INTUITION RIGHT.
BUT IT WAS WORTH IT... AND I WAS, WITH MICHELE'S HELP, CHANGING OUR POINT OF VIEW OF THE EARTH AND THE UNIVERSE.
I HAD TO INTERRUPT MY WORK AND LEAVE MY FAMILY AND MICHELE FOR A LECTURE TOUR ACROSS ALL OF EUROPE.
3
BY **1909** MY WORK WAS STARTING TO BE RECOGNIZED BY THE BY THE MOST PRESTIGIOUS INSTITUTIONS. I FINALLY WAS GIVEN A JOB AS A TEACHER IN ZURICH. THE FIRST REWARD AFTER SO MANY YEARS OF HARD WORK.

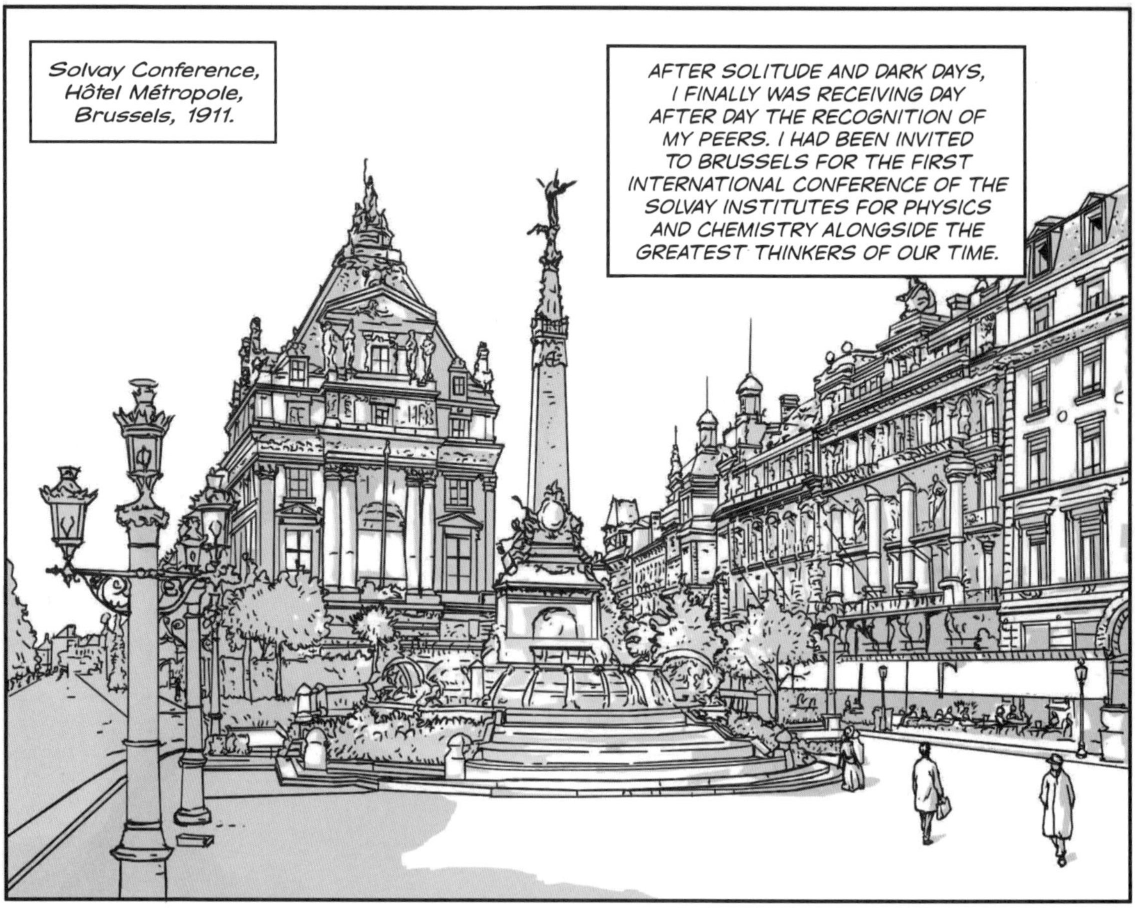

Solvay Conference, Hôtel Métropole, Brussels, 1911.
AFTER SOLITUDE AND DARK DAYS, I FINALLY WAS RECEIVING DAY AFTER DAY THE RECOGNITION OF MY PEERS. I HAD BEEN INVITED TO BRUSSELS FOR THE FIRST INTERNATIONAL CONFERENCE OF THE SOLVAY INSTITUTES FOR PHYSICS AND CHEMISTRY ALONGSIDE THE GREATEST THINKERS OF OUR TIME.

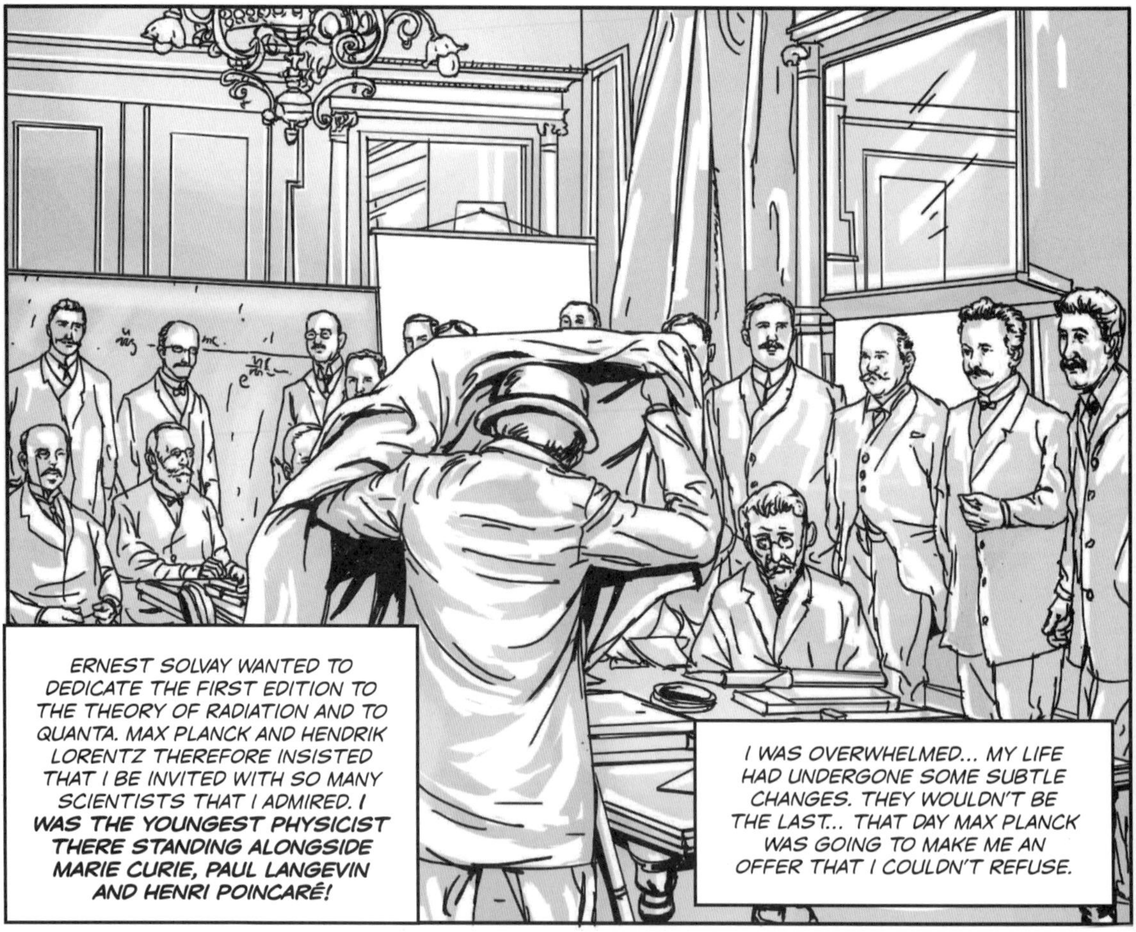

ERNEST SOLVAY WANTED TO DEDICATE THE FIRST EDITION TO THE THEORY OF RADIATION AND TO QUANTA. MAX PLANCK AND HENDRIK LORENTZ THEREFORE INSISTED THAT I BE INVITED WITH SO MANY SCIENTISTS THAT I ADMIRED. **I WAS THE YOUNGEST PHYSICIST THERE STANDING ALONGSIDE MARIE CURIE, PAUL LANGEVIN AND HENRI POINCARÉ!**
I WAS OVERWHELMED... MY LIFE HAD UNDERGONE SOME SUBTLE CHANGES. THEY WOULDN'T BE THE LAST... THAT DAY MAX PLANCK WAS GOING TO MAKE ME AN OFFER THAT I COULDN'T REFUSE.

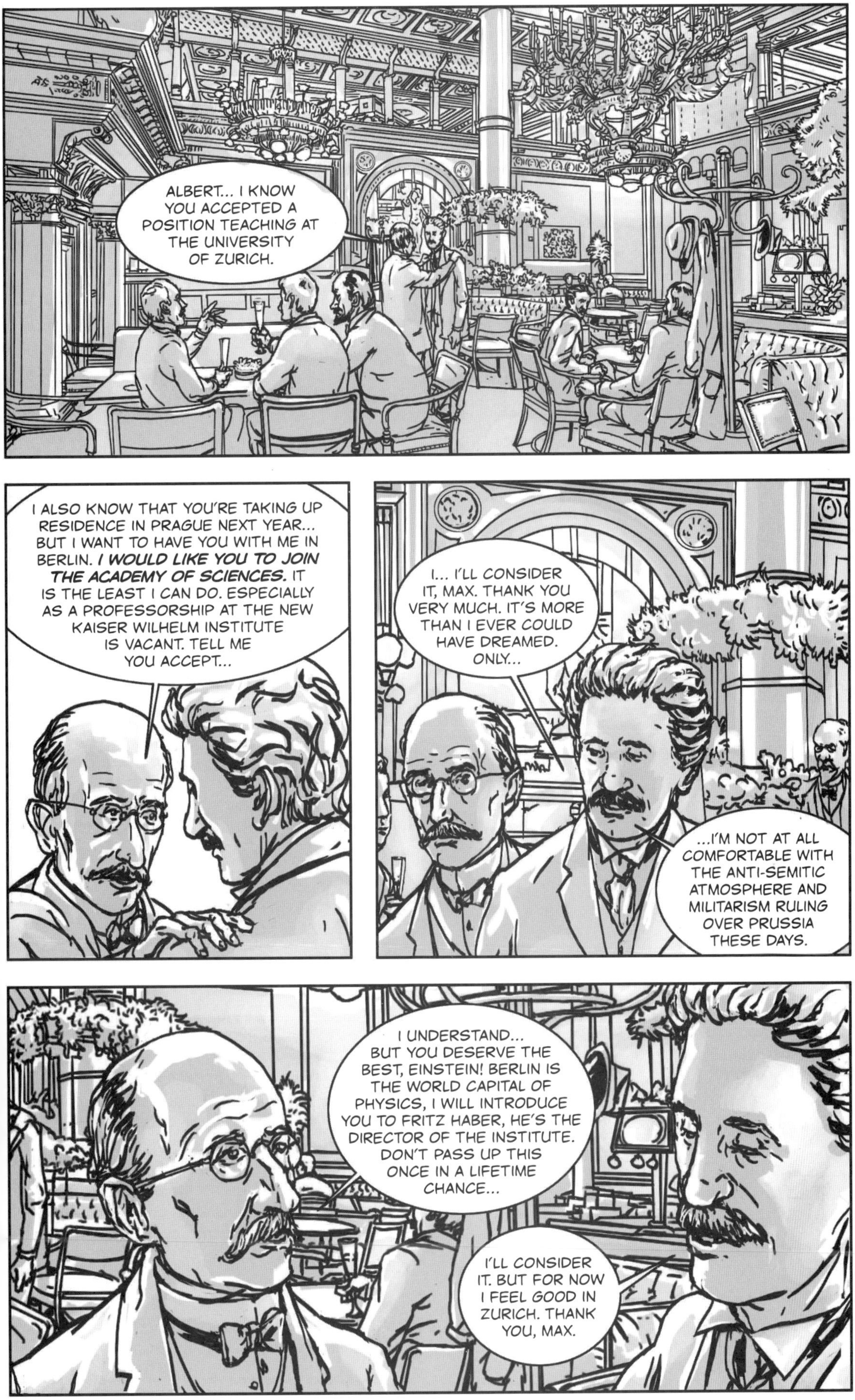
ALBERT... I KNOW YOU ACCEPTED A POSITION TEACHING AT THE UNIVERSITY OF ZURICH.
I ALSO KNOW THAT YOU'RE TAKING UP RESIDENCE IN PRAGUE NEXT YEAR... BUT I WANT TO HAVE YOU WITH ME IN BERLIN. ***I WOULD LIKE YOU TO JOIN THE ACADEMY OF SCIENCES.*** IT IS THE LEAST I CAN DO. ESPECIALLY AS A PROFESSORSHIP AT THE NEW KAISER WILHELM INSTITUTE IS VACANT. TELL ME YOU ACCEPT...
I... I'LL CONSIDER IT, MAX. THANK YOU VERY MUCH. IT'S MORE THAN I EVER COULD HAVE DREAMED. ONLY...
...I'M NOT AT ALL COMFORTABLE WITH THE ANTI-SEMITIC ATMOSPHERE AND MILITARISM RULING OVER PRUSSIA THESE DAYS.
I UNDERSTAND... BUT YOU DESERVE THE BEST, EINSTEIN! BERLIN IS THE WORLD CAPITAL OF PHYSICS, I WILL INTRODUCE YOU TO FRITZ HABER, HE'S THE DIRECTOR OF THE INSTITUTE. DON'T PASS UP THIS ONCE IN A LIFETIME CHANCE...
I'LL CONSIDER IT. BUT FOR NOW I FEEL GOOD IN ZURICH. THANK YOU, MAX.

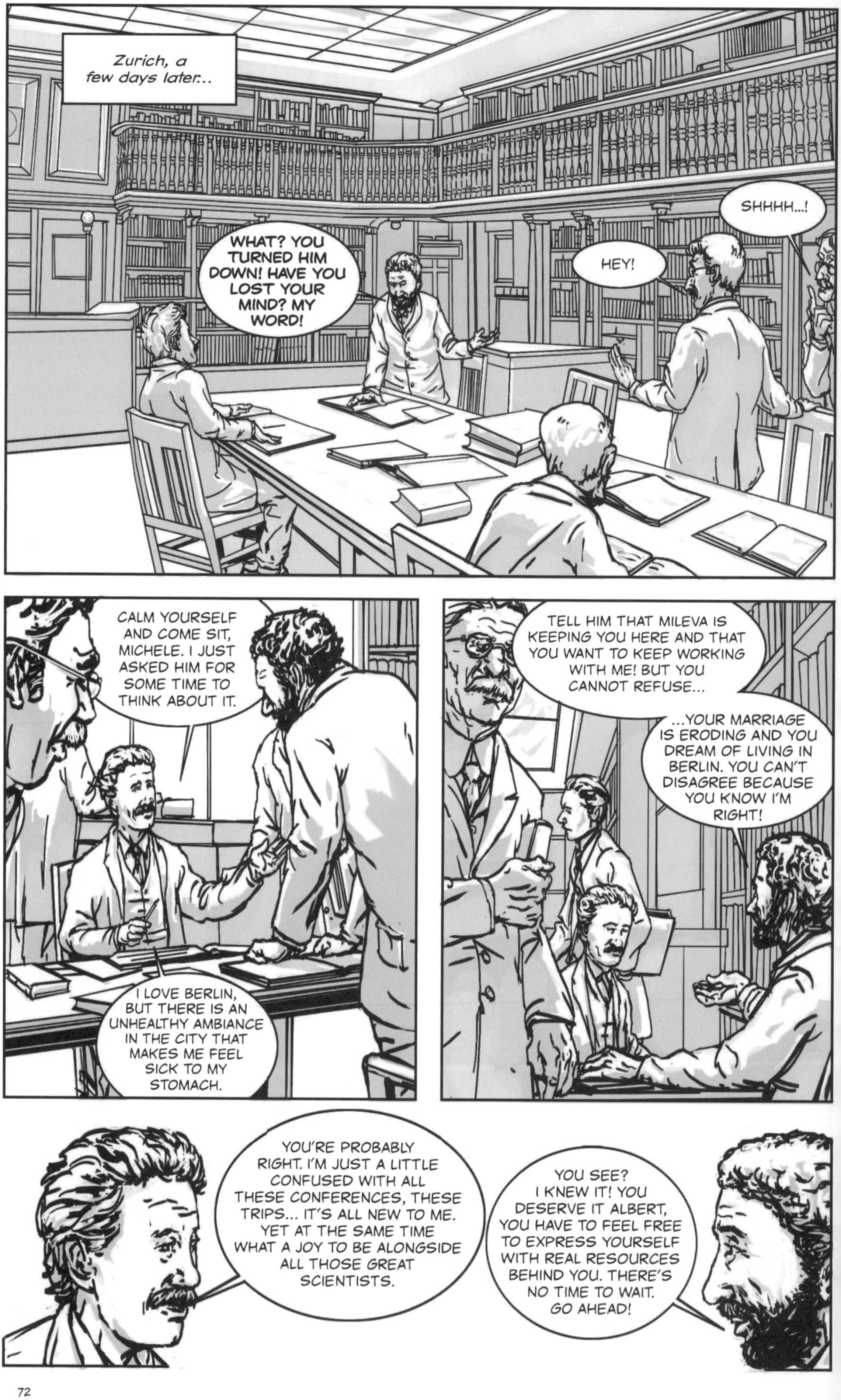
Zurich, a few days later...
WHAT? YOU TURNED HIM DOWN! HAVE YOU LOST YOUR MIND? MY WORD!
HEY!
SHHHH...!
CALM YOURSELF AND COME SIT, MICHELE. I JUST ASKED HIM FOR SOME TIME TO THINK ABOUT IT.
I LOVE BERLIN, BUT THERE IS AN UNHEALTHY AMBIANCE IN THE CITY THAT MAKES ME FEEL SICK TO MY STOMACH.
TELL HIM THAT MILEVA IS KEEPING YOU HERE AND THAT YOU WANT TO KEEP WORKING WITH ME! BUT YOU CANNOT REFUSE...
...YOUR MARRIAGE IS ERODING AND YOU DREAM OF LIVING IN BERLIN. YOU CAN'T DISAGREE BECAUSE YOU KNOW I'M RIGHT!
YOU'RE PROBABLY RIGHT. I'M JUST A LITTLE CONFUSED WITH ALL THESE CONFERENCES, THESE TRIPS... IT'S ALL NEW TO ME. YET AT THE SAME TIME WHAT A JOY TO BE ALONGSIDE ALL THOSE GREAT SCIENTISTS.
YOU SEE? I KNEW IT! YOU DESERVE IT ALBERT, YOU HAVE TO FEEL FREE TO EXPRESS YOURSELF WITH REAL RESOURCES BEHIND YOU. THERE'S NO TIME TO WAIT. GO AHEAD!

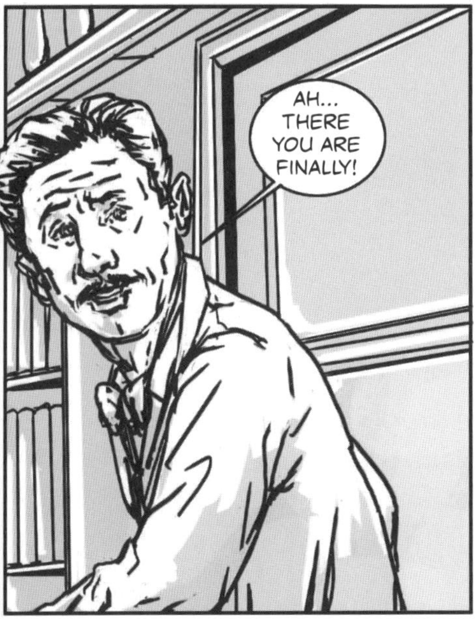
AH... THERE YOU ARE FINALLY!
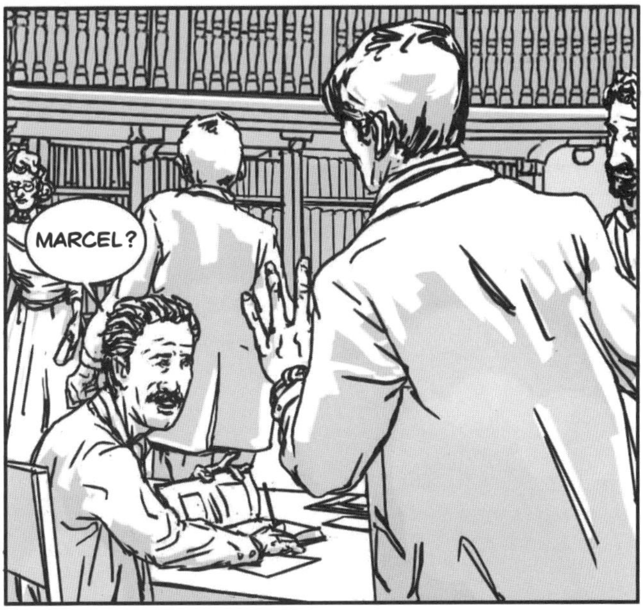
MARCEL?
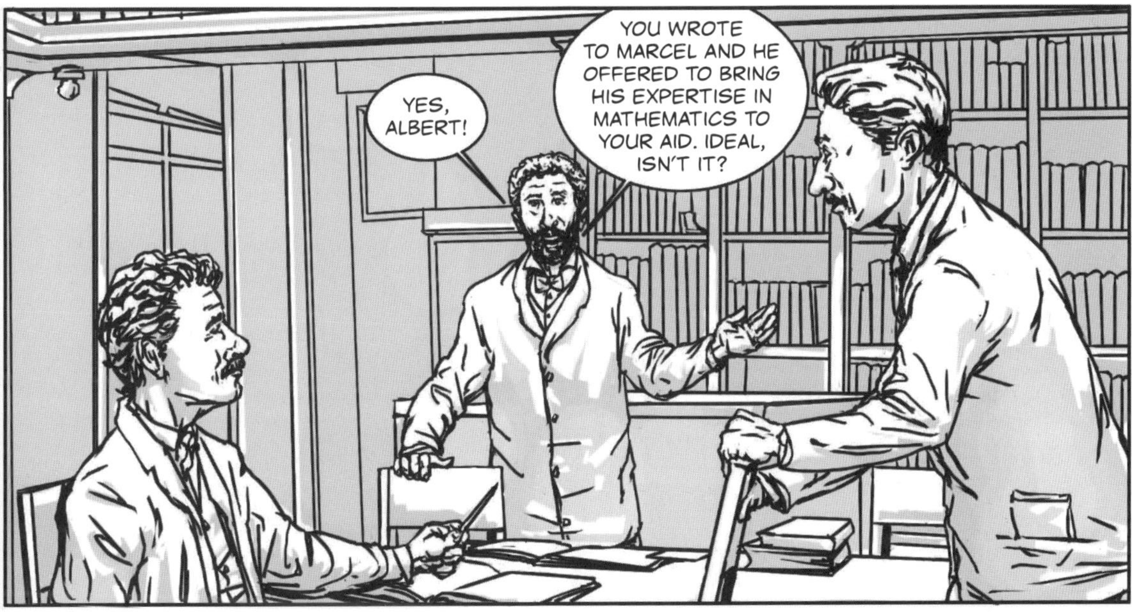
YES, ALBERT!
YOU WROTE TO MARCEL AND HE OFFERED TO BRING HIS EXPERTISE IN MATHEMATICS TO YOUR AID. IDEAL, ISN'T IT?
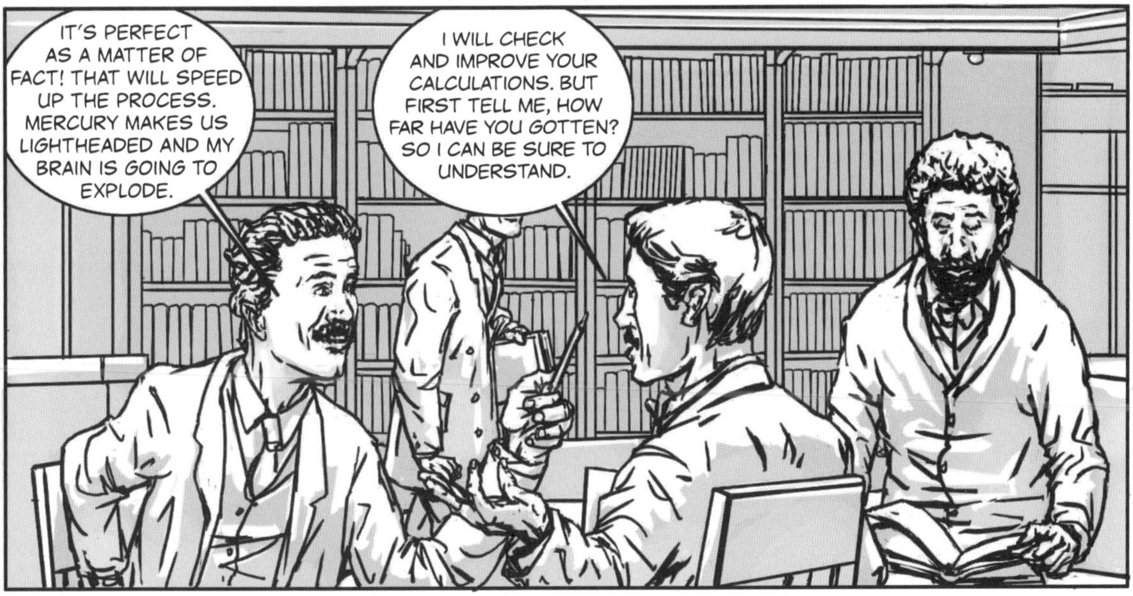
IT'S PERFECT AS A MATTER OF FACT! THAT WILL SPEED UP THE PROCESS. MERCURY MAKES US LIGHTHEADED AND MY BRAIN IS GOING TO EXPLODE.
I WILL CHECK AND IMPROVE YOUR CALCULATIONS. BUT FIRST TELL ME, HOW FAR HAVE YOU GOTTEN? SO I CAN BE SURE TO UNDERSTAND.

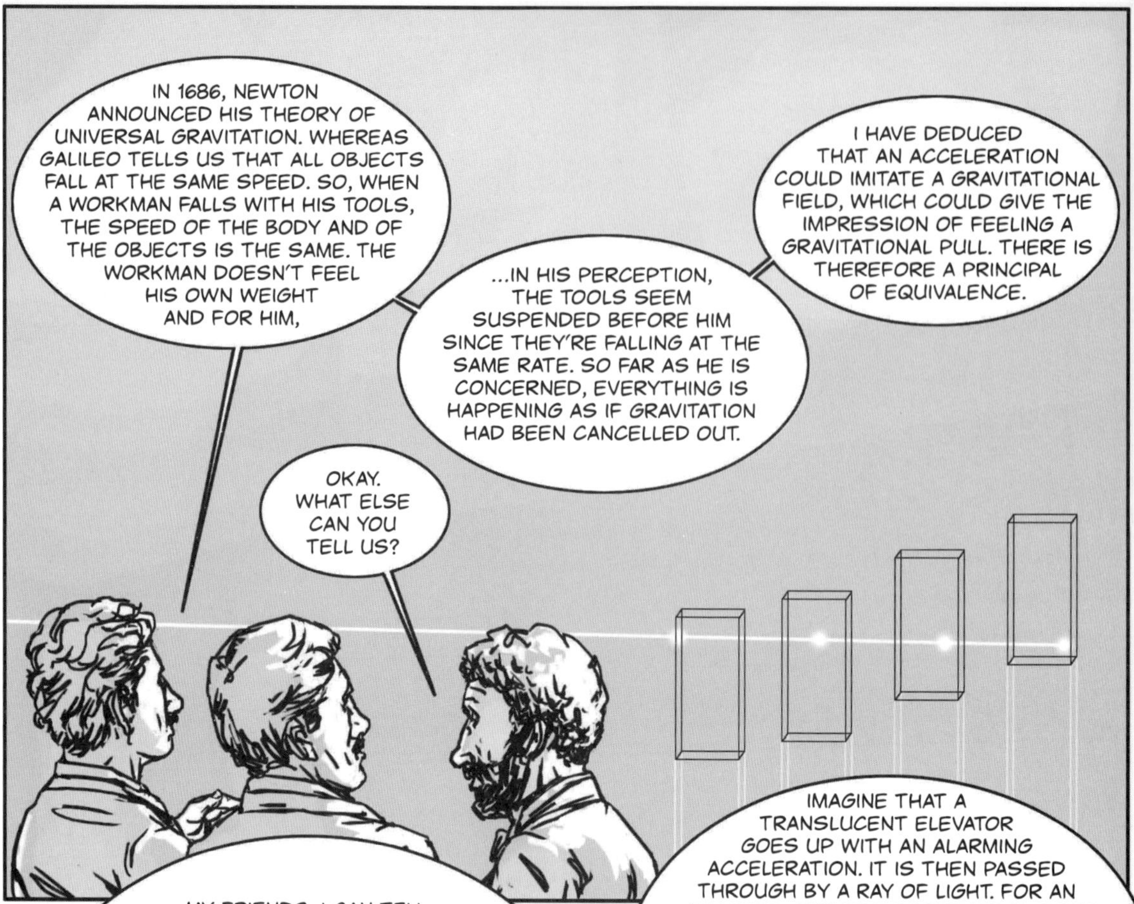
IN 1686, NEWTON ANNOUNCED HIS THEORY OF UNIVERSAL GRAVITATION. WHEREAS GALILEO TELLS US THAT ALL OBJECTS FALL AT THE SAME SPEED. SO, WHEN A WORKMAN FALLS WITH HIS TOOLS, THE SPEED OF THE BODY AND OF THE OBJECTS IS THE SAME. THE WORKMAN DOESN'T FEEL HIS OWN WEIGHT AND FOR HIM,
...IN HIS PERCEPTION, THE TOOLS SEEM SUSPENDED BEFORE HIM SINCE THEY'RE FALLING AT THE SAME RATE. SO FAR AS HE IS CONCERNED, EVERYTHING IS HAPPENING AS IF GRAVITATION HAD BEEN CANCELLED OUT.
I HAVE DEDUCED THAT AN ACCELERATION COULD IMITATE A GRAVITATIONAL FIELD, WHICH COULD GIVE THE IMPRESSION OF FEELING A GRAVITATIONAL PULL. THERE IS THEREFORE A PRINCIPAL OF EQUIVALENCE.
OKAY. WHAT ELSE CAN YOU TELL US?

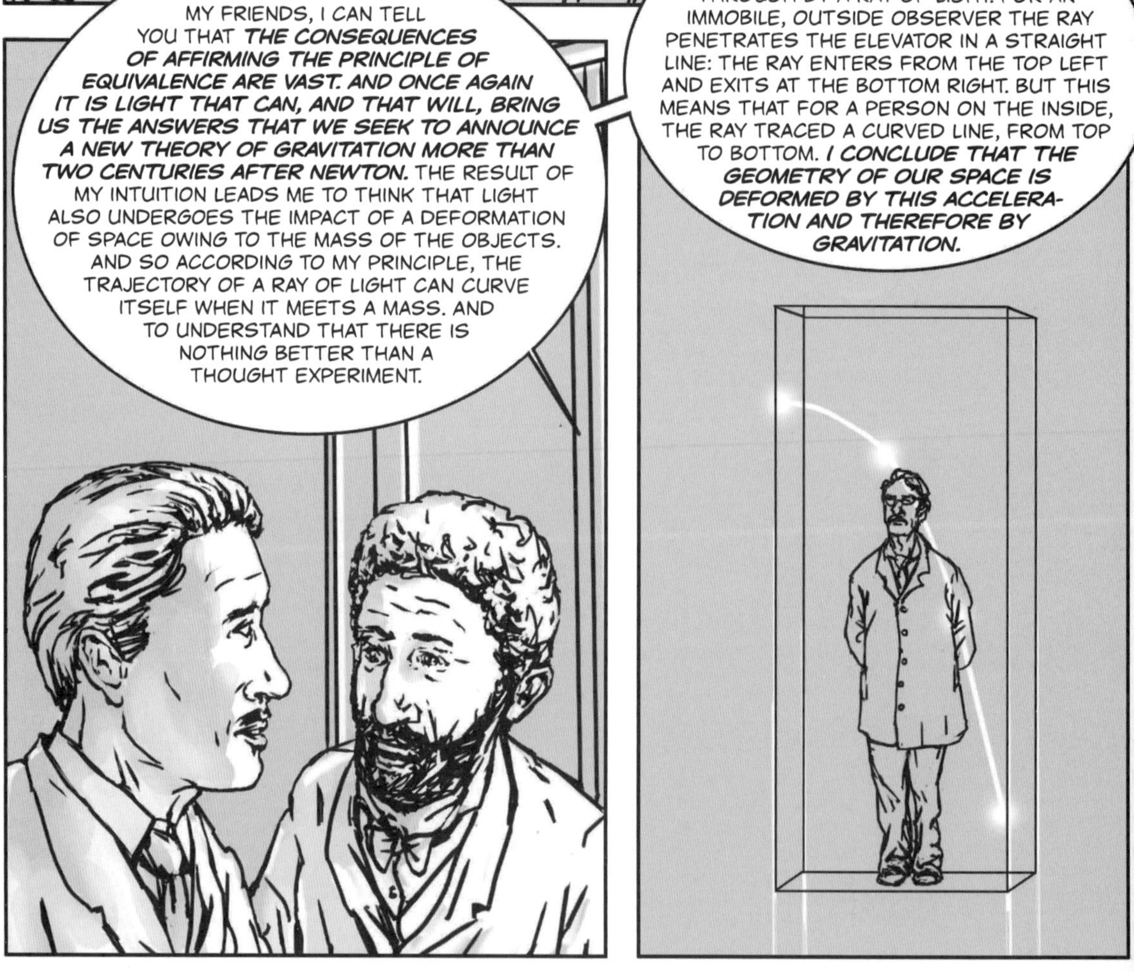
MY FRIENDS, I CAN TELL YOU THAT ***THE CONSEQUENCES OF AFFIRMING THE PRINCIPLE OF EQUIVALENCE ARE VAST. AND ONCE AGAIN IT IS LIGHT THAT CAN, AND THAT WILL, BRING US THE ANSWERS THAT WE SEEK TO ANNOUNCE A NEW THEORY OF GRAVITATION MORE THAN TWO CENTURIES AFTER NEWTON.*** THE RESULT OF MY INTUITION LEADS ME TO THINK THAT LIGHT ALSO UNDERGOES THE IMPACT OF A DEFORMATION OF SPACE OWING TO THE MASS OF THE OBJECTS. AND SO ACCORDING TO MY PRINCIPLE, THE TRAJECTORY OF A RAY OF LIGHT CAN CURVE ITSELF WHEN IT MEETS A MASS. AND TO UNDERSTAND THAT THERE IS NOTHING BETTER THAN A THOUGHT EXPERIMENT.
IMAGINE THAT A TRANSLUCENT ELEVATOR GOES UP WITH AN ALARMING ACCELERATION. IT IS THEN PASSED THROUGH BY A RAY OF LIGHT. FOR AN IMMOBILE, OUTSIDE OBSERVER THE RAY PENETRATES THE ELEVATOR IN A STRAIGHT LINE: THE RAY ENTERS FROM THE TOP LEFT AND EXITS AT THE BOTTOM RIGHT. BUT THIS MEANS THAT FOR A PERSON ON THE INSIDE, THE RAY TRACED A CURVED LINE, FROM TOP TO BOTTOM. ***I CONCLUDE THAT THE GEOMETRY OF OUR SPACE IS DEFORMED BY THIS ACCELERATION AND THEREFORE BY GRAVITATION.***

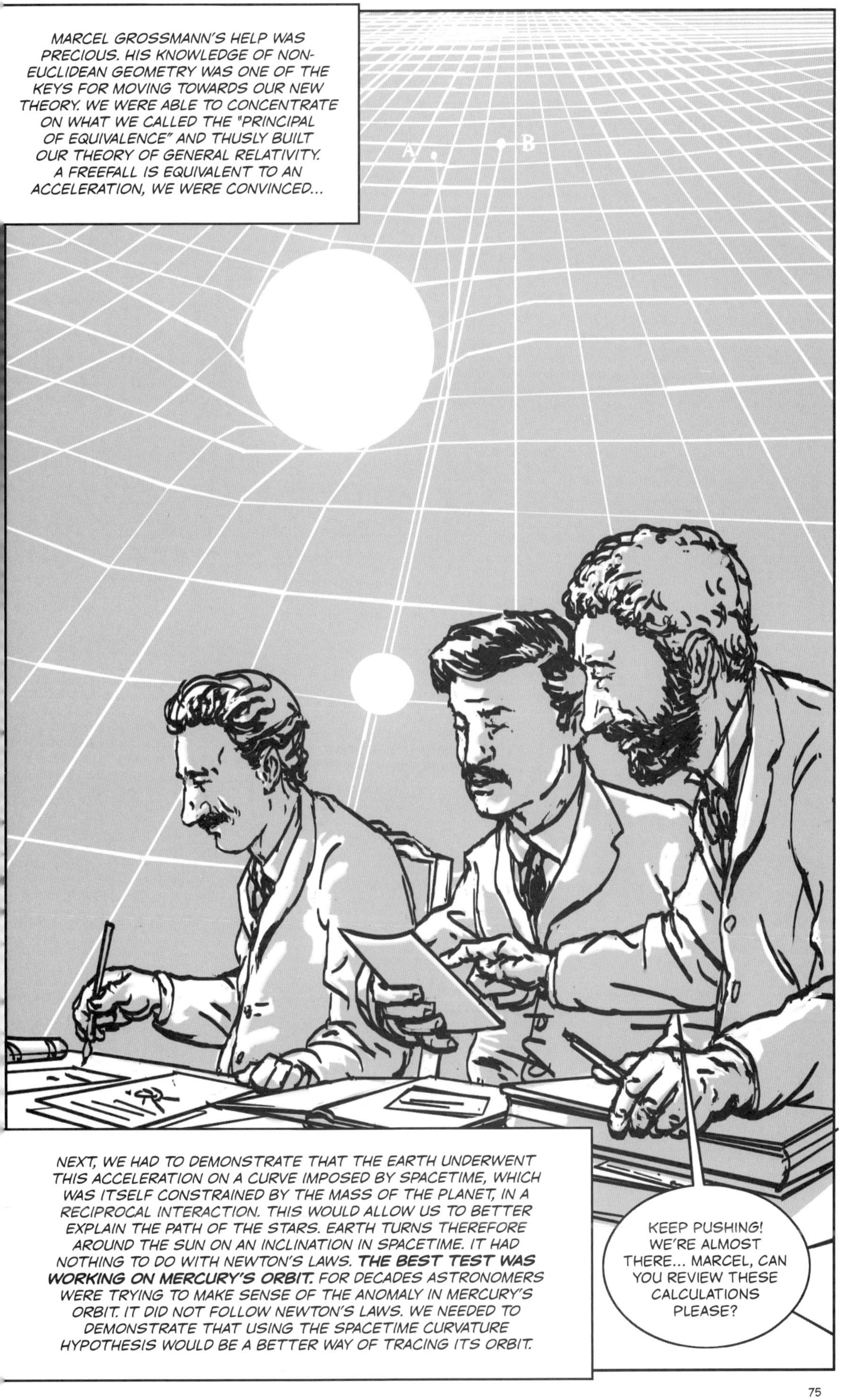
MARCEL GROSSMANN'S HELP WAS PRECIOUS. HIS KNOWLEDGE OF NON-EUCLIDEAN GEOMETRY WAS ONE OF THE KEYS FOR MOVING TOWARDS OUR NEW THEORY. WE WERE ABLE TO CONCENTRATE ON WHAT WE CALLED THE "PRINCIPAL OF EQUIVALENCE" AND THUSLY BUILT OUR THEORY OF GENERAL RELATIVITY. A FREEFALL IS EQUIVALENT TO AN ACCELERATION, WE WERE CONVINCED...
A
B
NEXT, WE HAD TO DEMONSTRATE THAT THE EARTH UNDERWENT THIS ACCELERATION ON A CURVE IMPOSED BY SPACETIME, WHICH WAS ITSELF CONSTRAINED BY THE MASS OF THE PLANET, IN A RECIPROCAL INTERACTION. THIS WOULD ALLOW US TO BETTER EXPLAIN THE PATH OF THE STARS. EARTH TURNS THEREFORE AROUND THE SUN ON AN INCLINATION IN SPACETIME. IT HAD NOTHING TO DO WITH NEWTON'S LAWS. **THE BEST TEST WAS WORKING ON MERCURY'S ORBIT.** FOR DECADES ASTRONOMERS WERE TRYING TO MAKE SENSE OF THE ANOMALY IN MERCURY'S ORBIT. IT DID NOT FOLLOW NEWTON'S LAWS. WE NEEDED TO DEMONSTRATE THAT USING THE SPACETIME CURVATURE HYPOTHESIS WOULD BE A BETTER WAY OF TRACING ITS ORBIT.
KEEP PUSHING! WE'RE ALMOST THERE... MARCEL, CAN YOU REVIEW THESE CALCULATIONS PLEASE?

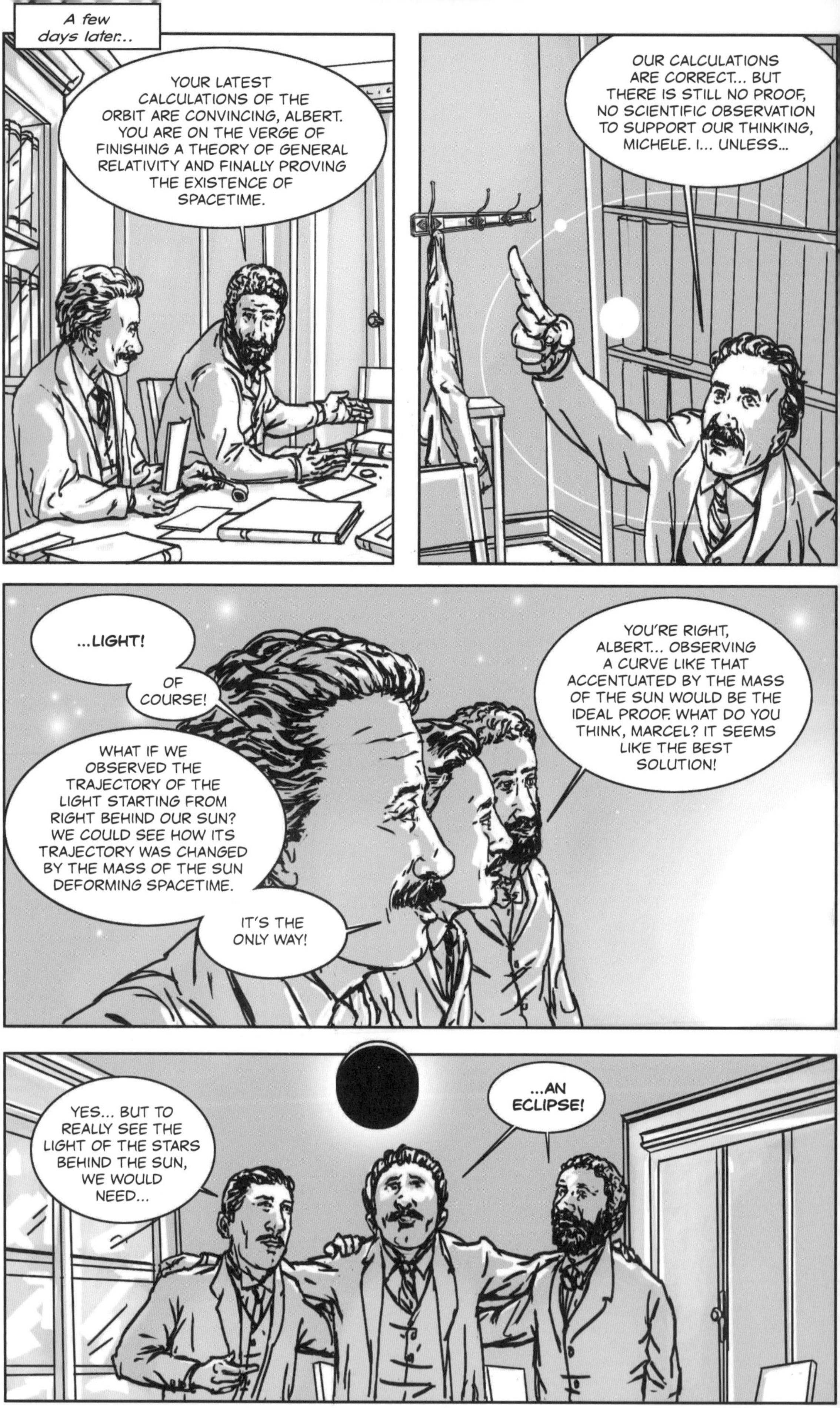
A few days later...
YOUR LATEST CALCULATIONS OF THE ORBIT ARE CONVINCING, ALBERT. YOU ARE ON THE VERGE OF FINISHING A THEORY OF GENERAL RELATIVITY AND FINALLY PROVING THE EXISTENCE OF SPACETIME.
OUR CALCULATIONS ARE CORRECT... BUT THERE IS STILL NO PROOF, NO SCIENTIFIC OBSERVATION TO SUPPORT OUR THINKING, MICHELE. I... UNLESS...
...LIGHT!
OF COURSE!
WHAT IF WE OBSERVED THE TRAJECTORY OF THE LIGHT STARTING FROM RIGHT BEHIND OUR SUN? WE COULD SEE HOW ITS TRAJECTORY WAS CHANGED BY THE MASS OF THE SUN DEFORMING SPACETIME.
IT'S THE ONLY WAY!
YOU'RE RIGHT, ALBERT... OBSERVING A CURVE LIKE THAT ACCENTUATED BY THE MASS OF THE SUN WOULD BE THE IDEAL PROOF. WHAT DO YOU THINK, MARCEL? IT SEEMS LIKE THE BEST SOLUTION!
YES... BUT TO REALLY SEE THE LIGHT OF THE STARS BEHIND THE SUN, WE WOULD NEED...
...AN ECLIPSE!

Berlin-Babelsberg Observatory, German Empire, 1912.

...OF COURSE! THIS MR. EINSTEIN IS CERTAINLY CORRECT...

DEAR PROFESSOR EINSTEIN, I WOULD BE HONORED TO SHARE MY ASTRONOMICAL RESULTS WITH YOU.

THE NEXT TOTAL ECLIPSE OF THE SUN WILL TAKE PLACE IN CRIMEA. IT COULD BE THE OPPORTUNITY TO FIND EXPERIMENTAL PROOF OF YOUR THEORIES IN REAL LIFE.

AS AN ASSISTANT, I FEAR THAT I DO NOT HAVE THE NECESSARY WEIGHT TO PUSH THROUGH A REQUEST FOR FUNDING TO MY SUPERIORS... BUT I AM SURE THAT I WILL BE ABLE TO MAKE IT HAPPEN AMONGST MY OWN FRIEND NETWORK...

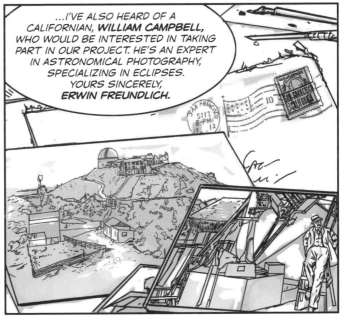

...I'VE ALSO HEARD OF A CALIFORNIAN, **WILLIAM CAMPBELL,** WHO WOULD BE INTERESTED IN TAKING PART IN OUR PROJECT. HE'S AN EXPERT IN ASTRONOMICAL PHOTOGRAPHY, SPECIALIZING IN ECLIPSES. YOURS SINCERELY, **ERWIN FREUNDLICH.**

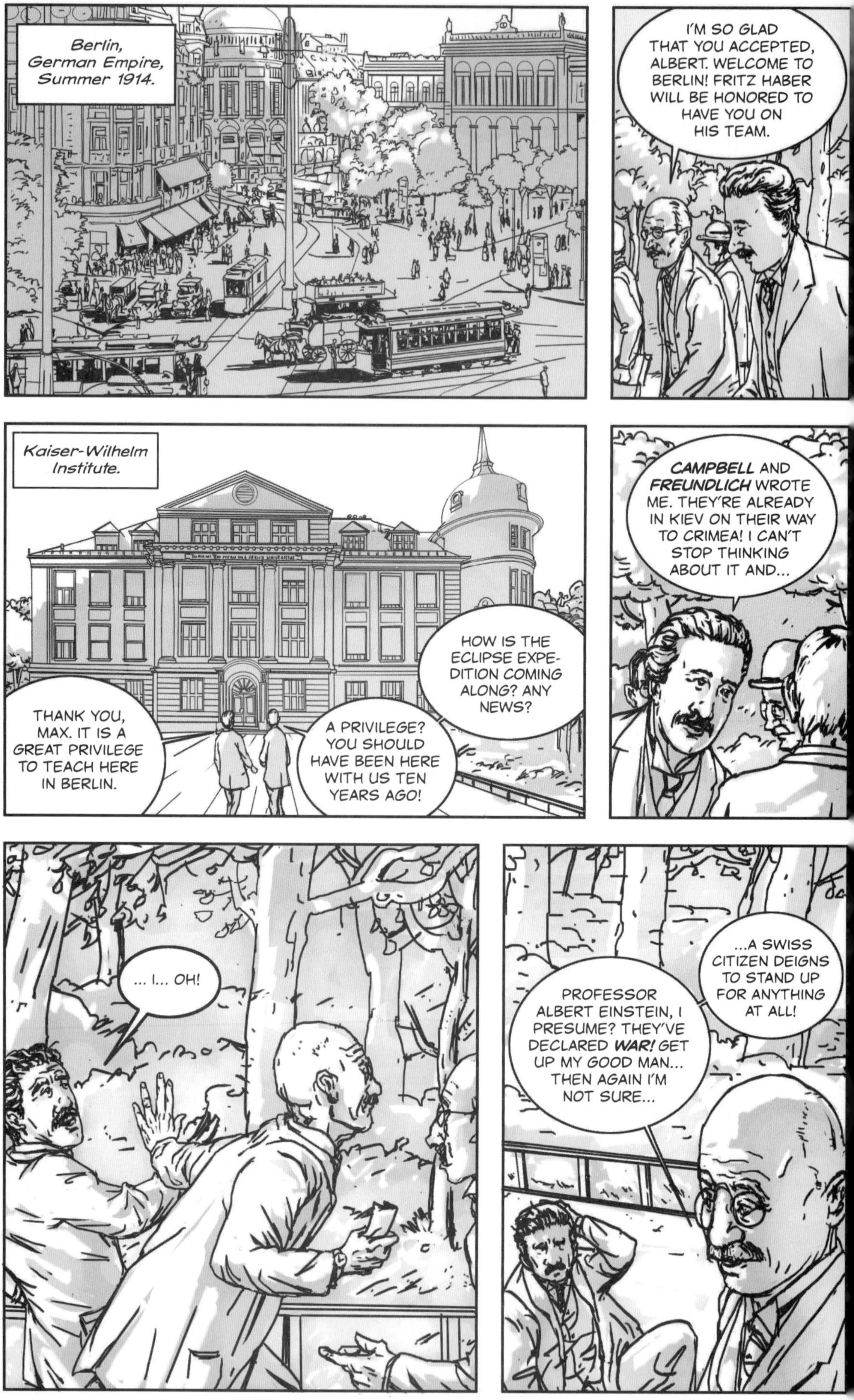
Berlin, German Empire, Summer 1914.
I'M SO GLAD THAT YOU ACCEPTED, ALBERT. WELCOME TO BERLIN! FRITZ HABER WILL BE HONORED TO HAVE YOU ON HIS TEAM.
Kaiser-Wilhelm Institute.
THANK YOU, MAX. IT IS A GREAT PRIVILEGE TO TEACH HERE IN BERLIN.
A PRIVILEGE? YOU SHOULD HAVE BEEN HERE WITH US TEN YEARS AGO!
HOW IS THE ECLIPSE EXPEDITION COMING ALONG? ANY NEWS?
CAMPBELL AND FREUNDLICH WROTE ME. THEY'RE ALREADY IN KIEV ON THEIR WAY TO CRIMEA! I CAN'T STOP THINKING ABOUT IT AND...
... I... OH!
PROFESSOR ALBERT EINSTEIN, I PRESUME? THEY'VE DECLARED WAR! GET UP MY GOOD MAN... THEN AGAIN I'M NOT SURE...
...A SWISS CITIZEN DEIGNS TO STAND UP FOR ANYTHING AT ALL!

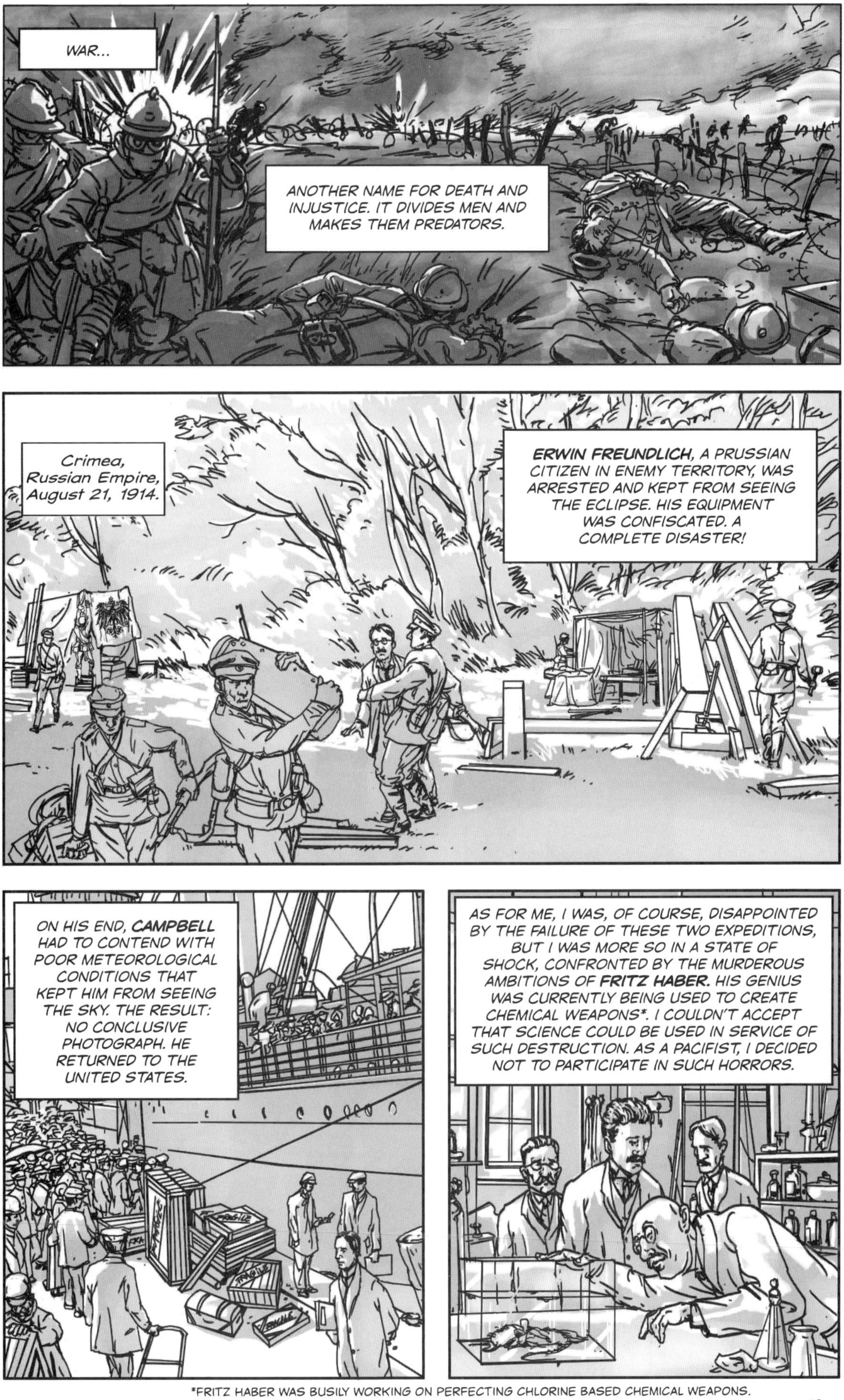
WAR...
ANOTHER NAME FOR DEATH AND INJUSTICE. IT DIVIDES MEN AND MAKES THEM PREDATORS.
Crimea, Russian Empire, August 21, 1914.
ERWIN FREUNDLICH, A PRUSSIAN CITIZEN IN ENEMY TERRITORY, WAS ARRESTED AND KEPT FROM SEEING THE ECLIPSE. HIS EQUIPMENT WAS CONFISCATED. A COMPLETE DISASTER!
ON HIS END, CAMPBELL HAD TO CONTEND WITH POOR METEOROLOGICAL CONDITIONS THAT KEPT HIM FROM SEEING THE SKY. THE RESULT: NO CONCLUSIVE PHOTOGRAPH. HE RETURNED TO THE UNITED STATES.
FRAGILE
FRAGILE
FRAGILE
AS FOR ME, I WAS, OF COURSE, DISAPPOINTED BY THE FAILURE OF THESE TWO EXPEDITIONS, BUT I WAS MORE SO IN A STATE OF SHOCK, CONFRONTED BY THE MURDEROUS AMBITIONS OF FRITZ HABER. HIS GENIUS WAS CURRENTLY BEING USED TO CREATE CHEMICAL WEAPONS*. I COULDN'T ACCEPT THAT SCIENCE COULD BE USED IN SERVICE OF SUCH DESTRUCTION. AS A PACIFIST, I DECIDED NOT TO PARTICIPATE IN SUCH HORRORS.

*FRITZ HABER WAS BUSILY WORKING ON PERFECTING CHLORINE BASED CHEMICAL WEAPONS.

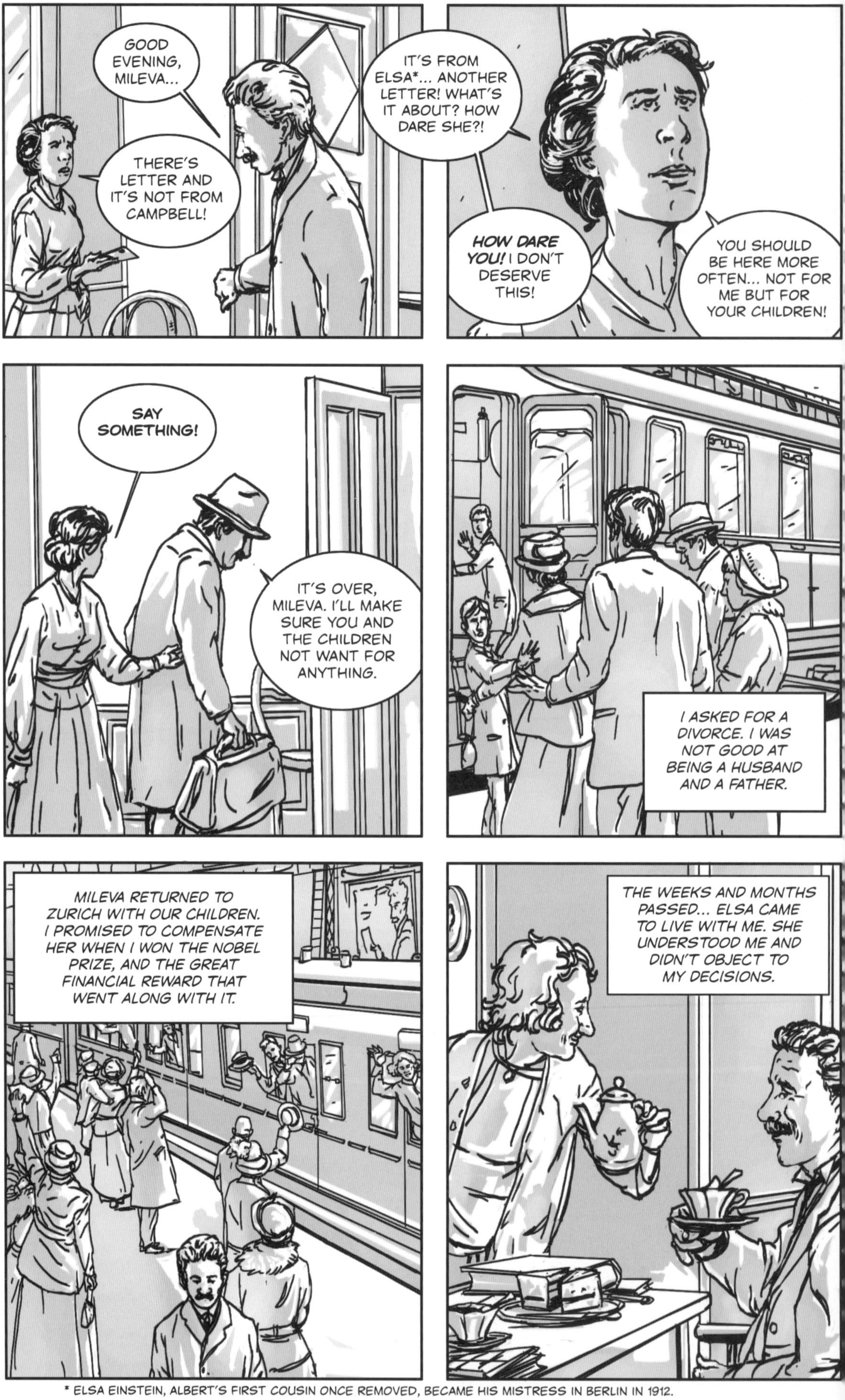
GOOD EVENING, MILEVA...
THERE'S LETTER AND IT'S NOT FROM CAMPBELL!
IT'S FROM ELSA*... ANOTHER LETTER! WHAT'S IT ABOUT? HOW DARE SHE?!
HOW DARE YOU! I DON'T DESERVE THIS!
YOU SHOULD BE HERE MORE OFTEN... NOT FOR ME BUT FOR YOUR CHILDREN!
SAY SOMETHING!
IT'S OVER, MILEVA. I'LL MAKE SURE YOU AND THE CHILDREN NOT WANT FOR ANYTHING.
I ASKED FOR A DIVORCE. I WAS NOT GOOD AT BEING A HUSBAND AND A FATHER.
MILEVA RETURNED TO ZURICH WITH OUR CHILDREN. I PROMISED TO COMPENSATE HER WHEN I WON THE NOBEL PRIZE, AND THE GREAT FINANCIAL REWARD THAT WENT ALONG WITH IT.
THE WEEKS AND MONTHS PASSED... ELSA CAME TO LIVE WITH ME. SHE UNDERSTOOD ME AND DIDN'T OBJECT TO MY DECISIONS.

* ELSA EINSTEIN, ALBERT'S FIRST COUSIN ONCE REMOVED, BECAME HIS MISTRESS IN BERLIN IN 1912.

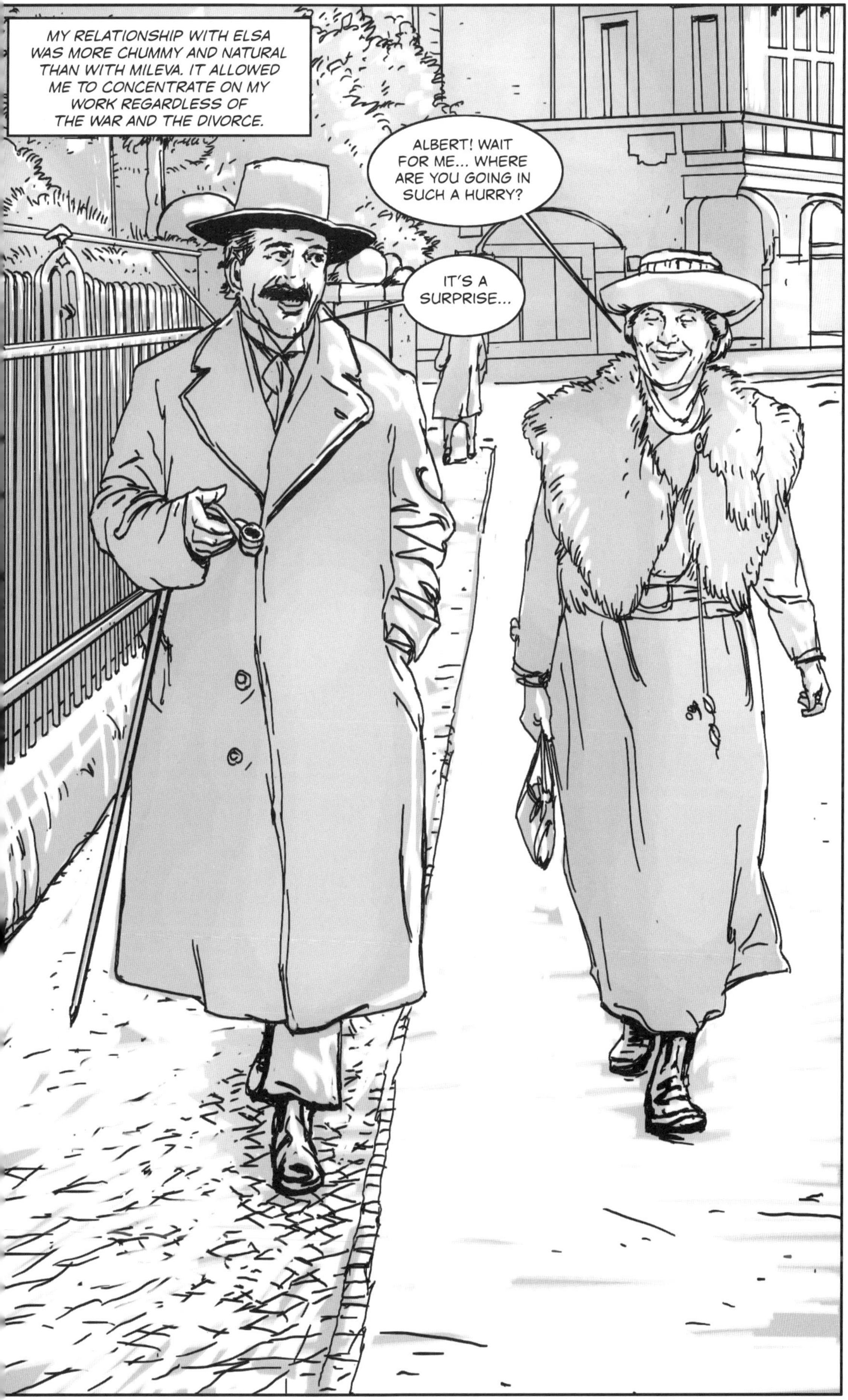
MY RELATIONSHIP WITH ELSA WAS MORE CHUMMY AND NATURAL THAN WITH MILEVA. IT ALLOWED ME TO CONCENTRATE ON MY WORK REGARDLESS OF THE WAR AND THE DIVORCE.
ALBERT! WAIT FOR ME... WHERE ARE YOU GOING IN SUCH A HURRY?
IT'S A SURPRISE...

SIMON ARCHENHOLD WILL BE THERE, HE'S AN OLD FRIEND! A PACIFIST LIKE ME AND CAMPBELL. ONE OF THE FIRST ASTRONOMERS TO HAVE PUT A CAMERA INTO A TELESCOPE OVER TWENTY YEARS AGO.

AND HE IS FIRST AND FOREMOST A GENEROUS SCIENTIST WHOSE MAIN OBJECTIVE IS SHARING HIS LATEST DISCOVERIES WITH THE PUBLIC.

I READ THAT IN THE PAPERS... SO, WE ARE GOING TO THE INAUGURATION OF THE GIANT TREPTOW TELESCOPE?

YOU COULDN'T HIDE ANYTHING FROM ELSA... IT WAS AT THIS INAUGURATION, JUNE 2, 1915, IN BERLIN, THAT I HELD MY FIRST PUBLIC LECTURE ON THE THEORY OF GENERAL RELATIVITY. THERE WERE STILL A FEW CALCULATIONS TO FINISH, BUT THE ESSENTIAL WAS THERE AND THE AUDIENCE WAS NOT FOUND LACKING.

PROFESSOR! YOUR THEORY ALLOWS US TO UNDERSTAND PARTS OF THE UNIVERSE AND ITS LAWS... BUT IT IS NOT YET UNANIMOUSLY RECOGNIZED BY YOUR PEERS. HOW DO YOU PLAN TO PROVE IT?

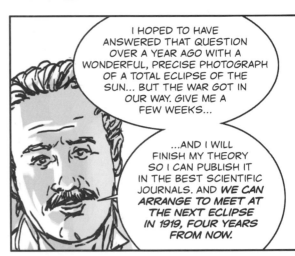

I HOPED TO HAVE ANSWERED THAT QUESTION OVER A YEAR AGO WITH A WONDERFUL, PRECISE PHOTOGRAPH OF A TOTAL ECLIPSE OF THE SUN... BUT THE WAR GOT IN OUR WAY. GIVE ME A FEW WEEKS...

...AND I WILL FINISH MY THEORY SO I CAN PUBLISH IT IN THE BEST SCIENTIFIC JOURNALS. AND *WE CAN ARRANGE TO MEET AT THE NEXT ECLIPSE IN 1919, FOUR YEARS FROM NOW.*

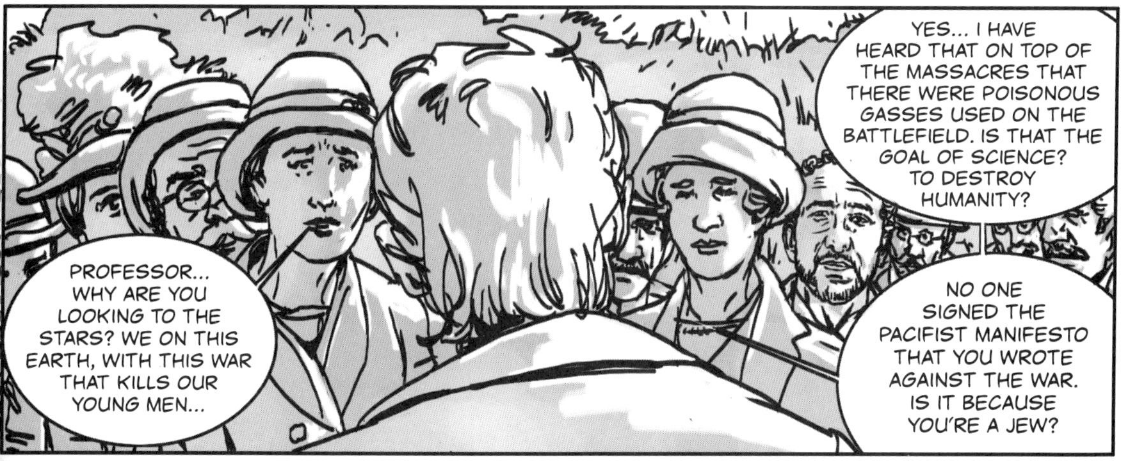
YES... I HAVE HEARD THAT ON TOP OF THE MASSACRES THAT THERE WERE POISONOUS GASSES USED ON THE BATTLEFIELD. IS THAT THE GOAL OF SCIENCE? TO DESTROY HUMANITY?
PROFESSOR... WHY ARE YOU LOOKING TO THE STARS? WE ON THIS EARTH, WITH THIS WAR THAT KILLS OUR YOUNG MEN...
NO ONE SIGNED THE PACIFIST MANIFESTO THAT YOU WROTE AGAINST THE WAR. IS IT BECAUSE YOU'RE A JEW?

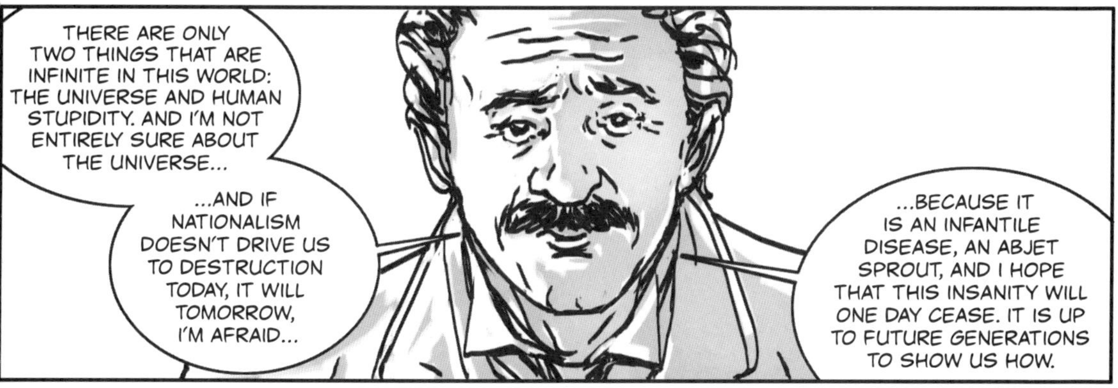
THERE ARE ONLY TWO THINGS THAT ARE INFINITE IN THIS WORLD: THE UNIVERSE AND HUMAN STUPIDITY. AND I'M NOT ENTIRELY SURE ABOUT THE UNIVERSE...
...AND IF NATIONALISM DOESN'T DRIVE US TO DESTRUCTION TODAY, IT WILL TOMORROW, I'M AFRAID...
...BECAUSE IT IS AN INFANTILE DISEASE, AN ABJET SPROUT, AND I HOPE THAT THIS INSANITY WILL ONE DAY CEASE. IT IS UP TO FUTURE GENERATIONS TO SHOW US HOW.

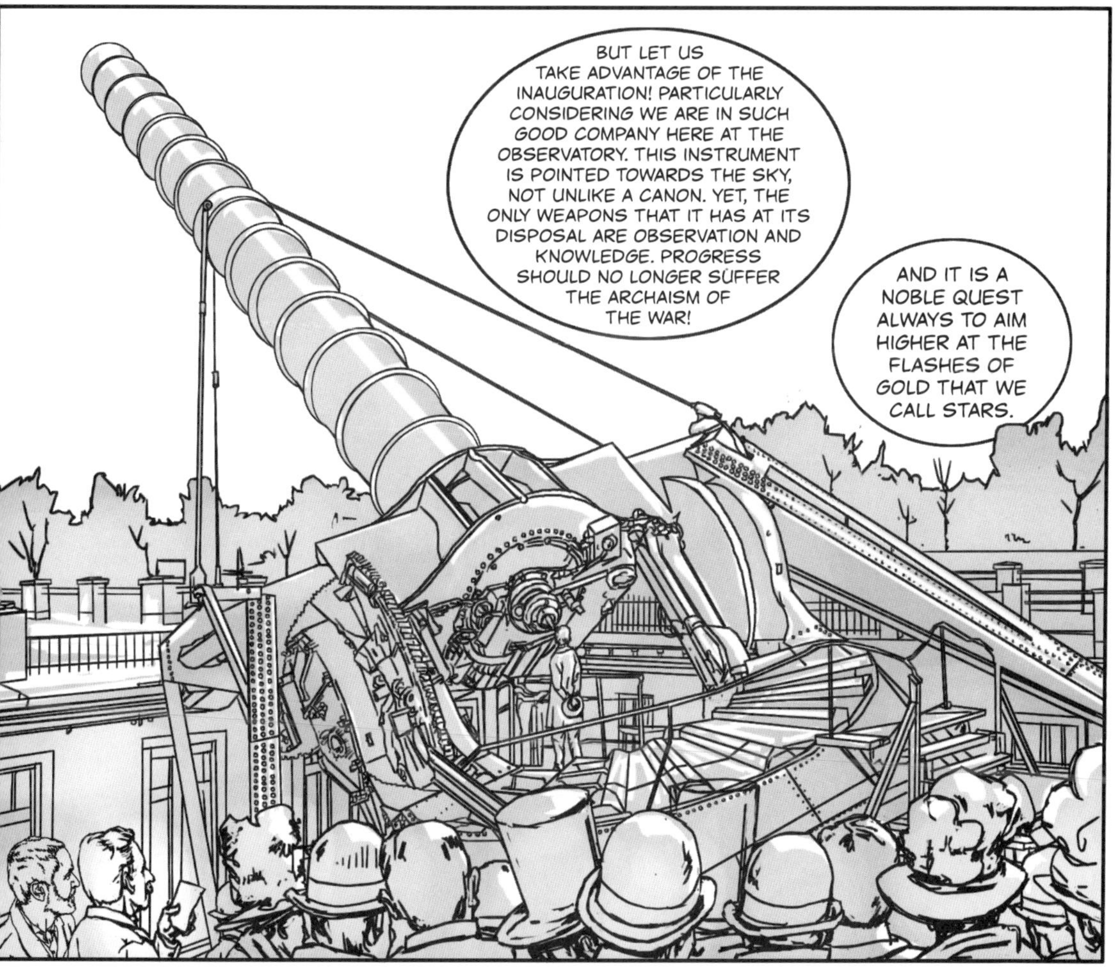
BUT LET US TAKE ADVANTAGE OF THE INAUGURATION! PARTICULARLY CONSIDERING WE ARE IN SUCH GOOD COMPANY HERE AT THE OBSERVATORY. THIS INSTRUMENT IS POINTED TOWARDS THE SKY, NOT UNLIKE A CANON. YET, THE ONLY WEAPONS THAT IT HAS AT ITS DISPOSAL ARE OBSERVATION AND KNOWLEDGE. PROGRESS SHOULD NO LONGER SUFFER THE ARCHAISM OF THE WAR!
AND IT IS A NOBLE QUEST ALWAYS TO AIM HIGHER AT THE FLASHES OF GOLD THAT WE CALL STARS.

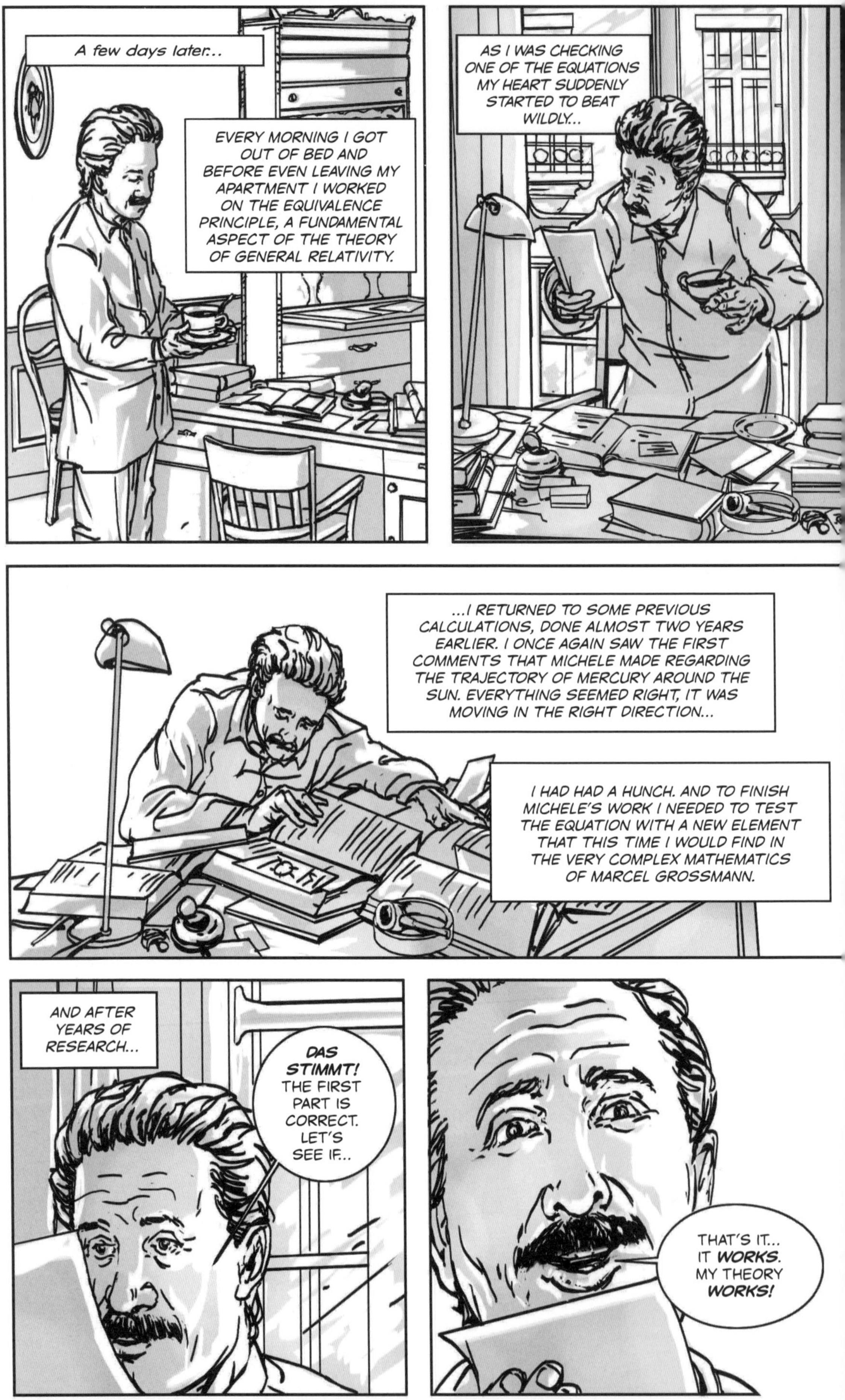
A few days later...
EVERY MORNING I GOT OUT OF BED AND BEFORE EVEN LEAVING MY APARTMENT I WORKED ON THE EQUIVALENCE PRINCIPLE, A FUNDAMENTAL ASPECT OF THE THEORY OF GENERAL RELATIVITY.
AS I WAS CHECKING ONE OF THE EQUATIONS MY HEART SUDDENLY STARTED TO BEAT WILDLY...
...I RETURNED TO SOME PREVIOUS CALCULATIONS, DONE ALMOST TWO YEARS EARLIER. I ONCE AGAIN SAW THE FIRST COMMENTS THAT MICHELE MADE REGARDING THE TRAJECTORY OF MERCURY AROUND THE SUN. EVERYTHING SEEMED RIGHT, IT WAS MOVING IN THE RIGHT DIRECTION...
I HAD HAD A HUNCH. AND TO FINISH MICHELE'S WORK I NEEDED TO TEST THE EQUATION WITH A NEW ELEMENT THAT THIS TIME I WOULD FIND IN THE VERY COMPLEX MATHEMATICS OF MARCEL GROSSMANN.
AND AFTER YEARS OF RESEARCH...
DAS STIMMT! THE FIRST PART IS CORRECT. LET'S SEE IF...
THAT'S IT... IT **WORKS**. MY THEORY **WORKS!**

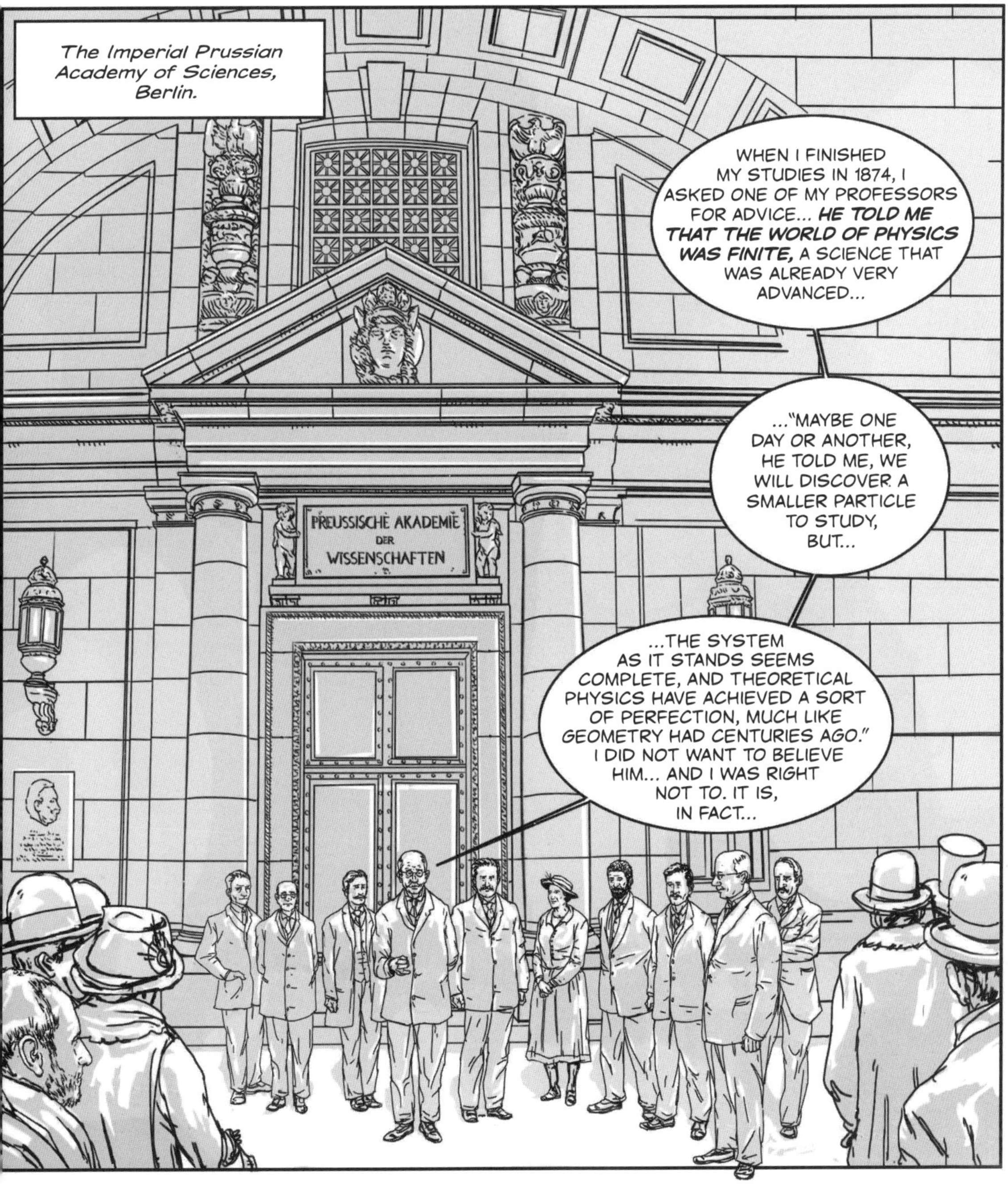
The Imperial Prussian Academy of Sciences, Berlin.
WHEN I FINISHED MY STUDIES IN 1874, I ASKED ONE OF MY PROFESSORS FOR ADVICE... **HE TOLD ME THAT THE WORLD OF PHYSICS WAS FINITE,** A SCIENCE THAT WAS ALREADY VERY ADVANCED...
..."MAYBE ONE DAY OR ANOTHER, HE TOLD ME, WE WILL DISCOVER A SMALLER PARTICLE TO STUDY, BUT...
...THE SYSTEM AS IT STANDS SEEMS COMPLETE, AND THEORETICAL PHYSICS HAVE ACHIEVED A SORT OF PERFECTION, MUCH LIKE GEOMETRY HAD CENTURIES AGO." I DID NOT WANT TO BELIEVE HIM... AND I WAS RIGHT NOT TO. IT IS, IN FACT...
PREUSSISCHE AKADEMIE DER WISSENSCHAFTEN

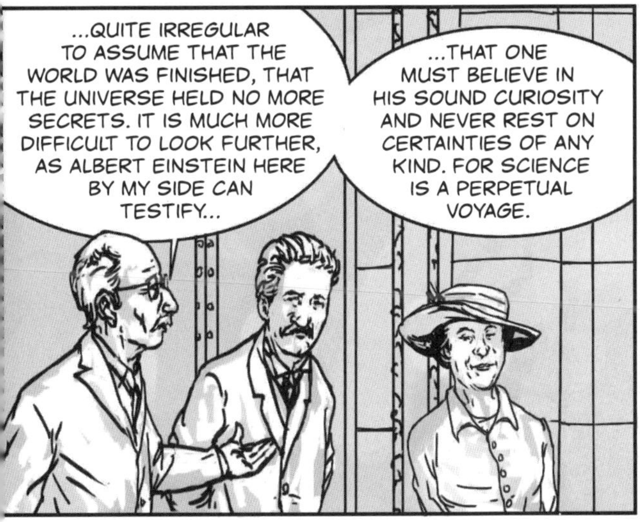
...QUITE IRREGULAR TO ASSUME THAT THE WORLD WAS FINISHED, THAT THE UNIVERSE HELD NO MORE SECRETS. IT IS MUCH MORE DIFFICULT TO LOOK FURTHER, AS ALBERT EINSTEIN HERE BY MY SIDE CAN TESTIFY...
...THAT ONE MUST BELIEVE IN HIS SOUND CURIOSITY AND NEVER REST ON CERTAINTIES OF ANY KIND. FOR SCIENCE IS A PERPETUAL VOYAGE.

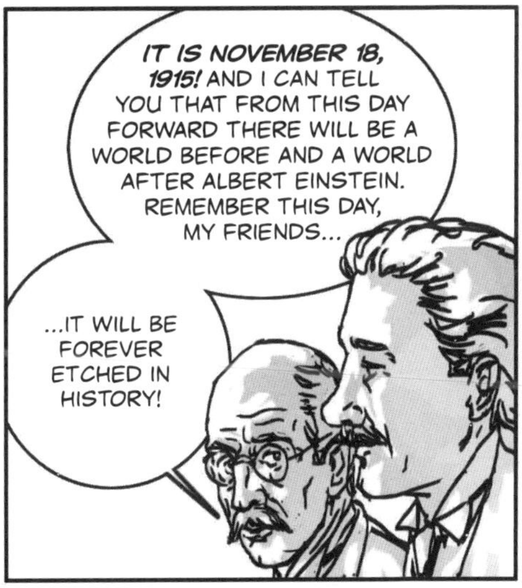
IT IS NOVEMBER 18, 1915! AND I CAN TELL YOU THAT FROM THIS DAY FORWARD THERE WILL BE A WORLD BEFORE AND A WORLD AFTER ALBERT EINSTEIN. REMEMBER THIS DAY, MY FRIENDS...
...IT WILL BE FOREVER ETCHED IN HISTORY!

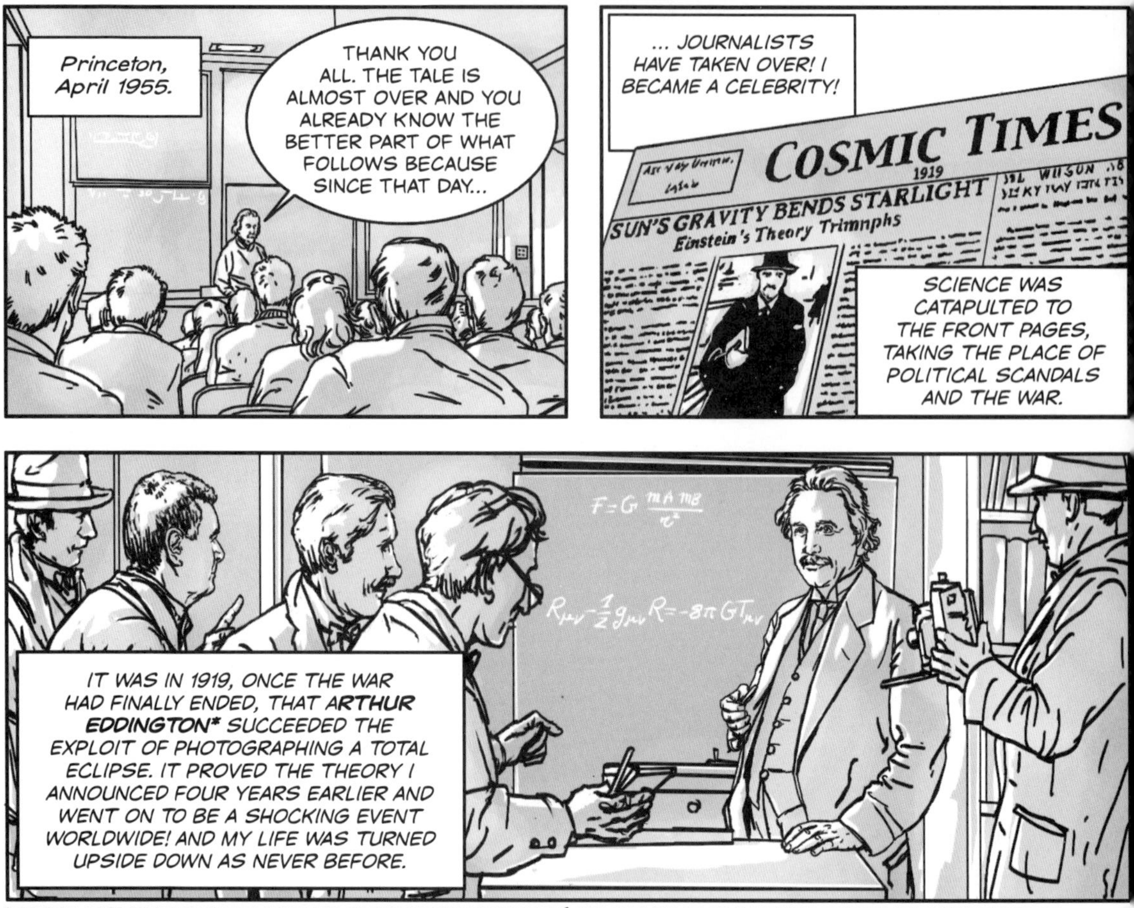
Princeton, April 1955.
THANK YOU ALL. THE TALE IS ALMOST OVER AND YOU ALREADY KNOW THE BETTER PART OF WHAT FOLLOWS BECAUSE SINCE THAT DAY...
... JOURNALISTS HAVE TAKEN OVER! I BECAME A CELEBRITY!
COSMIC TIMES
1919
SUN'S GRAVITY BENDS STARLIGHT
Einstein's Theory Trimnphs
SCIENCE WAS CATAPULTED TO THE FRONT PAGES, TAKING THE PLACE OF POLITICAL SCANDALS AND THE WAR.
$F = G\frac{m_A m_B}{r^2}$
$R_{\mu\nu} - \frac{1}{2} g_{\mu\nu} R = -8\pi G T_{\mu\nu}$
IT WAS IN 1919, ONCE THE WAR HAD FINALLY ENDED, THAT ARTHUR EDDINGTON* SUCCEEDED THE EXPLOIT OF PHOTOGRAPHING A TOTAL ECLIPSE. IT PROVED THE THEORY I ANNOUNCED FOUR YEARS EARLIER AND WENT ON TO BE A SHOCKING EVENT WORLDWIDE! AND MY LIFE WAS TURNED UPSIDE DOWN AS NEVER BEFORE.

* BRITISH ASTROPHYSICIST WHO BROUGHT AN EXPEDITION TO SAO TOMÉ OFF THE COAST OF GABON TO CONFIRM EINSTEIN'S THEORIES

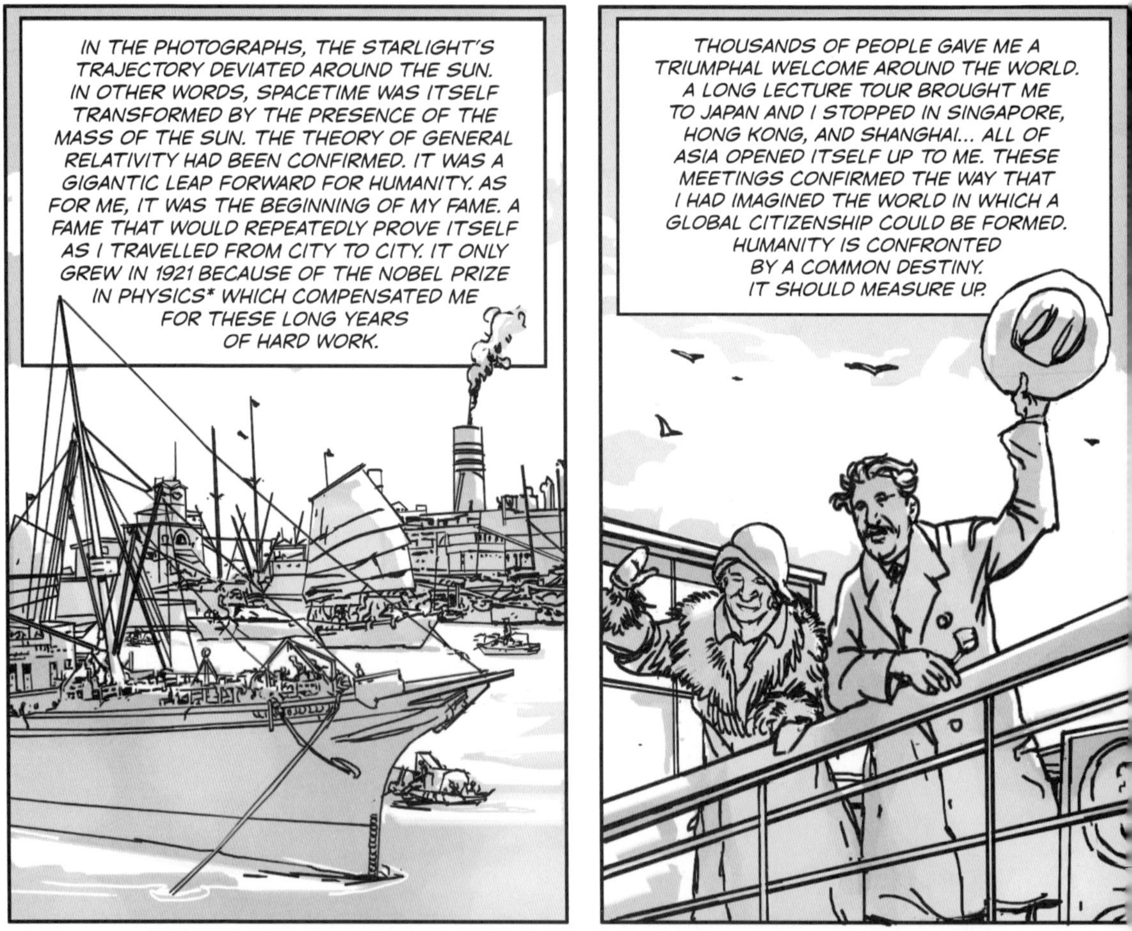
IN THE PHOTOGRAPHS, THE STARLIGHT'S TRAJECTORY DEVIATED AROUND THE SUN. IN OTHER WORDS, SPACETIME WAS ITSELF TRANSFORMED BY THE PRESENCE OF THE MASS OF THE SUN. THE THEORY OF GENERAL RELATIVITY HAD BEEN CONFIRMED. IT WAS A GIGANTIC LEAP FORWARD FOR HUMANITY. AS FOR ME, IT WAS THE BEGINNING OF MY FAME. A FAME THAT WOULD REPEATEDLY PROVE ITSELF AS I TRAVELLED FROM CITY TO CITY. IT ONLY GREW IN 1921 BECAUSE OF THE NOBEL PRIZE IN PHYSICS* WHICH COMPENSATED ME FOR THESE LONG YEARS OF HARD WORK.
THOUSANDS OF PEOPLE GAVE ME A TRIUMPHAL WELCOME AROUND THE WORLD. A LONG LECTURE TOUR BROUGHT ME TO JAPAN AND I STOPPED IN SINGAPORE, HONG KONG, AND SHANGHAI... ALL OF ASIA OPENED ITSELF UP TO ME. THESE MEETINGS CONFIRMED THE WAY THAT I HAD IMAGINED THE WORLD IN WHICH A GLOBAL CITIZENSHIP COULD BE FORMED. HUMANITY IS CONFRONTED BY A COMMON DESTINY. IT SHOULD MEASURE UP.

*THE NOBEL PRIZE WAS AWARDED TO ALBERT EINSTEIN FOR HIS WORK ON THE PHOTOELECTRIC EFFECT.

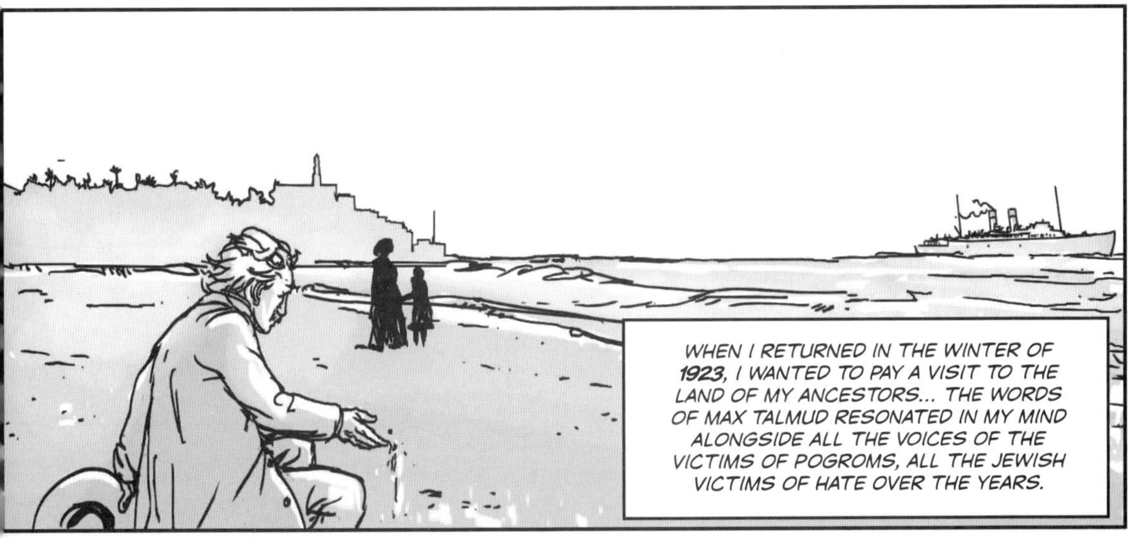
WHEN I RETURNED IN THE WINTER OF 1923, I WANTED TO PAY A VISIT TO THE LAND OF MY ANCESTORS... THE WORDS OF MAX TALMUD RESONATED IN MY MIND ALONGSIDE ALL THE VOICES OF THE VICTIMS OF POGROMS, ALL THE JEWISH VICTIMS OF HATE OVER THE YEARS.

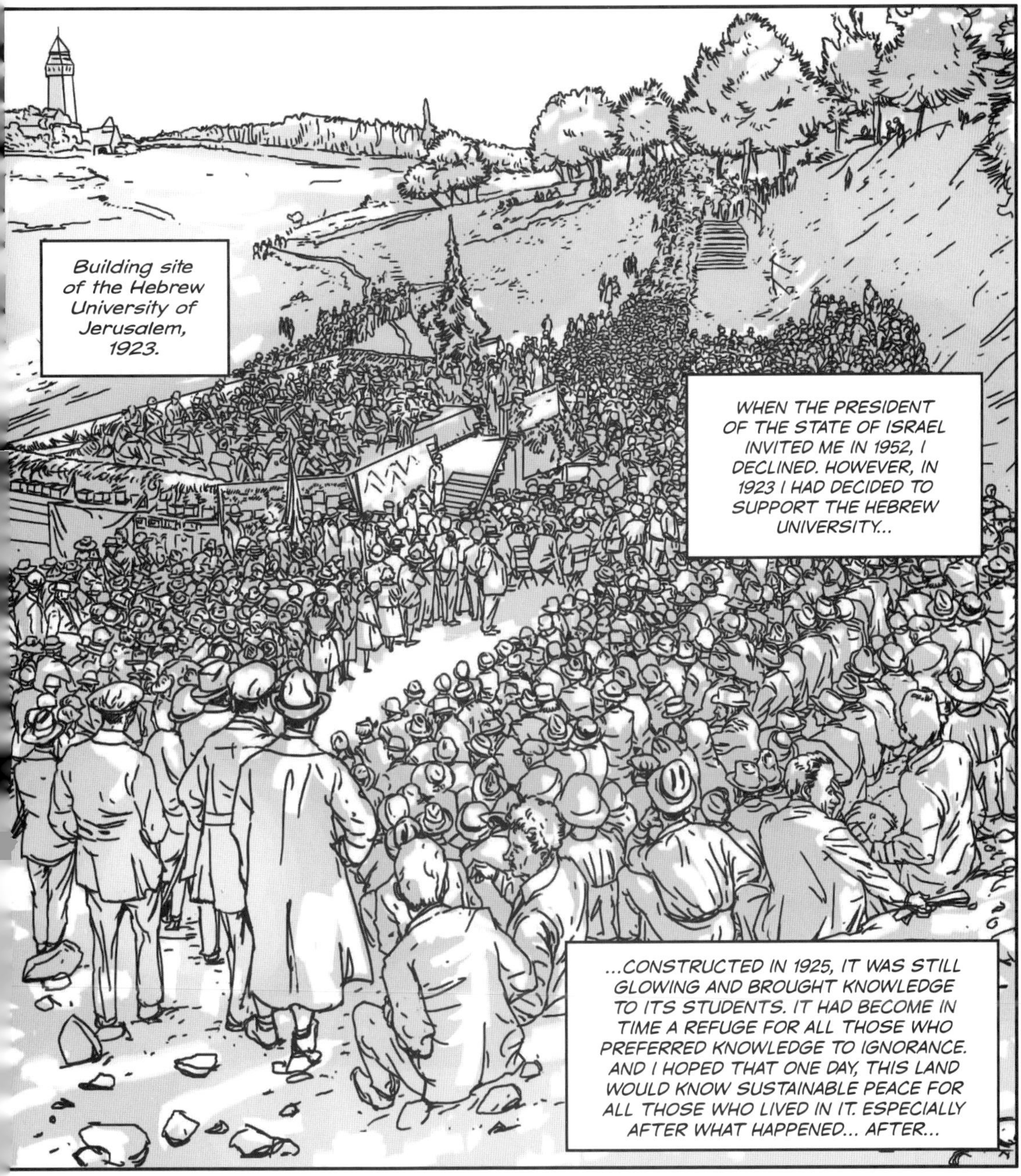
Building site of the Hebrew University of Jerusalem, 1923.
WHEN THE PRESIDENT OF THE STATE OF ISRAEL INVITED ME IN 1952, I DECLINED. HOWEVER, IN 1923 I HAD DECIDED TO SUPPORT THE HEBREW UNIVERSITY...
...CONSTRUCTED IN 1925, IT WAS STILL GLOWING AND BROUGHT KNOWLEDGE TO ITS STUDENTS. IT HAD BECOME IN TIME A REFUGE FOR ALL THOSE WHO PREFERRED KNOWLEDGE TO IGNORANCE. AND I HOPED THAT ONE DAY, THIS LAND WOULD KNOW SUSTAINABLE PEACE FOR ALL THOSE WHO LIVED IN IT. ESPECIALLY AFTER WHAT HAPPENED... AFTER...

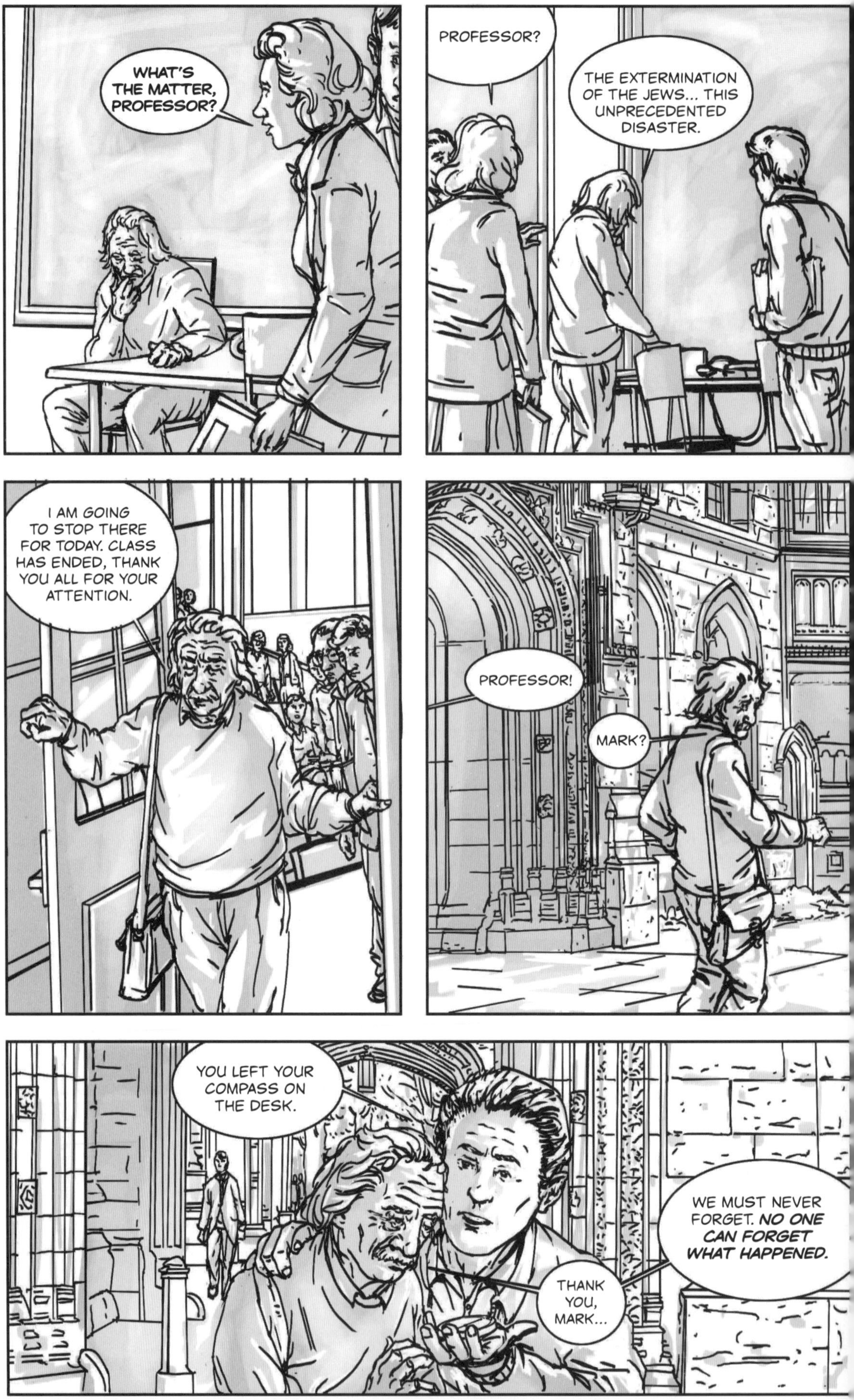
WHAT'S THE MATTER, PROFESSOR?
PROFESSOR?
THE EXTERMINATION OF THE JEWS... THIS UNPRECEDENTED DISASTER.
I AM GOING TO STOP THERE FOR TODAY. CLASS HAS ENDED, THANK YOU ALL FOR YOUR ATTENTION.
PROFESSOR!
MARK?
YOU LEFT YOUR COMPASS ON THE DESK.
WE MUST NEVER FORGET. ***NO ONE CAN FORGET WHAT HAPPENED.***
THANK YOU, MARK...

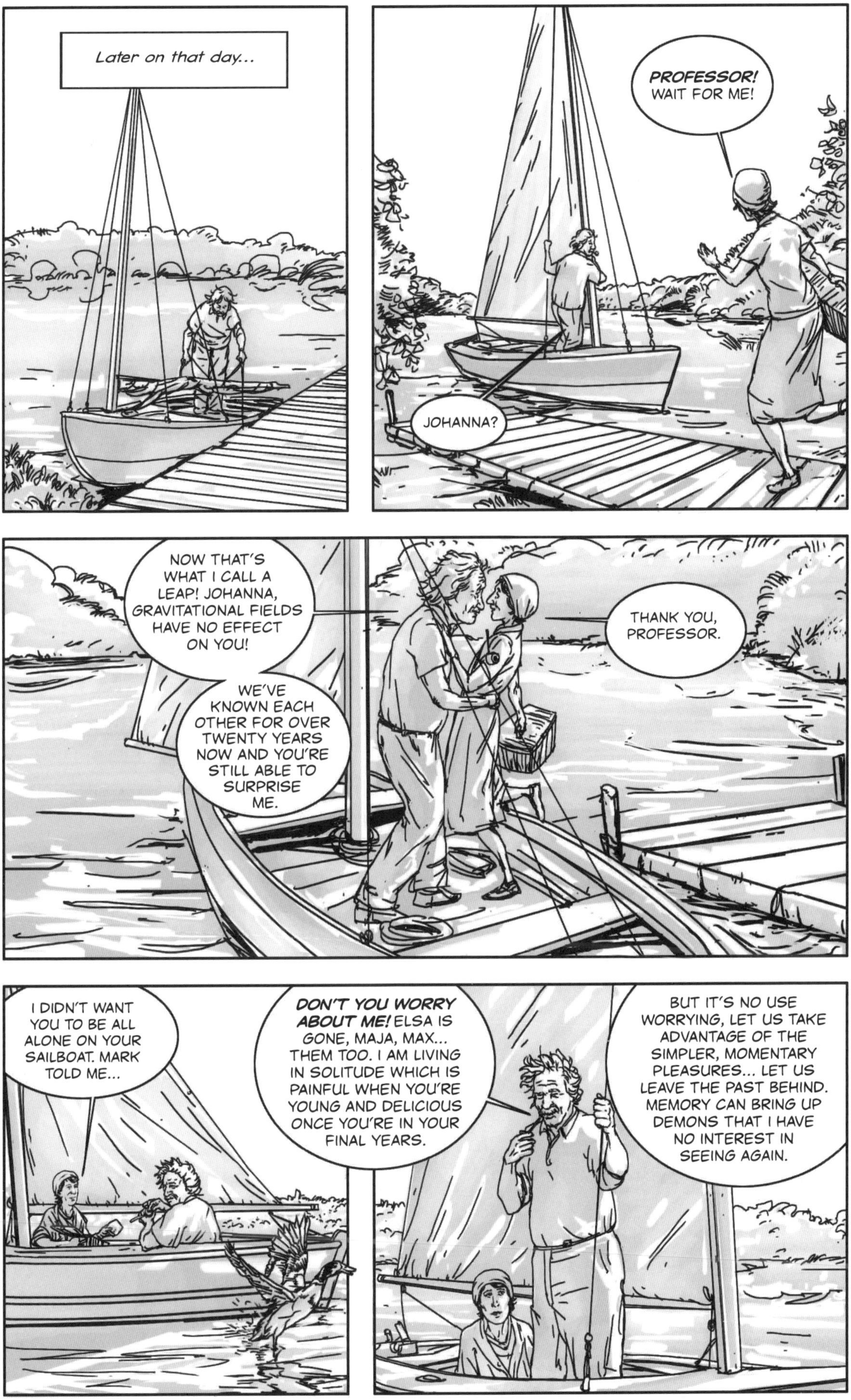
Later on that day...
PROFESSOR! WAIT FOR ME!
JOHANNA?
NOW THAT'S WHAT I CALL A LEAP! JOHANNA, GRAVITATIONAL FIELDS HAVE NO EFFECT ON YOU!
WE'VE KNOWN EACH OTHER FOR OVER TWENTY YEARS NOW AND YOU'RE STILL ABLE TO SURPRISE ME.
THANK YOU, PROFESSOR.
I DIDN'T WANT YOU TO BE ALL ALONE ON YOUR SAILBOAT. MARK TOLD ME...
DON'T YOU WORRY ABOUT ME! ELSA IS GONE, MAJA, MAX... THEM TOO. I AM LIVING IN SOLITUDE WHICH IS PAINFUL WHEN YOU'RE YOUNG AND DELICIOUS ONCE YOU'RE IN YOUR FINAL YEARS.
BUT IT'S NO USE WORRYING, LET US TAKE ADVANTAGE OF THE SIMPLER, MOMENTARY PLEASURES... LET US LEAVE THE PAST BEHIND. MEMORY CAN BRING UP DEMONS THAT I HAVE NO INTEREST IN SEEING AGAIN.

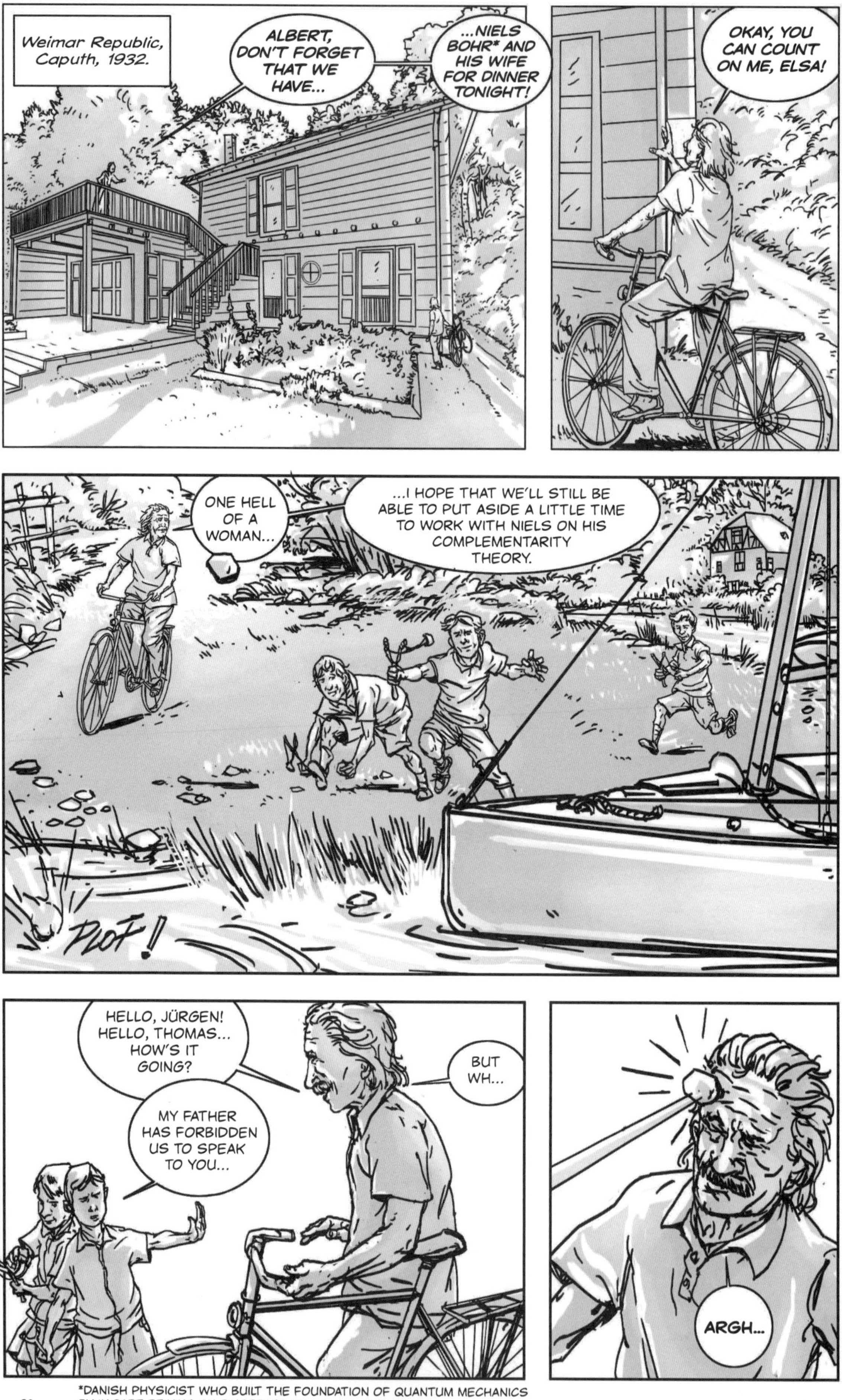
Weimar Republic, Caputh, 1932.
ALBERT, DON'T FORGET THAT WE HAVE...
...NIELS BOHR* AND HIS WIFE FOR DINNER TONIGHT!
OKAY, YOU CAN COUNT ON ME, ELSA!
ONE HELL OF A WOMAN...
...I HOPE THAT WE'LL STILL BE ABLE TO PUT ASIDE A LITTLE TIME TO WORK WITH NIELS ON HIS COMPLEMENTARITY THEORY.
PLOF!
HELLO, JÜRGEN! HELLO, THOMAS... HOW'S IT GOING?
BUT WH...
MY FATHER HAS FORBIDDEN US TO SPEAK TO YOU...
ARGH...

*DANISH PHYSICIST WHO BUILT THE FOUNDATION OF QUANTUM MECHANICS BY IN PART RELYING ON EINSTEIN'S WORK ON LIGHT QUANTA.

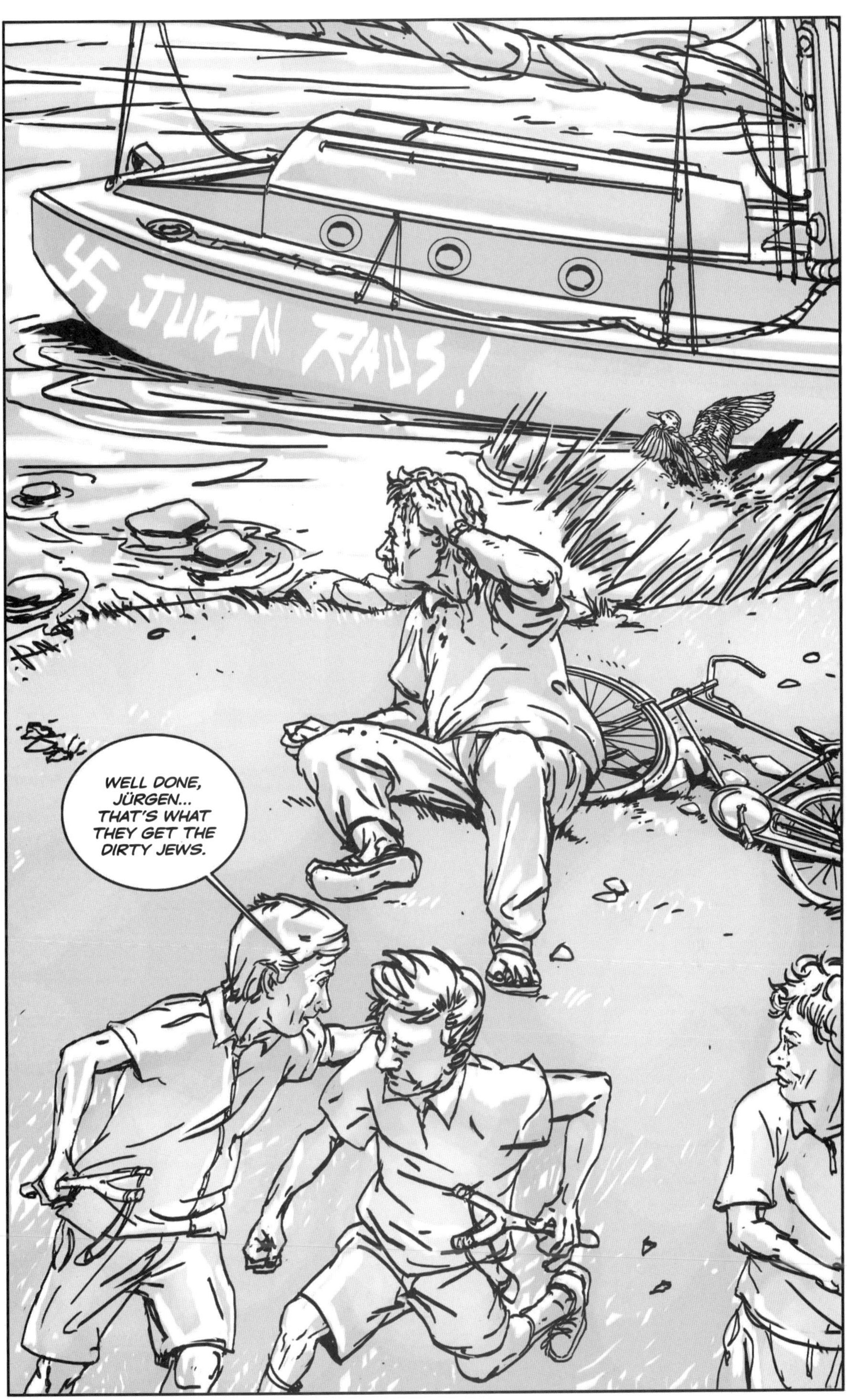
JUDEN RAUS!
WELL DONE, JÜRGEN... THAT'S WHAT THEY GET THE DIRTY JEWS.

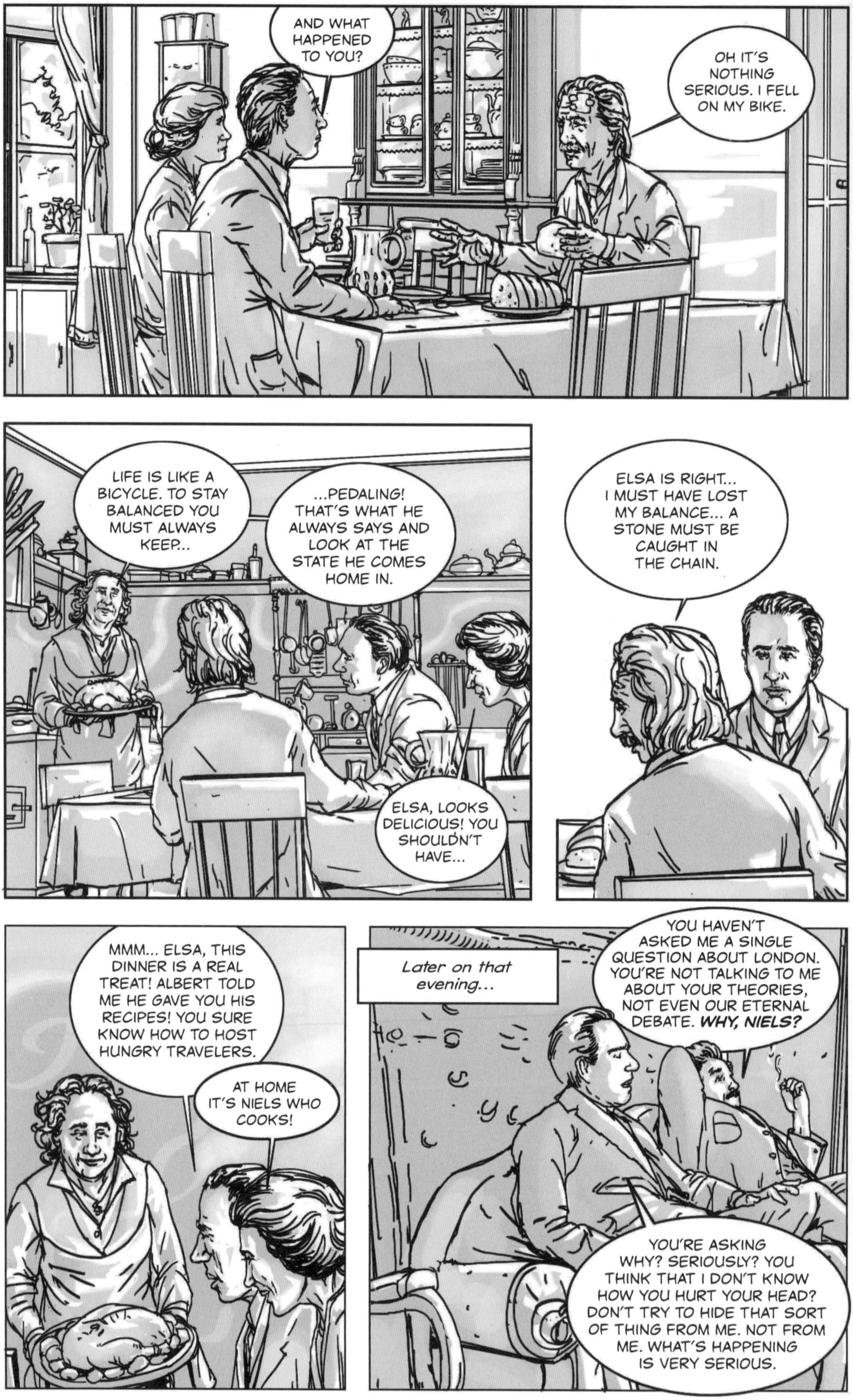
AND WHAT HAPPENED TO YOU?
OH IT'S NOTHING SERIOUS. I FELL ON MY BIKE.
LIFE IS LIKE A BICYCLE. TO STAY BALANCED YOU MUST ALWAYS KEEP...
...PEDALING! THAT'S WHAT HE ALWAYS SAYS AND LOOK AT THE STATE HE COMES HOME IN.
ELSA, LOOKS DELICIOUS! YOU SHOULDN'T HAVE...
ELSA IS RIGHT... I MUST HAVE LOST MY BALANCE... A STONE MUST BE CAUGHT IN THE CHAIN.
MMM... ELSA, THIS DINNER IS A REAL TREAT! ALBERT TOLD ME HE GAVE YOU HIS RECIPES! YOU SURE KNOW HOW TO HOST HUNGRY TRAVELERS.
AT HOME IT'S NIELS WHO COOKS!
Later on that evening...
YOU HAVEN'T ASKED ME A SINGLE QUESTION ABOUT LONDON. YOU'RE NOT TALKING TO ME ABOUT YOUR THEORIES, NOT EVEN OUR ETERNAL DEBATE. ***WHY, NIELS?***
YOU'RE ASKING WHY? SERIOUSLY? YOU THINK THAT I DON'T KNOW HOW YOU HURT YOUR HEAD? DON'T TRY TO HIDE THAT SORT OF THING FROM ME. NOT FROM ME. WHAT'S HAPPENING IS VERY SERIOUS.

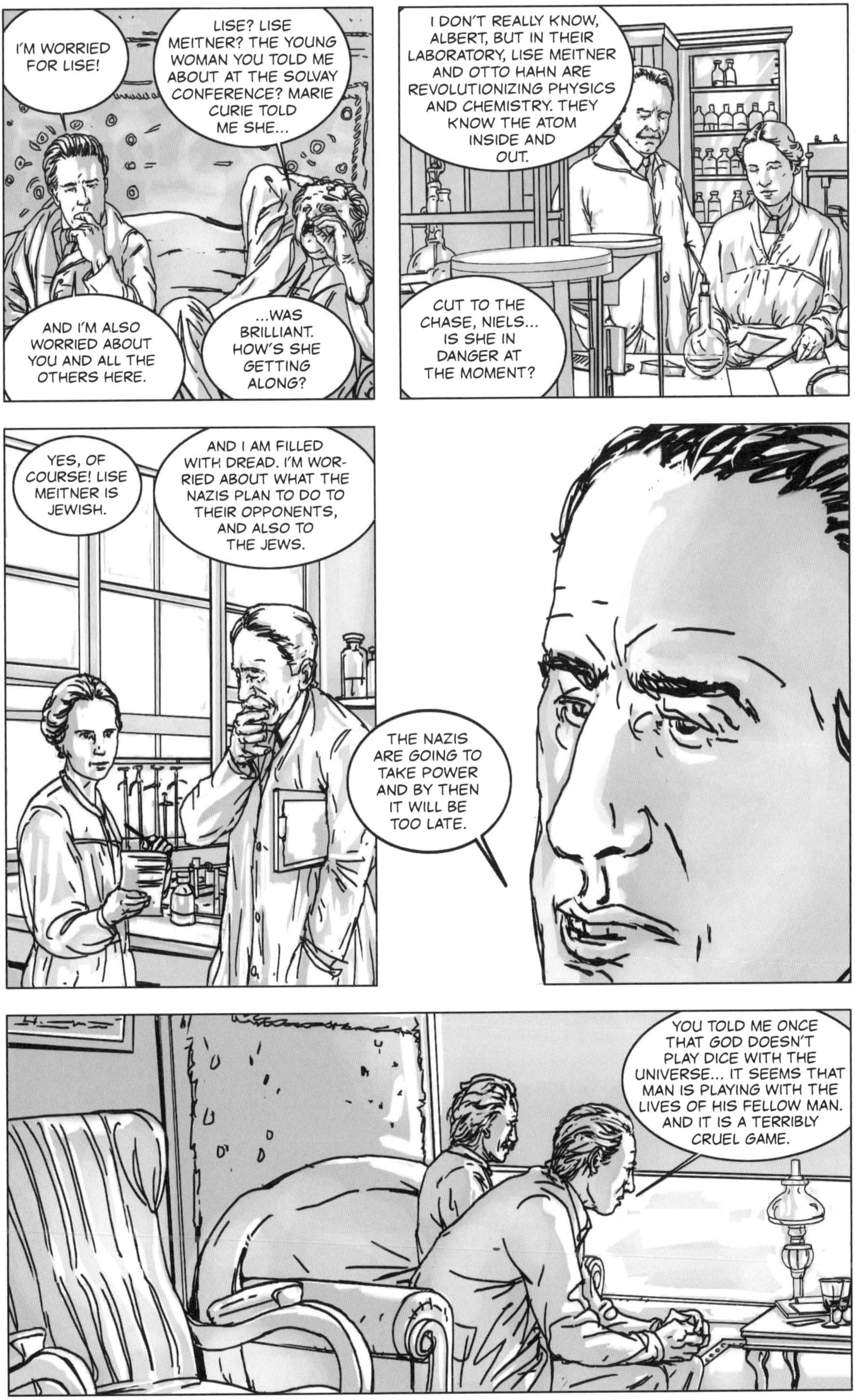
I'M WORRIED FOR LISE!
LISE? LISE MEITNER? THE YOUNG WOMAN YOU TOLD ME ABOUT AT THE SOLVAY CONFERENCE? MARIE CURIE TOLD ME SHE...
AND I'M ALSO WORRIED ABOUT YOU AND ALL THE OTHERS HERE.
...WAS BRILLIANT. HOW'S SHE GETTING ALONG?
I DON'T REALLY KNOW, ALBERT, BUT IN THEIR LABORATORY, LISE MEITNER AND OTTO HAHN ARE REVOLUTIONIZING PHYSICS AND CHEMISTRY. THEY KNOW THE ATOM INSIDE AND OUT.
CUT TO THE CHASE, NIELS... IS SHE IN DANGER AT THE MOMENT?
YES, OF COURSE! LISE MEITNER IS JEWISH.
AND I AM FILLED WITH DREAD. I'M WORRIED ABOUT WHAT THE NAZIS PLAN TO DO TO THEIR OPPONENTS, AND ALSO TO THE JEWS.
THE NAZIS ARE GOING TO TAKE POWER AND BY THEN IT WILL BE TOO LATE.
YOU TOLD ME ONCE THAT GOD DOESN'T PLAY DICE WITH THE UNIVERSE... IT SEEMS THAT MAN IS PLAYING WITH THE LIVES OF HIS FELLOW MAN. AND IT IS A TERRIBLY CRUEL GAME.

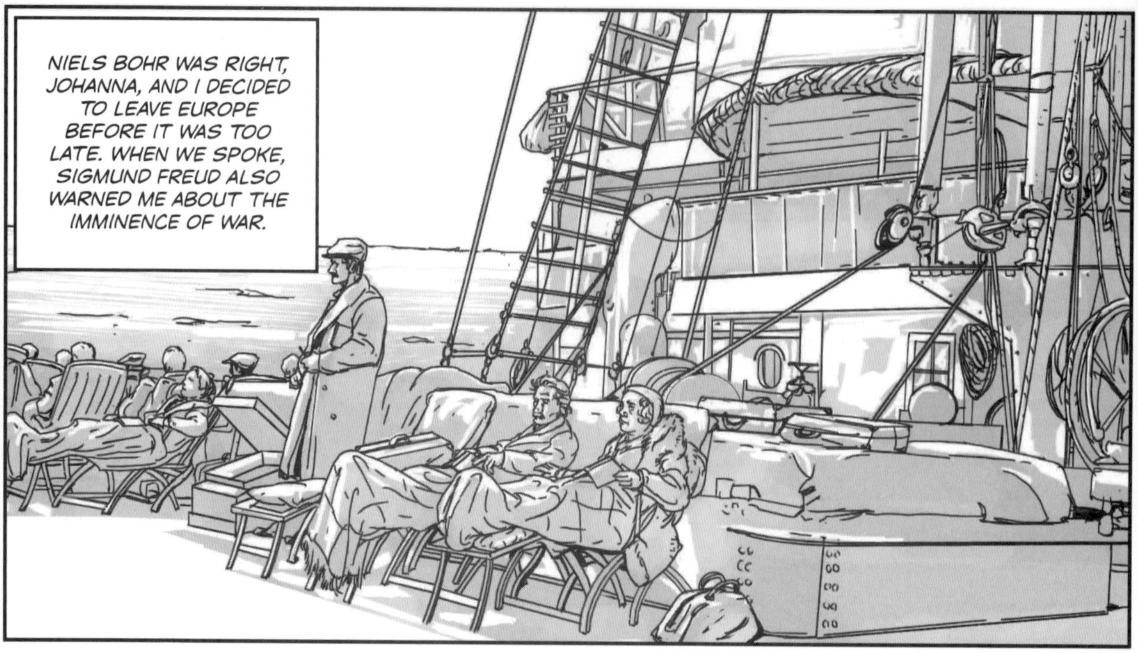
NIELS BOHR WAS RIGHT, JOHANNA, AND I DECIDED TO LEAVE EUROPE BEFORE IT WAS TOO LATE. WHEN WE SPOKE, SIGMUND FREUD ALSO WARNED ME ABOUT THE IMMINENCE OF WAR.

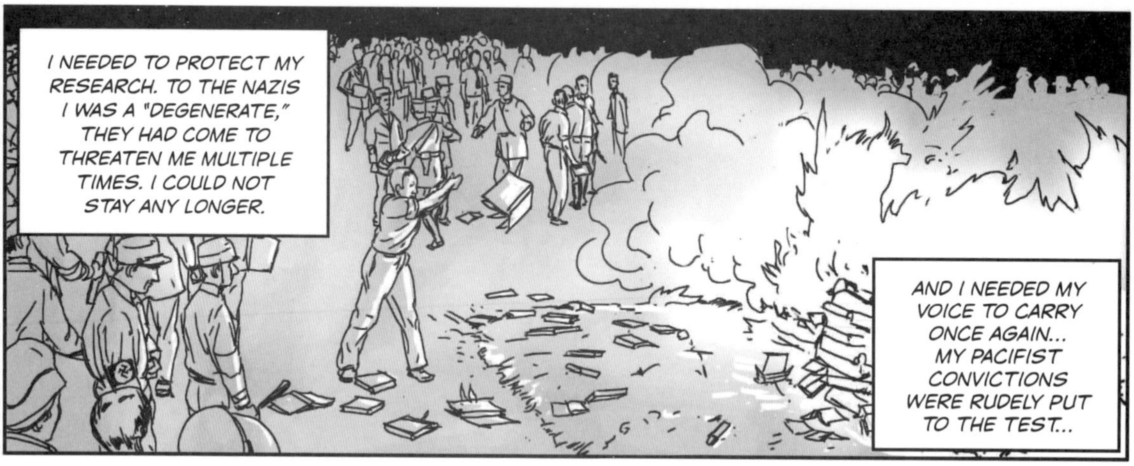
I NEEDED TO PROTECT MY RESEARCH. TO THE NAZIS I WAS A "DEGENERATE," THEY HAD COME TO THREATEN ME MULTIPLE TIMES. I COULD NOT STAY ANY LONGER.
AND I NEEDED MY VOICE TO CARRY ONCE AGAIN... MY PACIFIST CONVICTIONS WERE RUDELY PUT TO THE TEST...

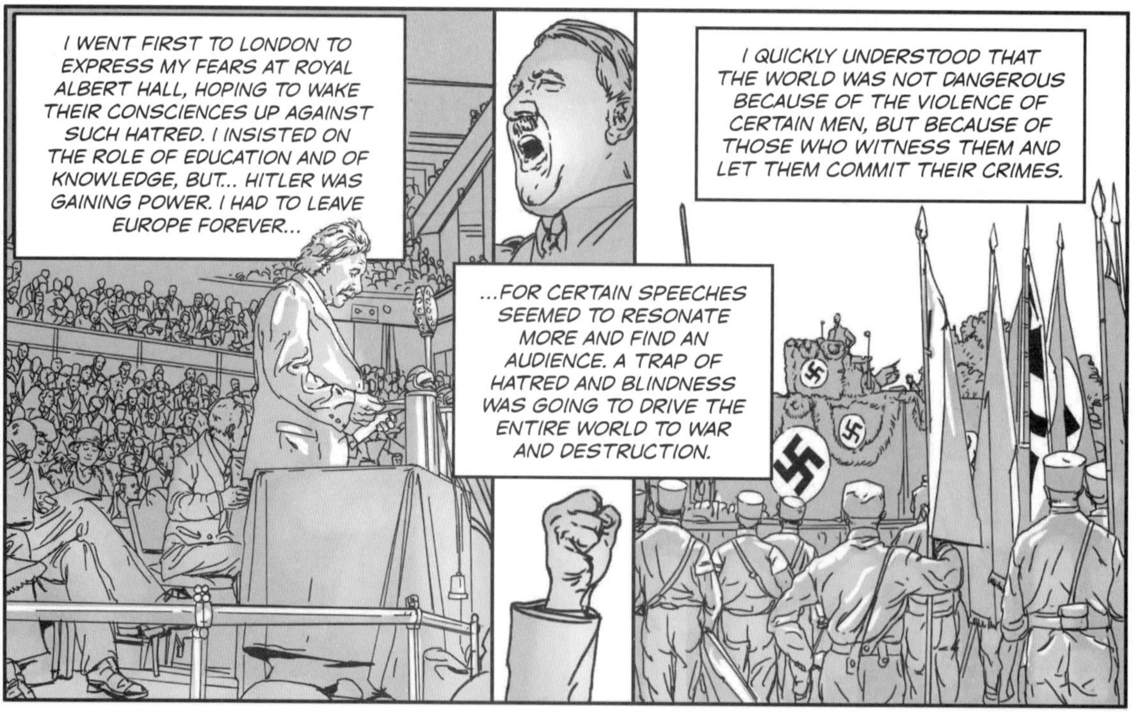
I WENT FIRST TO LONDON TO EXPRESS MY FEARS AT ROYAL ALBERT HALL, HOPING TO WAKE THEIR CONSCIENCES UP AGAINST SUCH HATRED. I INSISTED ON THE ROLE OF EDUCATION AND OF KNOWLEDGE, BUT... HITLER WAS GAINING POWER. I HAD TO LEAVE EUROPE FOREVER...
...FOR CERTAIN SPEECHES SEEMED TO RESONATE MORE AND FIND AN AUDIENCE. A TRAP OF HATRED AND BLINDNESS WAS GOING TO DRIVE THE ENTIRE WORLD TO WAR AND DESTRUCTION.
I QUICKLY UNDERSTOOD THAT THE WORLD WAS NOT DANGEROUS BECAUSE OF THE VIOLENCE OF CERTAIN MEN, BUT BECAUSE OF THOSE WHO WITNESS THEM AND LET THEM COMMIT THEIR CRIMES.

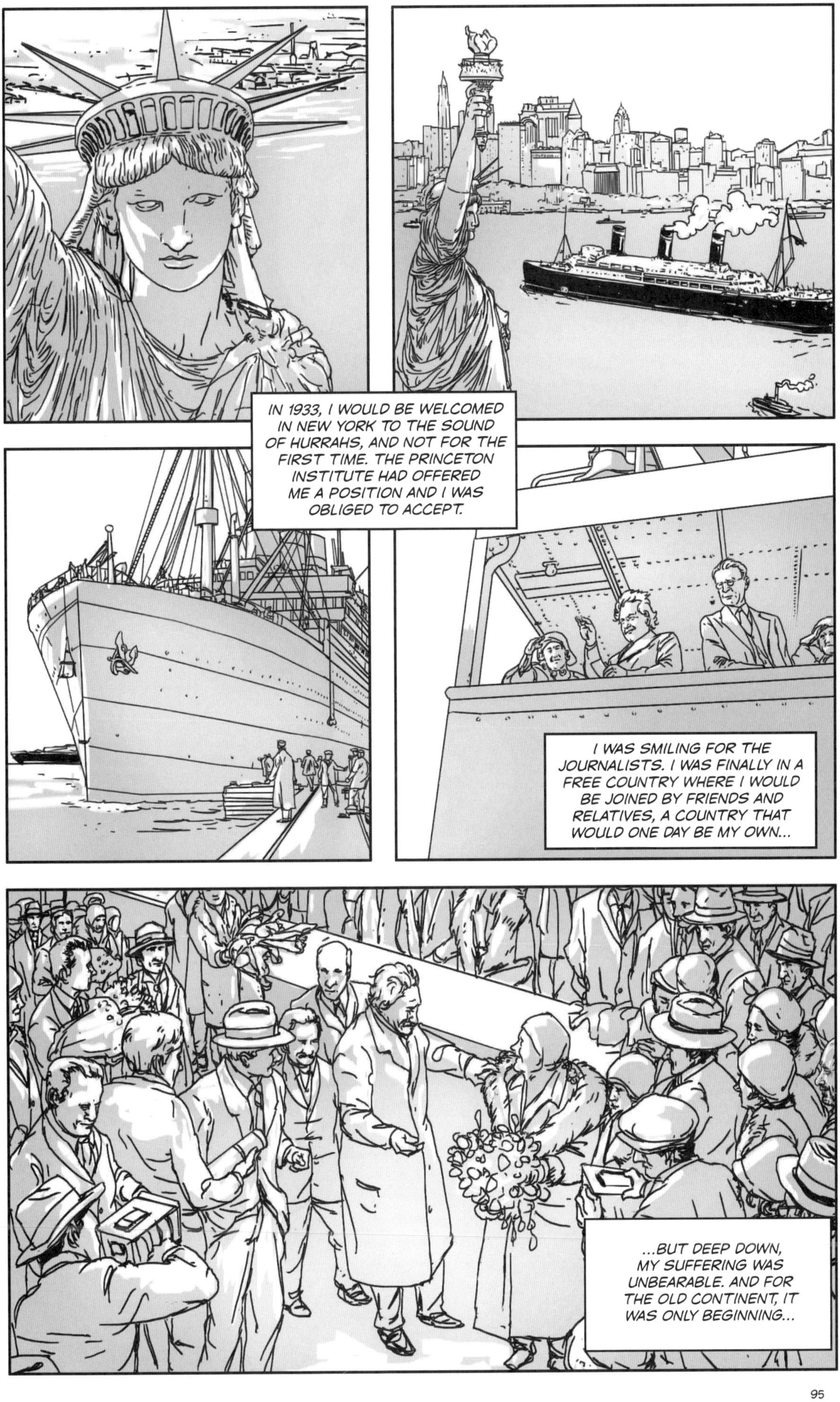
IN 1933, I WOULD BE WELCOMED IN NEW YORK TO THE SOUND OF HURRAHS, AND NOT FOR THE FIRST TIME. THE PRINCETON INSTITUTE HAD OFFERED ME A POSITION AND I WAS OBLIGED TO ACCEPT.
I WAS SMILING FOR THE JOURNALISTS. I WAS FINALLY IN A FREE COUNTRY WHERE I WOULD BE JOINED BY FRIENDS AND RELATIVES, A COUNTRY THAT WOULD ONE DAY BE MY OWN...
...BUT DEEP DOWN, MY SUFFERING WAS UNBEARABLE. AND FOR THE OLD CONTINENT, IT WAS ONLY BEGINNING...

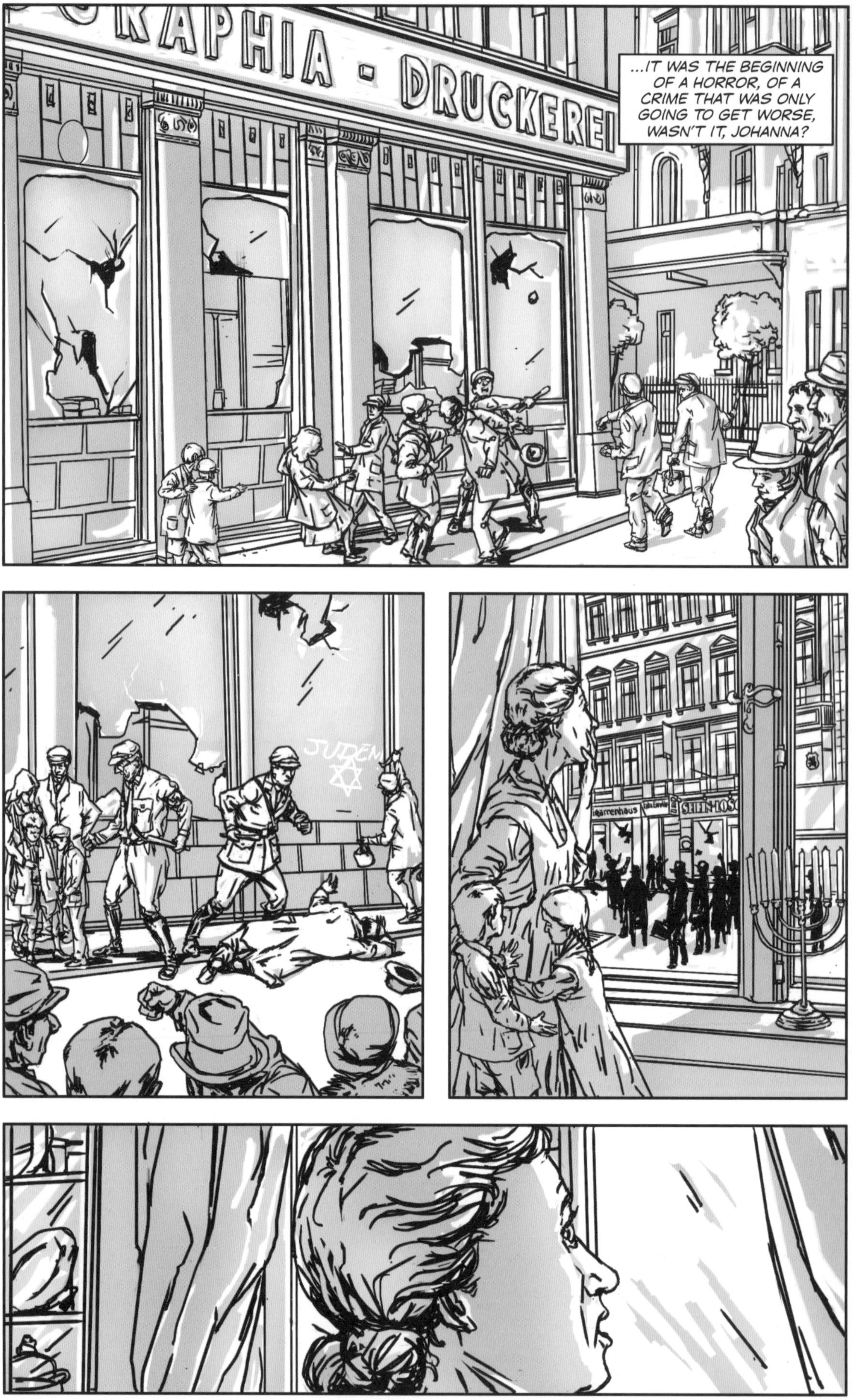
...IT WAS THE BEGINNING OF A HORROR, OF A CRIME THAT WAS ONLY GOING TO GET WORSE, WASN'T IT, JOHANNA?
DRUCKEREI
JUDEN

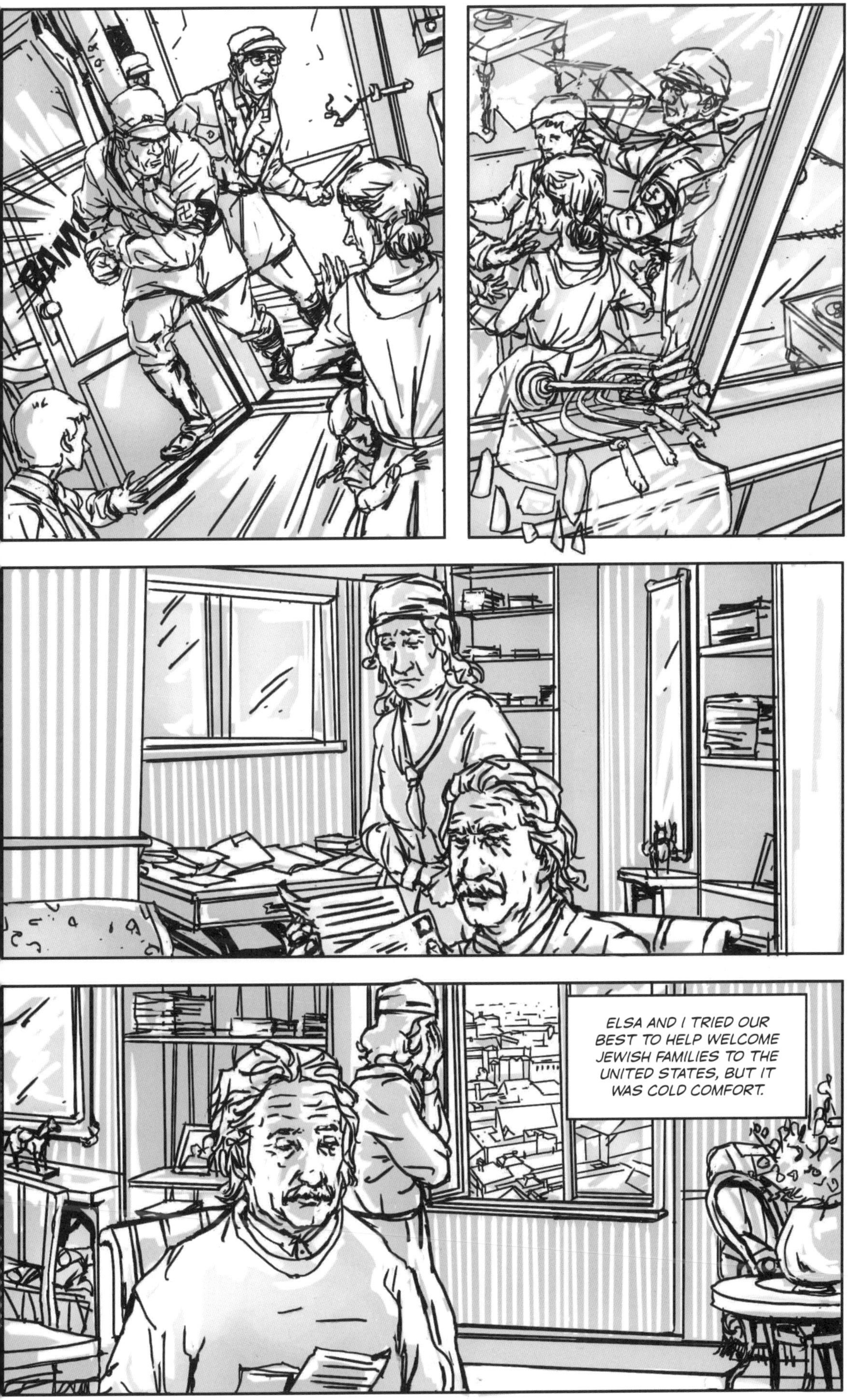
BAM!
ELSA AND I TRIED OUR BEST TO HELP WELCOME JEWISH FAMILIES TO THE UNITED STATES, BUT IT WAS COLD COMFORT.

I WAS COMING OFF SEVERAL LONG, DARK YEARS AND IT WAS FAR FROM BEING OVER... IN 1936, ELSA LEFT ME FOR ANOTHER WORLD. I DIDN'T GET A CHANCE TO SAY A REAL GOODBYE. MARCEL GROSSMANN, MY OLD FRIEND, FOLLOWED CLOSELY BEHIND HER...

AS FOR LISE MEITNER, THE NAZIS QUICKLY UNDERSTOOD THAT HER RESEARCH COULD BE USEFUL TO THEM. PARTICULARLY WHEN IN 1938 SHE DISCOVERED A SUBSTANCE EVEN MORE DENSE THAN URANIUM...

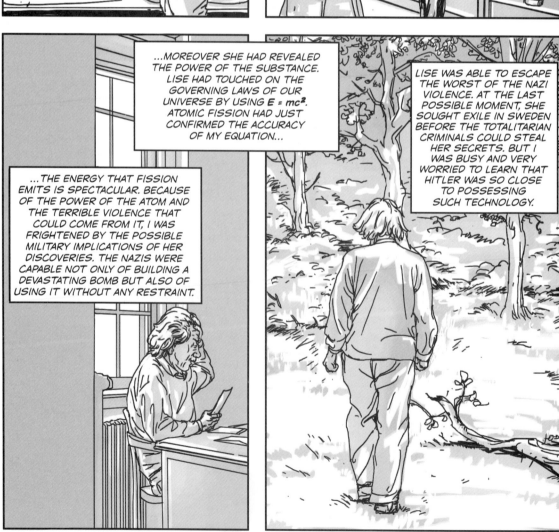

...MOREOVER SHE HAD REVEALED THE POWER OF THE SUBSTANCE. LISE HAD TOUCHED ON THE GOVERNING LAWS OF OUR UNIVERSE BY USING $E = mc^2$. ATOMIC FISSION HAD JUST CONFIRMED THE ACCURACY OF MY EQUATION...

...THE ENERGY THAT FISSION EMITS IS SPECTACULAR. BECAUSE OF THE POWER OF THE ATOM AND THE TERRIBLE VIOLENCE THAT COULD COME FROM IT, I WAS FRIGHTENED BY THE POSSIBLE MILITARY IMPLICATIONS OF HER DISCOVERIES. THE NAZIS WERE CAPABLE NOT ONLY OF BUILDING A DEVASTATING BOMB BUT ALSO OF USING IT WITHOUT ANY RESTRAINT.

LISE WAS ABLE TO ESCAPE THE WORST OF THE NAZI VIOLENCE. AT THE LAST POSSIBLE MOMENT, SHE SOUGHT EXILE IN SWEDEN BEFORE THE TOTALITARIAN CRIMINALS COULD STEAL HER SECRETS. BUT I WAS BUSY AND VERY WORRIED TO LEARN THAT HITLER WAS SO CLOSE TO POSSESSING SUCH TECHNOLOGY.

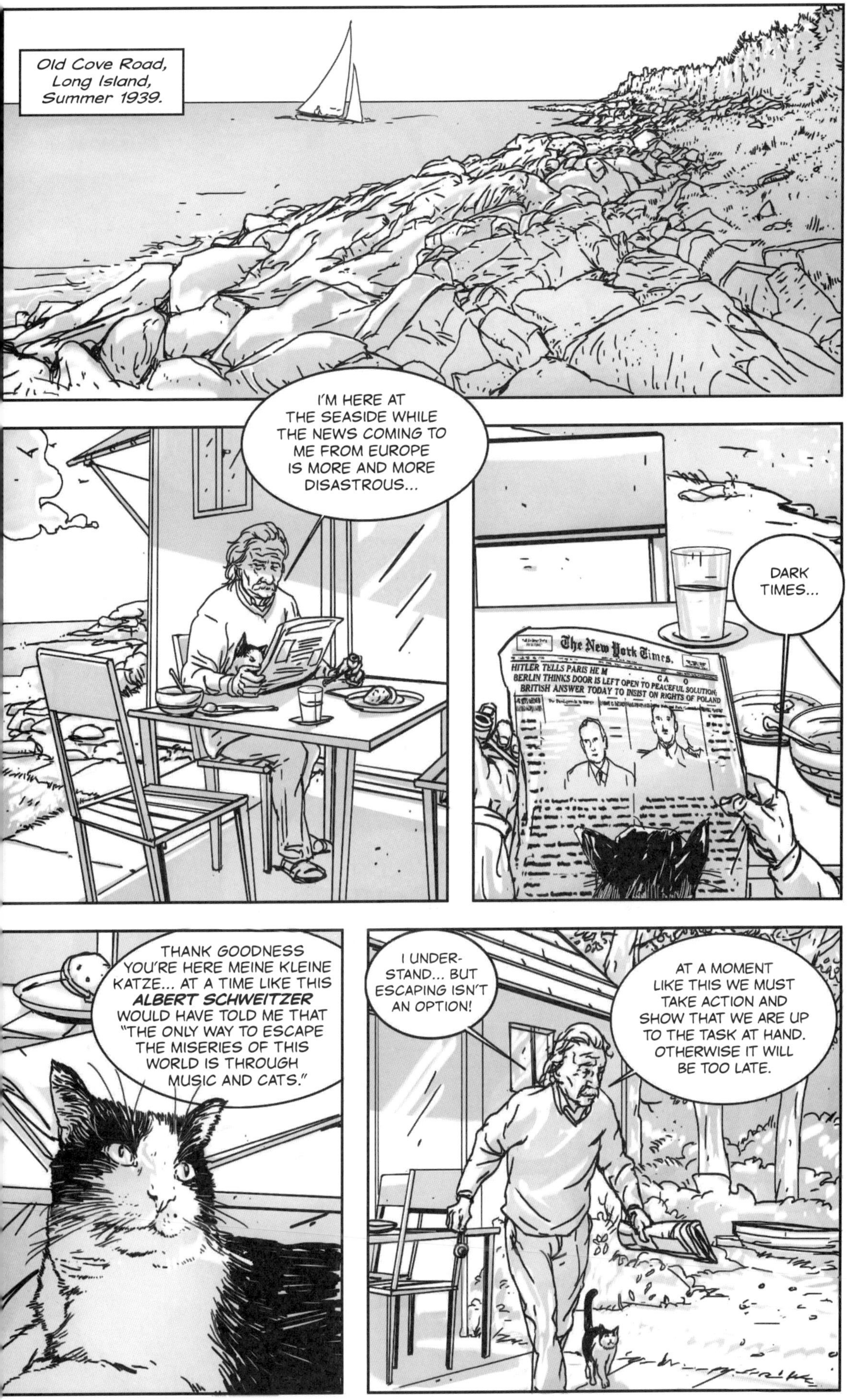
Old Cove Road, Long Island, Summer 1939.
I'M HERE AT THE SEASIDE WHILE THE NEWS COMING TO ME FROM EUROPE IS MORE AND MORE DISASTROUS...
The New York Times.
BERLIN THINKS DOOR IS LEFT OPEN TO PEACEFUL SOLUTION;
BRITISH ANSWER TODAY TO INSIST ON RIGHTS OF POLAND
DARK TIMES...
THANK GOODNESS YOU'RE HERE MEINE KLEINE KATZE... AT A TIME LIKE THIS ***ALBERT SCHWEITZER*** WOULD HAVE TOLD ME THAT "THE ONLY WAY TO ESCAPE THE MISERIES OF THIS WORLD IS THROUGH MUSIC AND CATS."
I UNDERSTAND... BUT ESCAPING ISN'T AN OPTION!
AT A MOMENT LIKE THIS WE MUST TAKE ACTION AND SHOW THAT WE ARE UP TO THE TASK AT HAND. OTHERWISE IT WILL BE TOO LATE.

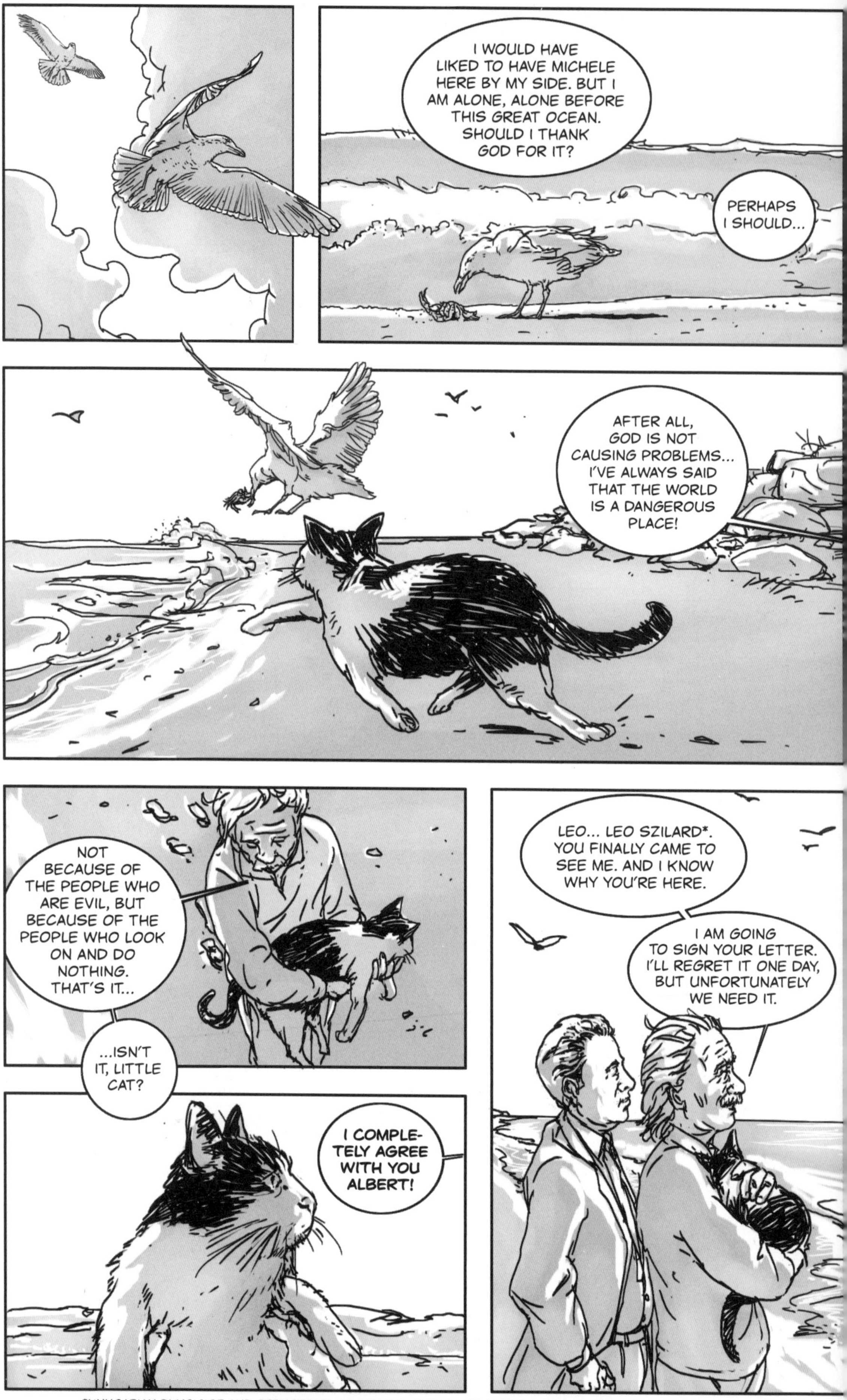
I WOULD HAVE LIKED TO HAVE MICHELE HERE BY MY SIDE. BUT I AM ALONE, ALONE BEFORE THIS GREAT OCEAN. SHOULD I THANK GOD FOR IT?
PERHAPS I SHOULD...
AFTER ALL, GOD IS NOT CAUSING PROBLEMS... I'VE ALWAYS SAID THAT THE WORLD IS A DANGEROUS PLACE!
NOT BECAUSE OF THE PEOPLE WHO ARE EVIL, BUT BECAUSE OF THE PEOPLE WHO LOOK ON AND DO NOTHING. THAT'S IT...
...ISN'T IT, LITTLE CAT?
I COMPLE-TELY AGREE WITH YOU ALBERT!
LEO... LEO SZILARD*. YOU FINALLY CAME TO SEE ME. AND I KNOW WHY YOU'RE HERE.
I AM GOING TO SIGN YOUR LETTER. I'LL REGRET IT ONE DAY, BUT UNFORTUNATELY WE NEED IT.

*HUNGARIAN PHYSICIST AND REFUGEE TO THE UNITED STATES. HE IS THE FIRST, ALONG WITH ENRICO FERMI, TO COME UP WITH A TECHNICAL APPROACH TO MANAGING NUCLEAR ENERGY.

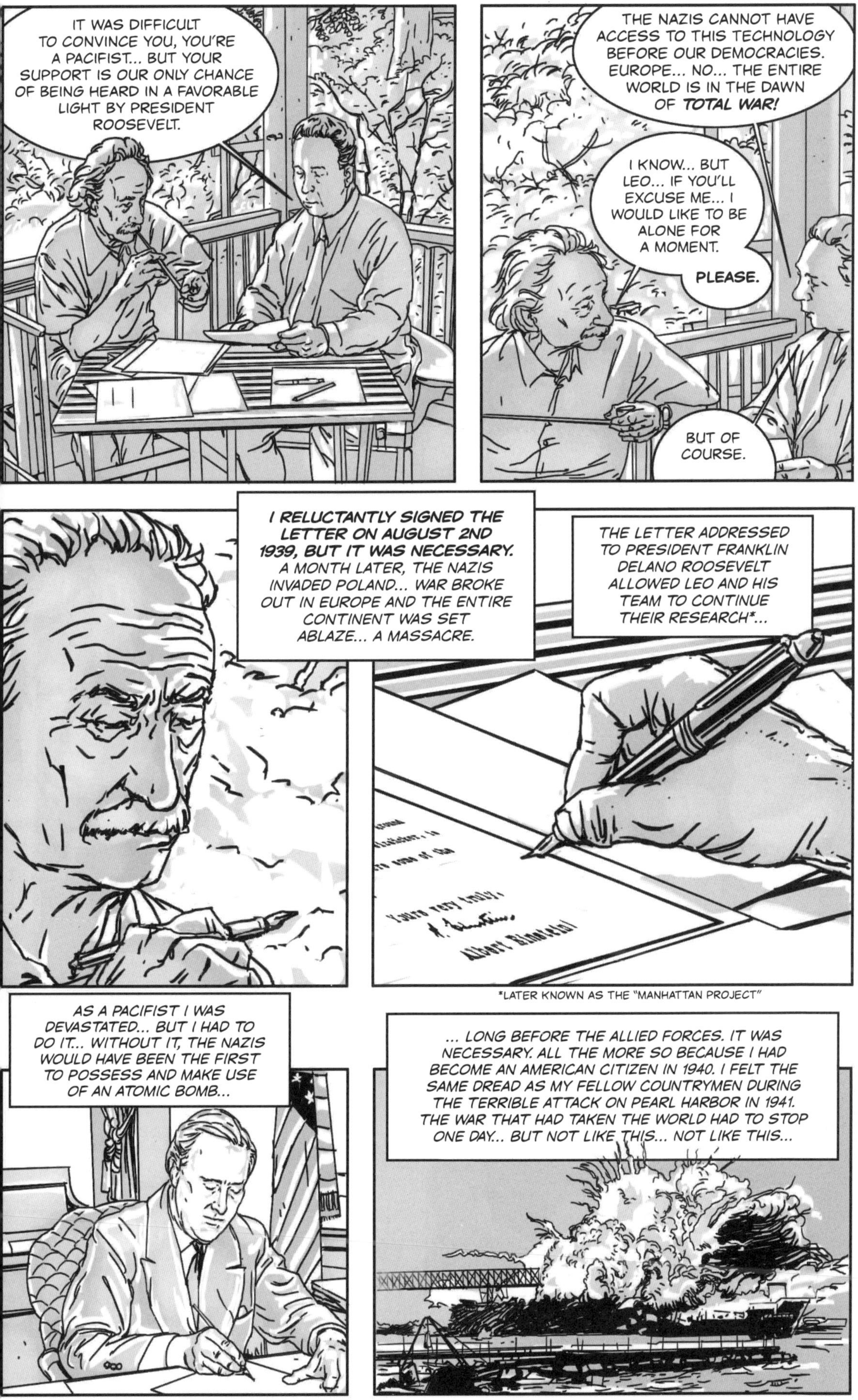
IT WAS DIFFICULT TO CONVINCE YOU, YOU'RE A PACIFIST... BUT YOUR SUPPORT IS OUR ONLY CHANCE OF BEING HEARD IN A FAVORABLE LIGHT BY PRESIDENT ROOSEVELT.
THE NAZIS CANNOT HAVE ACCESS TO THIS TECHNOLOGY BEFORE OUR DEMOCRACIES. EUROPE... NO... THE ENTIRE WORLD IS IN THE DAWN OF TOTAL WAR!
I KNOW... BUT LEO... IF YOU'LL EXCUSE ME... I WOULD LIKE TO BE ALONE FOR A MOMENT.
PLEASE.
BUT OF COURSE.
I RELUCTANTLY SIGNED THE LETTER ON AUGUST 2ND 1939, BUT IT WAS NECESSARY. A MONTH LATER, THE NAZIS INVADED POLAND... WAR BROKE OUT IN EUROPE AND THE ENTIRE CONTINENT WAS SET ABLAZE... A MASSACRE.
THE LETTER ADDRESSED TO PRESIDENT FRANKLIN DELANO ROOSEVELT ALLOWED LEO AND HIS TEAM TO CONTINUE THEIR RESEARCH*...
Yours very truly,
Albert Einstein
*LATER KNOWN AS THE "MANHATTAN PROJECT"
AS A PACIFIST I WAS DEVASTATED... BUT I HAD TO DO IT... WITHOUT IT, THE NAZIS WOULD HAVE BEEN THE FIRST TO POSSESS AND MAKE USE OF AN ATOMIC BOMB...
... LONG BEFORE THE ALLIED FORCES. IT WAS NECESSARY. ALL THE MORE SO BECAUSE I HAD BECOME AN AMERICAN CITIZEN IN 1940. I FELT THE SAME DREAD AS MY FELLOW COUNTRYMEN DURING THE TERRIBLE ATTACK ON PEARL HARBOR IN 1941. THE WAR THAT HAD TAKEN THE WORLD HAD TO STOP ONE DAY... BUT NOT LIKE THIS... NOT LIKE THIS...

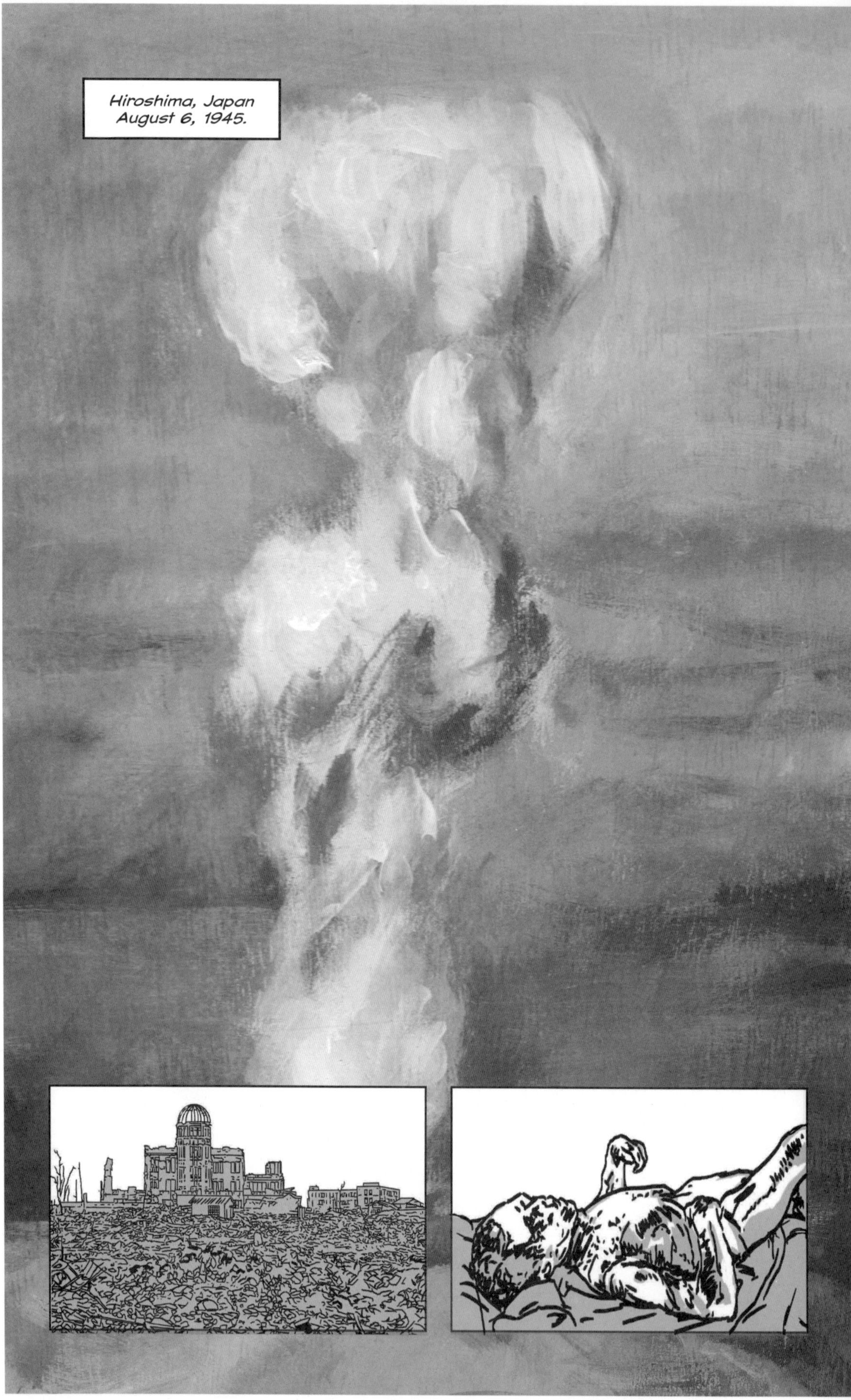
Hiroshima, Japan
August 6, 1945.

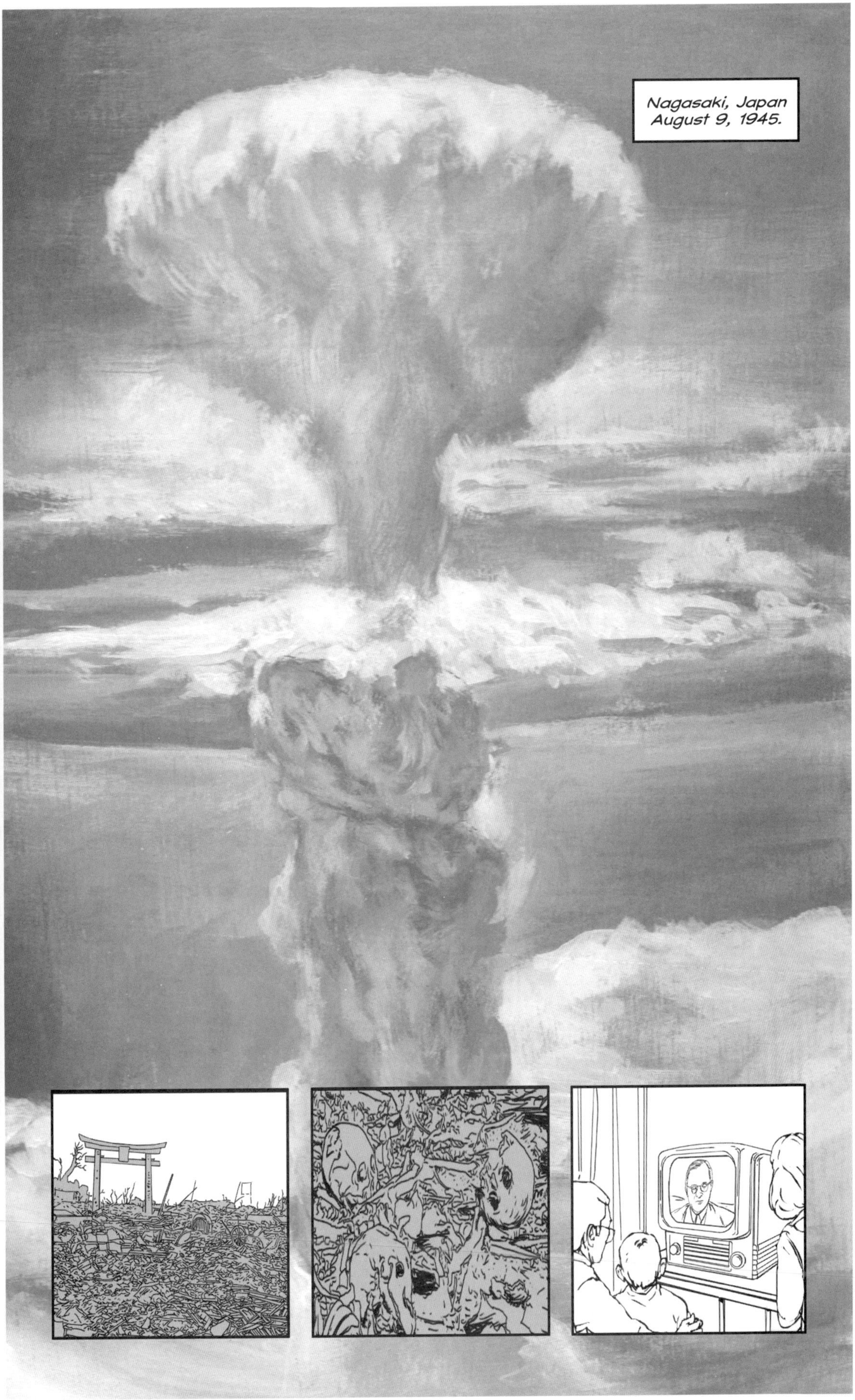
Nagasaki, Japan
August 9, 1945.

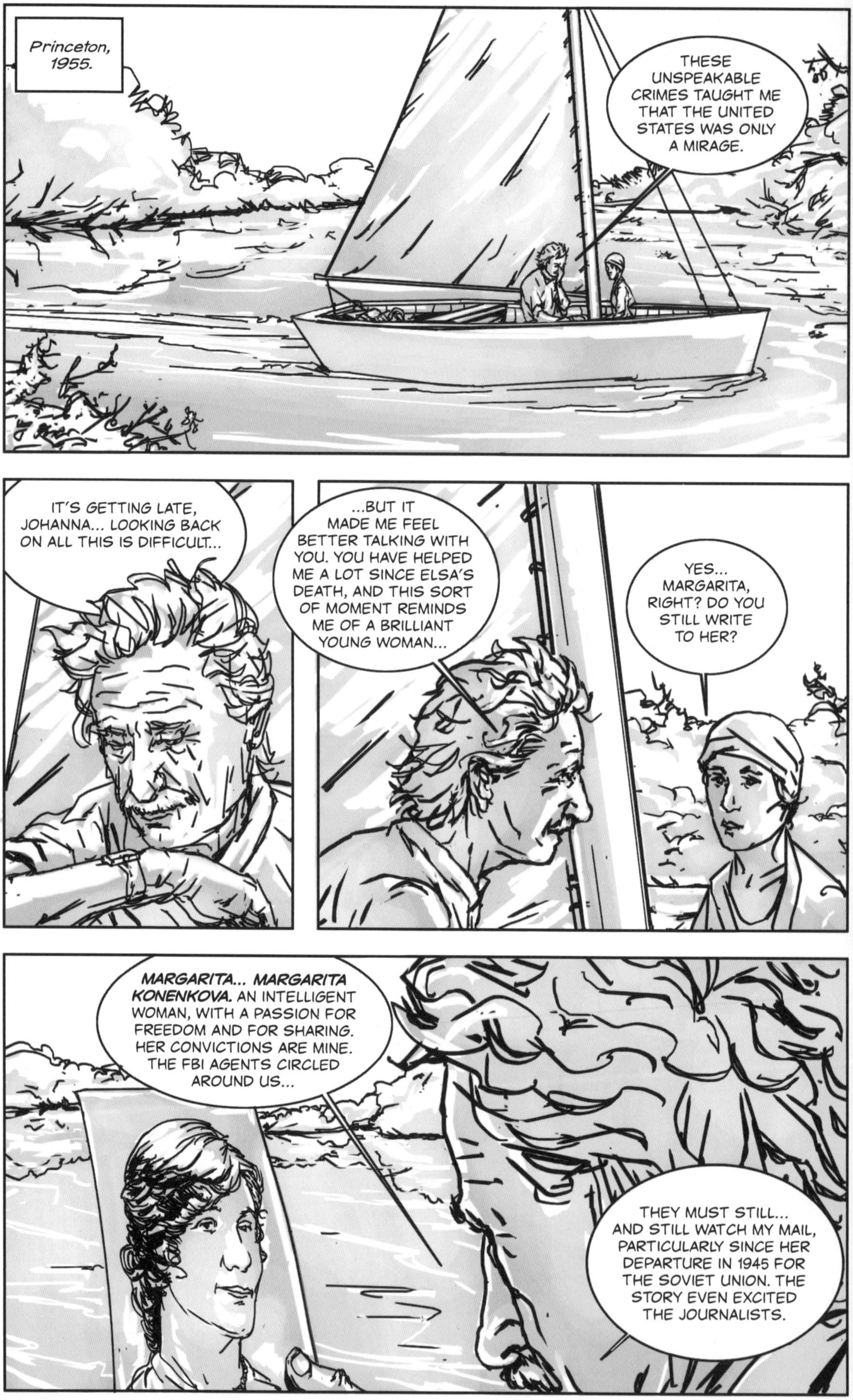
Princeton, 1955.
THESE UNSPEAKABLE CRIMES TAUGHT ME THAT THE UNITED STATES WAS ONLY A MIRAGE.
IT'S GETTING LATE, JOHANNA... LOOKING BACK ON ALL THIS IS DIFFICULT...
...BUT IT MADE ME FEEL BETTER TALKING WITH YOU. YOU HAVE HELPED ME A LOT SINCE ELSA'S DEATH, AND THIS SORT OF MOMENT REMINDS ME OF A BRILLIANT YOUNG WOMAN...
YES... MARGARITA, RIGHT? DO YOU STILL WRITE TO HER?
MARGARITA... MARGARITA KONENKOVA. AN INTELLIGENT WOMAN, WITH A PASSION FOR FREEDOM AND FOR SHARING. HER CONVICTIONS ARE MINE. THE FBI AGENTS CIRCLED AROUND US...
THEY MUST STILL... AND STILL WATCH MY MAIL, PARTICULARLY SINCE HER DEPARTURE IN 1945 FOR THE SOVIET UNION. THE STORY EVEN EXCITED THE JOURNALISTS.

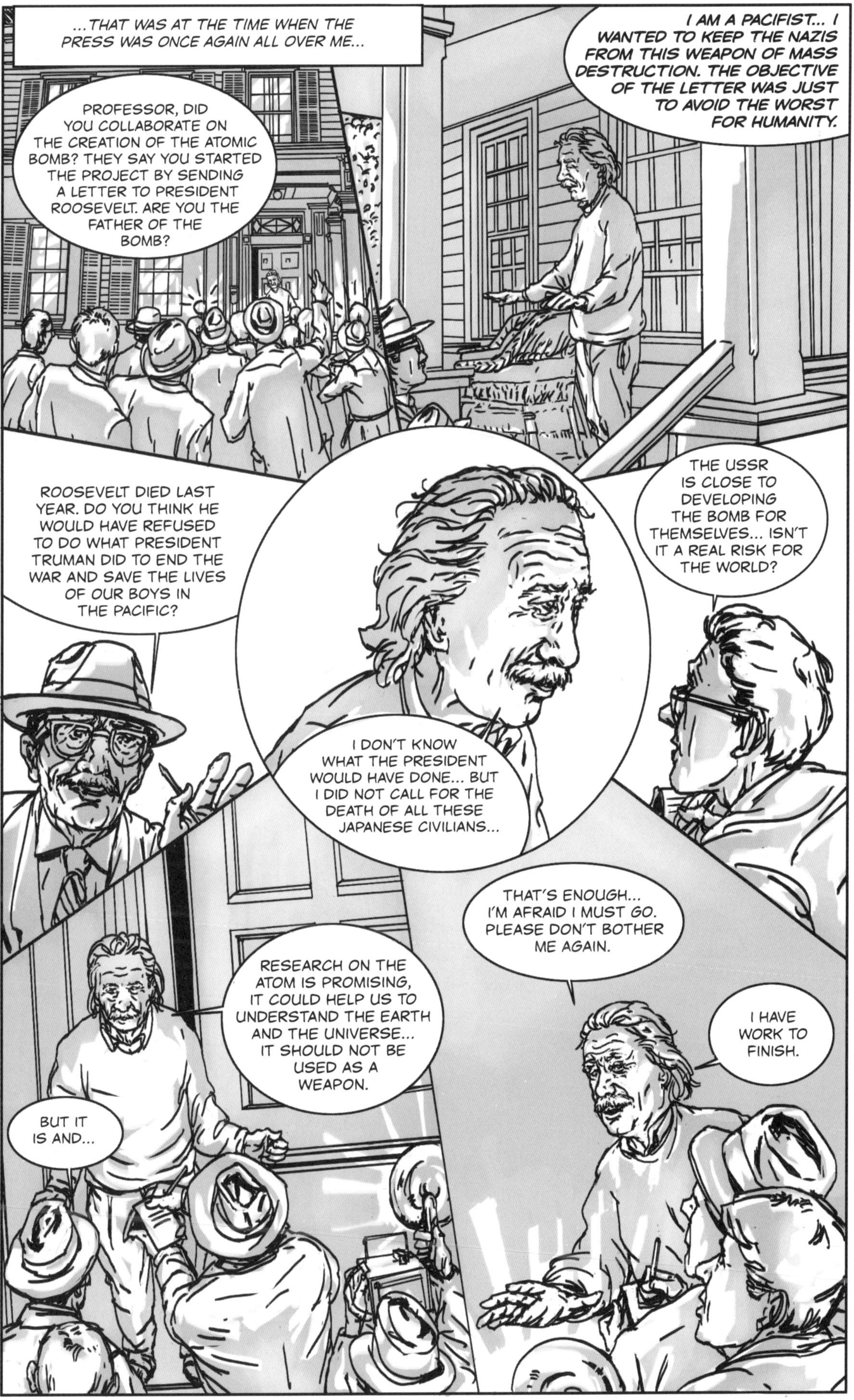
...THAT WAS AT THE TIME WHEN THE PRESS WAS ONCE AGAIN ALL OVER ME...
PROFESSOR, DID YOU COLLABORATE ON THE CREATION OF THE ATOMIC BOMB? THEY SAY YOU STARTED THE PROJECT BY SENDING A LETTER TO PRESIDENT ROOSEVELT. ARE YOU THE FATHER OF THE BOMB?
I AM A PACIFIST... I WANTED TO KEEP THE NAZIS FROM THIS WEAPON OF MASS DESTRUCTION. THE OBJECTIVE OF THE LETTER WAS JUST TO AVOID THE WORST FOR HUMANITY.
ROOSEVELT DIED LAST YEAR. DO YOU THINK HE WOULD HAVE REFUSED TO DO WHAT PRESIDENT TRUMAN DID TO END THE WAR AND SAVE THE LIVES OF OUR BOYS IN THE PACIFIC?
THE USSR IS CLOSE TO DEVELOPING THE BOMB FOR THEMSELVES... ISN'T IT A REAL RISK FOR THE WORLD?
I DON'T KNOW WHAT THE PRESIDENT WOULD HAVE DONE... BUT I DID NOT CALL FOR THE DEATH OF ALL THESE JAPANESE CIVILIANS...
RESEARCH ON THE ATOM IS PROMISING, IT COULD HELP US TO UNDERSTAND THE EARTH AND THE UNIVERSE... IT SHOULD NOT BE USED AS A WEAPON.
BUT IT IS AND...
THAT'S ENOUGH... I'M AFRAID I MUST GO. PLEASE DON'T BOTHER ME AGAIN.
I HAVE WORK TO FINISH.

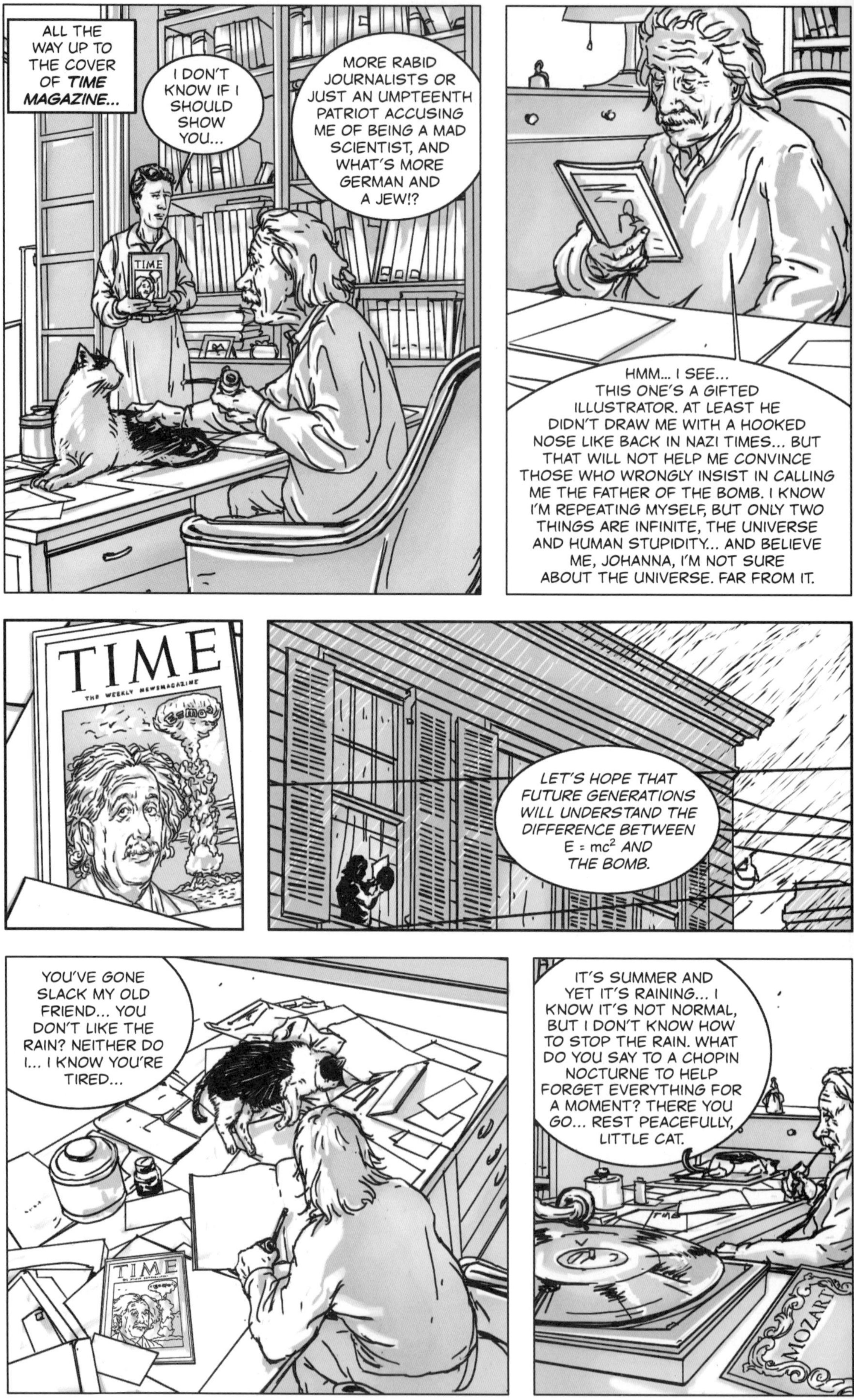

ALL THE WAY UP TO THE COVER OF **TIME MAGAZINE...**
I DON'T KNOW IF I SHOULD SHOW YOU...
MORE RABID JOURNALISTS OR JUST AN UMPTEENTH PATRIOT ACCUSING ME OF BEING A MAD SCIENTIST, AND WHAT'S MORE GERMAN AND A JEW!?
HMM... I SEE... THIS ONE'S A GIFTED ILLUSTRATOR. AT LEAST HE DIDN'T DRAW ME WITH A HOOKED NOSE LIKE BACK IN NAZI TIMES... BUT THAT WILL NOT HELP ME CONVINCE THOSE WHO WRONGLY INSIST IN CALLING ME THE FATHER OF THE BOMB. I KNOW I'M REPEATING MYSELF, BUT ONLY TWO THINGS ARE INFINITE, THE UNIVERSE AND HUMAN STUPIDITY... AND BELIEVE ME, JOHANNA, I'M NOT SURE ABOUT THE UNIVERSE. FAR FROM IT.
TIME
THE WEEKLY NEWSMAGAZINE
LET'S HOPE THAT FUTURE GENERATIONS WILL UNDERSTAND THE DIFFERENCE BETWEEN E = mc² *AND THE BOMB.*
YOU'VE GONE SLACK MY OLD FRIEND... YOU DON'T LIKE THE RAIN? NEITHER DO I... I KNOW YOU'RE TIRED...
TIME
IT'S SUMMER AND YET IT'S RAINING... I KNOW IT'S NOT NORMAL, BUT I DON'T KNOW HOW TO STOP THE RAIN. WHAT DO YOU SAY TO A CHOPIN NOCTURNE TO HELP FORGET EVERYTHING FOR A MOMENT? THERE YOU GO... REST PEACEFULLY, LITTLE CAT.
MOZART

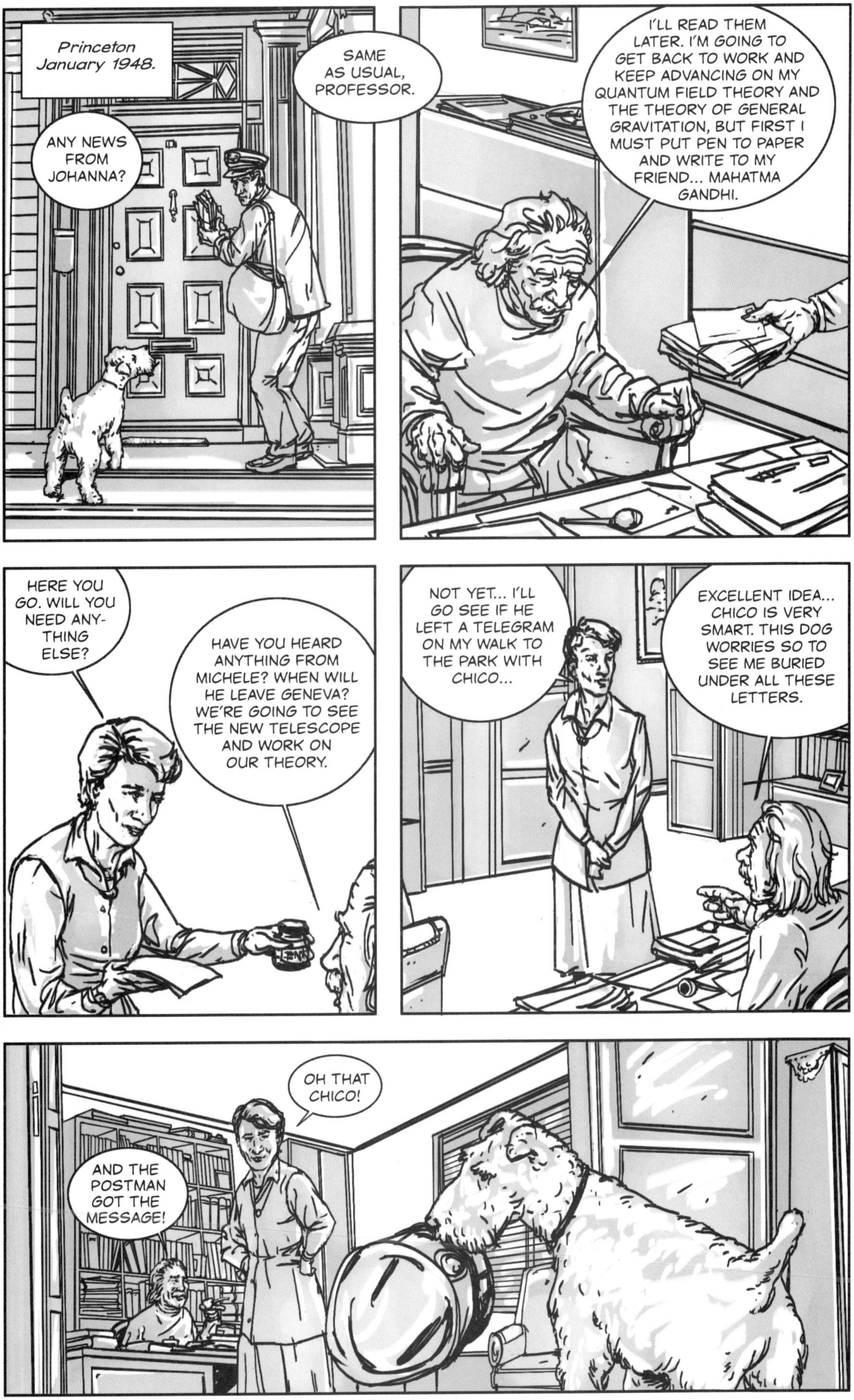
Princeton
January 1948.
ANY NEWS FROM JOHANNA?
SAME AS USUAL, PROFESSOR.
I'LL READ THEM LATER. I'M GOING TO GET BACK TO WORK AND KEEP ADVANCING ON MY QUANTUM FIELD THEORY AND THE THEORY OF GENERAL GRAVITATION, BUT FIRST I MUST PUT PEN TO PAPER AND WRITE TO MY FRIEND... MAHATMA GANDHI.
HERE YOU GO. WILL YOU NEED ANY-THING ELSE?
HAVE YOU HEARD ANYTHING FROM MICHELE? WHEN WILL HE LEAVE GENEVA? WE'RE GOING TO SEE THE NEW TELESCOPE AND WORK ON OUR THEORY.
NOT YET... I'LL GO SEE IF HE LEFT A TELEGRAM ON MY WALK TO THE PARK WITH CHICO...
EXCELLENT IDEA... CHICO IS VERY SMART. THIS DOG WORRIES SO TO SEE ME BURIED UNDER ALL THESE LETTERS.
OH THAT CHICO!
AND THE POSTMAN GOT THE MESSAGE!

A LITTLE WHILE LATER, JOHANNA, YOU INFORMED ME OF THE ASSASSINATION OF *GANDHI*. I WAS DEVASTATED.

I SAW HIS WISDOM FIRSTHAND IN OUR RICH CORRESPONDENCE. I COULD EXORCISE MY SUFFERING OVER THE WAR AND THE DISCOVERY OF THE CAMPS. IT ALLOWED ME TO MAINTAIN MY FAITH IN HUMANITY DESPITE ALL THAT INSANITY...

IN MY OPINION, GANDHI EMBODIED THE GREATEST POLITICAL GENIUS OF OUR CIVILIZATION. HE DEFINED A CONCRETE SENSE OF POLICY AND WAS ABLE TO EXTRACT INEXHAUSTIBLE HEROISM FROM EVERY MAN ONCE HE DISCOVERED A GOAL AND A VALUE WITHIN HIS GRASP. I THINK THAT WAS WHY I, WHEN THEY ASKED ME TO BE THE PRESIDENT OF THE NEW ISRAELI STATE, I REFUSED. I WAS HONORED, BUT I REFUSED...

...BECAUSE WE SHOULD STRIVE TO PRACTICE NON-VIOLENCE IN CONSCIOUS AND RATIONAL WAYS, IN THE WAY WHERE WE ARE NOT USING IT TO DEFEND A CAUSE OR ACTIONS WE THINK ARE BAD.

EVEN IN THE NEXT LIFE, HIS SPIRIT RESIDED WITHIN ME, HIS AURA HAS REMAINED INTACT. I UNDERSTOOD THAT ONE SHOULD NOT LEAVE THIS WORLD...

...AND MEN PRISONERS OF DEATH... THE SPIRAL OF DEATH MADE UNIQUELY OF VIOLENCE AND OF HATE. *NON-VIOLENCE IS NOT PASSIVITY, IT'S A CONSCIOUS ACTION.*

AND I WAS SURELY GOING TO REACT TO THE ABSURDITY OF THE WORLD TO MAKE REAL HIS POETRY AND INSPIRE YOUTH IN SEARCH OF A REVIVAL.

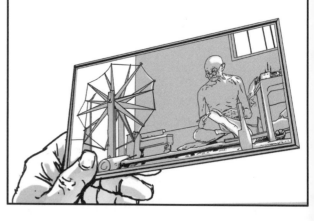

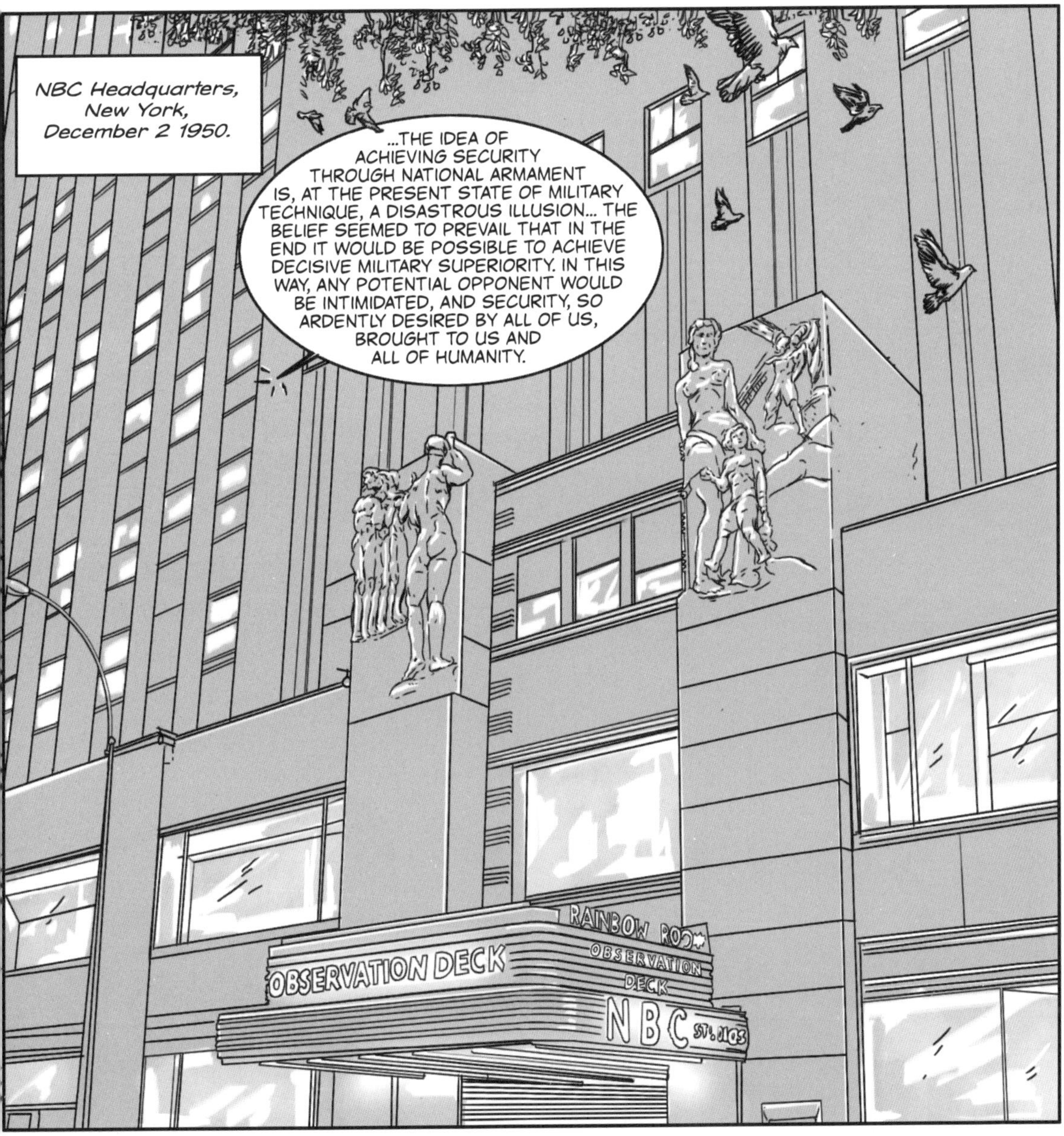
NBC Headquarters, New York, December 2 1950.
...THE IDEA OF ACHIEVING SECURITY THROUGH NATIONAL ARMAMENT IS, AT THE PRESENT STATE OF MILITARY TECHNIQUE, A DISASTROUS ILLUSION... THE BELIEF SEEMED TO PREVAIL THAT IN THE END IT WOULD BE POSSIBLE TO ACHIEVE DECISIVE MILITARY SUPERIORITY. IN THIS WAY, ANY POTENTIAL OPPONENT WOULD BE INTIMIDATED, AND SECURITY, SO ARDENTLY DESIRED BY ALL OF US, BROUGHT TO US AND ALL OF HUMANITY.
OBSERVATION DECK
OBSERVATION DECK
NBC

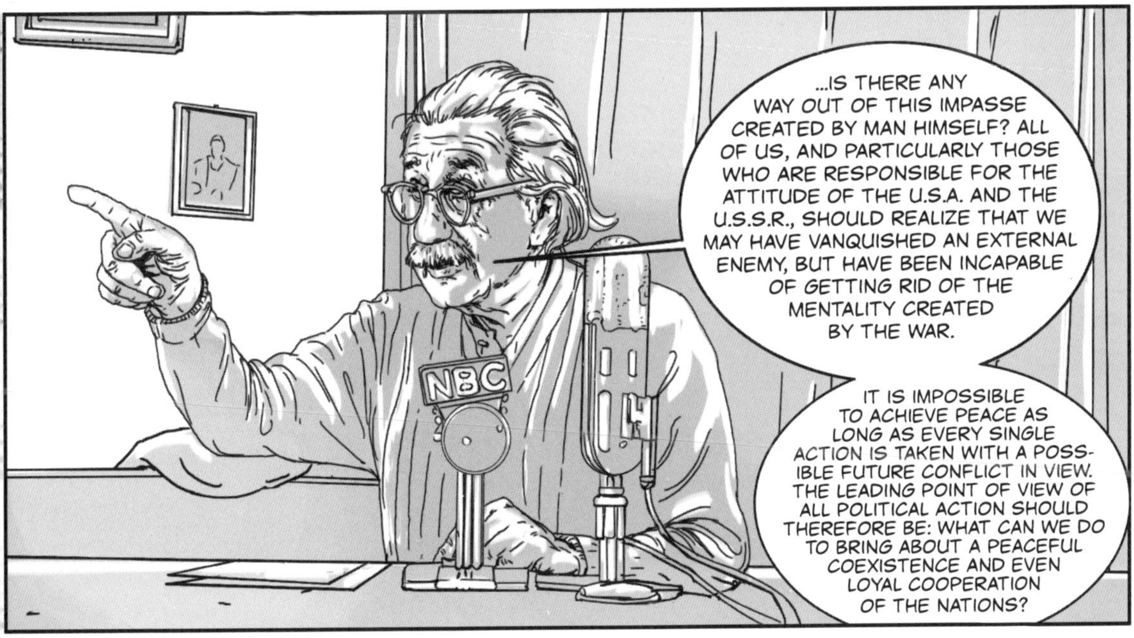
...IS THERE ANY WAY OUT OF THIS IMPASSE CREATED BY MAN HIMSELF? ALL OF US, AND PARTICULARLY THOSE WHO ARE RESPONSIBLE FOR THE ATTITUDE OF THE U.S.A. AND THE U.S.S.R., SHOULD REALIZE THAT WE MAY HAVE VANQUISHED AN EXTERNAL ENEMY, BUT HAVE BEEN INCAPABLE OF GETTING RID OF THE MENTALITY CREATED BY THE WAR.
IT IS IMPOSSIBLE TO ACHIEVE PEACE AS LONG AS EVERY SINGLE ACTION IS TAKEN WITH A POSS-IBLE FUTURE CONFLICT IN VIEW. THE LEADING POINT OF VIEW OF ALL POLITICAL ACTION SHOULD THEREFORE BE: WHAT CAN WE DO TO BRING ABOUT A PEACEFUL COEXISTENCE AND EVEN LOYAL COOPERATION OF THE NATIONS?
NBC

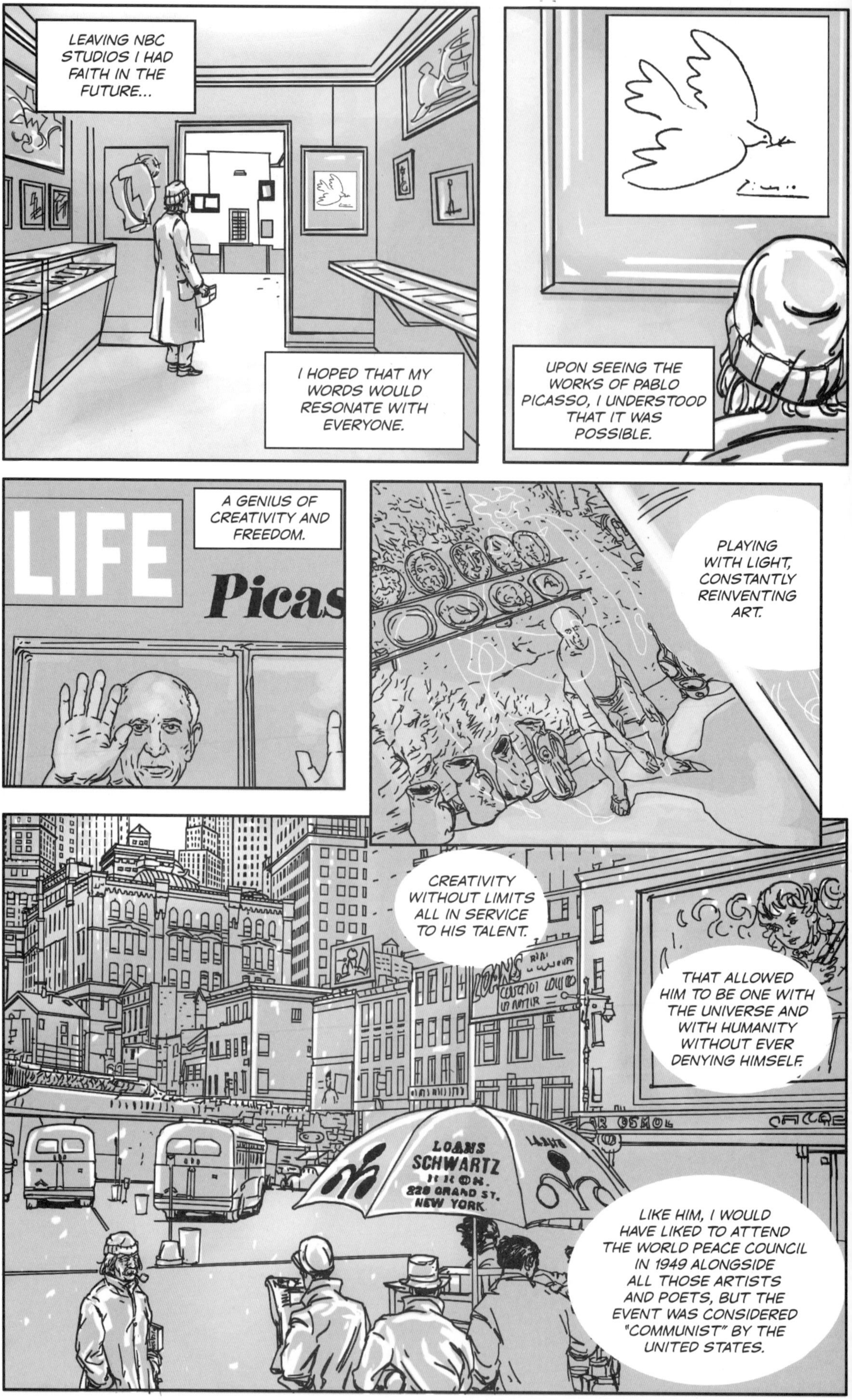
LEAVING NBC STUDIOS I HAD FAITH IN THE FUTURE...
I HOPED THAT MY WORDS WOULD RESONATE WITH EVERYONE.
UPON SEEING THE WORKS OF PABLO PICASSO, I UNDERSTOOD THAT IT WAS POSSIBLE.
LIFE
A GENIUS OF CREATIVITY AND FREEDOM.
Picas
PLAYING WITH LIGHT, CONSTANTLY REINVENTING ART.
CREATIVITY WITHOUT LIMITS ALL IN SERVICE TO HIS TALENT.
THAT ALLOWED HIM TO BE ONE WITH THE UNIVERSE AND WITH HUMANITY WITHOUT EVER DENYING HIMSELF.
LOANS
SCHWARTZ
828 GRAND ST.
NEW YORK
LIKE HIM, I WOULD HAVE LIKED TO ATTEND THE WORLD PEACE COUNCIL IN 1949 ALONGSIDE ALL THOSE ARTISTS AND POETS, BUT THE EVENT WAS CONSIDERED "COMMUNIST" BY THE UNITED STATES.

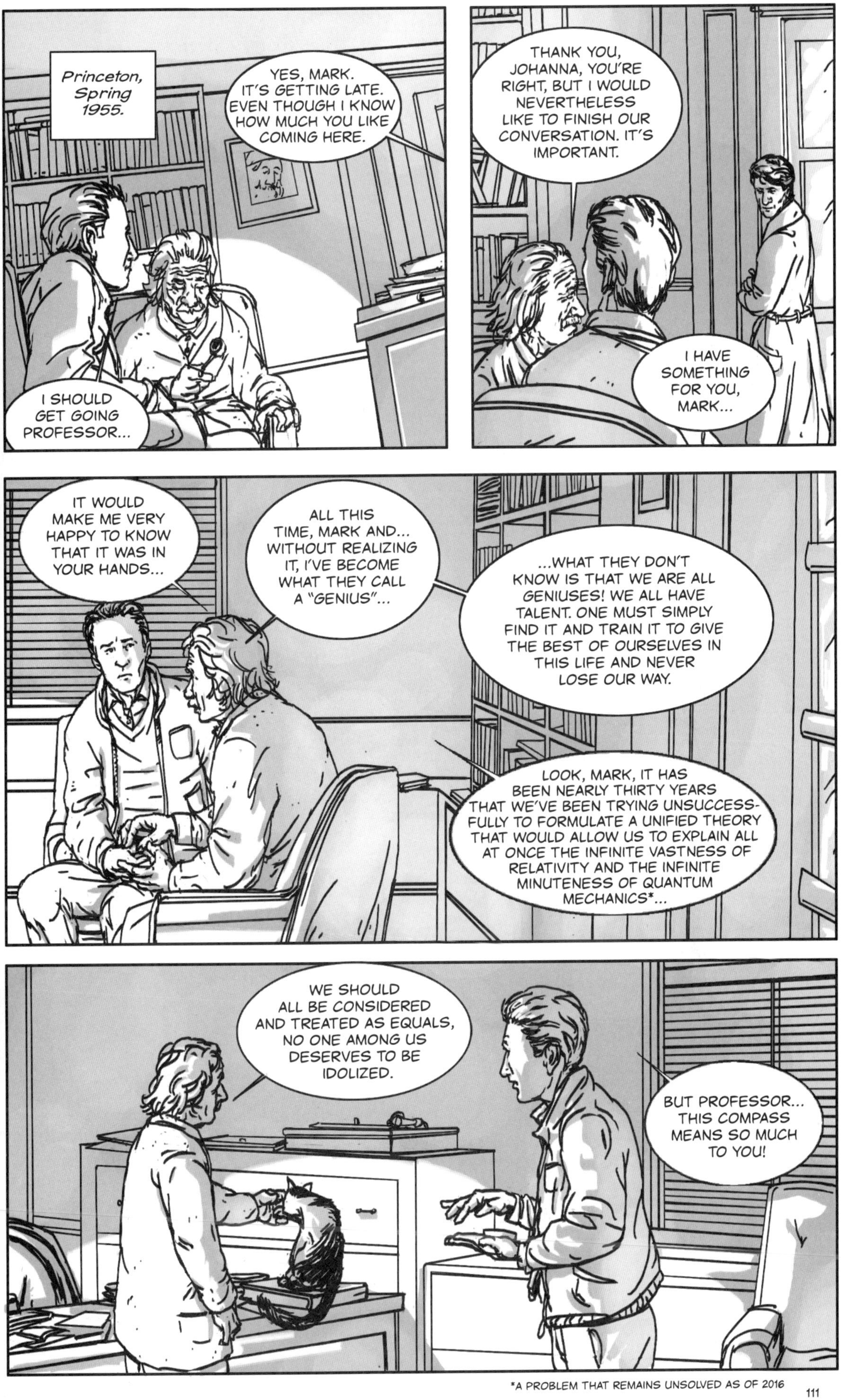
Princeton, Spring 1955.
YES, MARK. IT'S GETTING LATE. EVEN THOUGH I KNOW HOW MUCH YOU LIKE COMING HERE.
I SHOULD GET GOING PROFESSOR...
THANK YOU, JOHANNA, YOU'RE RIGHT, BUT I WOULD NEVERTHELESS LIKE TO FINISH OUR CONVERSATION. IT'S IMPORTANT.
I HAVE SOMETHING FOR YOU, MARK...
IT WOULD MAKE ME VERY HAPPY TO KNOW THAT IT WAS IN YOUR HANDS...
ALL THIS TIME, MARK AND... WITHOUT REALIZING IT, I'VE BECOME WHAT THEY CALL A "GENIUS"...
...WHAT THEY DON'T KNOW IS THAT WE ARE ALL GENIUSES! WE ALL HAVE TALENT. ONE MUST SIMPLY FIND IT AND TRAIN IT TO GIVE THE BEST OF OURSELVES IN THIS LIFE AND NEVER LOSE OUR WAY.
LOOK, MARK, IT HAS BEEN NEARLY THIRTY YEARS THAT WE'VE BEEN TRYING UNSUCCESSFULLY TO FORMULATE A UNIFIED THEORY THAT WOULD ALLOW US TO EXPLAIN ALL AT ONCE THE INFINITE VASTNESS OF RELATIVITY AND THE INFINITE MINUTENESS OF QUANTUM MECHANICS*...
WE SHOULD ALL BE CONSIDERED AND TREATED AS EQUALS, NO ONE AMONG US DESERVES TO BE IDOLIZED.
BUT PROFESSOR... THIS COMPASS MEANS SO MUCH TO YOU!

*A PROBLEM THAT REMAINS UNSOLVED AS OF 2016

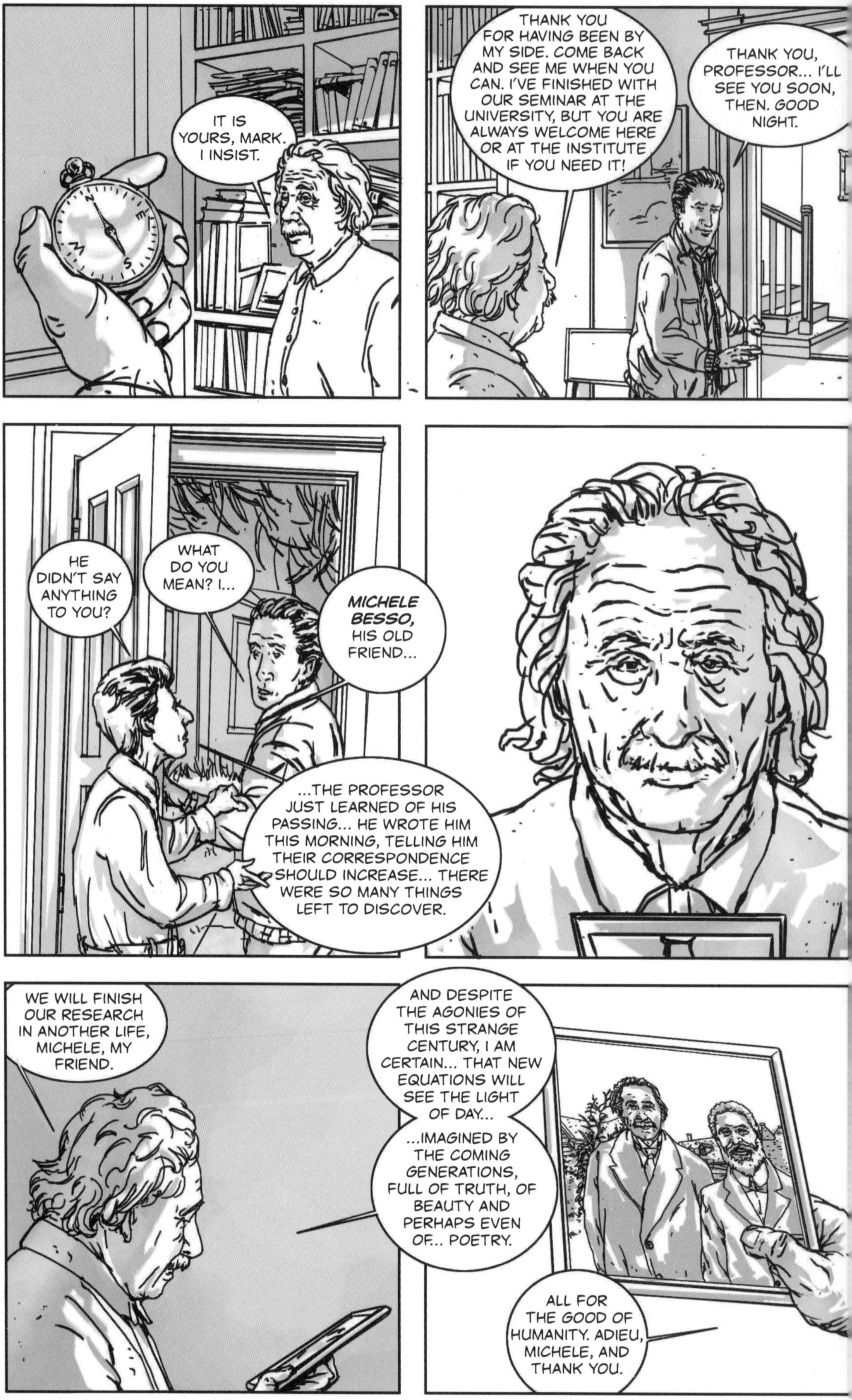
IT IS YOURS, MARK. I INSIST.
THANK YOU FOR HAVING BEEN BY MY SIDE. COME BACK AND SEE ME WHEN YOU CAN. I'VE FINISHED WITH OUR SEMINAR AT THE UNIVERSITY, BUT YOU ARE ALWAYS WELCOME HERE OR AT THE INSTITUTE IF YOU NEED IT!
THANK YOU, PROFESSOR... I'LL SEE YOU SOON, THEN. GOOD NIGHT.
HE DIDN'T SAY ANYTHING TO YOU?
WHAT DO YOU MEAN? I...
MICHELE BESSO, HIS OLD FRIEND...
...THE PROFESSOR JUST LEARNED OF HIS PASSING... HE WROTE HIM THIS MORNING, TELLING HIM THEIR CORRESPONDENCE SHOULD INCREASE... THERE WERE SO MANY THINGS LEFT TO DISCOVER.
WE WILL FINISH OUR RESEARCH IN ANOTHER LIFE, MICHELE, MY FRIEND.
AND DESPITE THE AGONIES OF THIS STRANGE CENTURY, I AM CERTAIN... THAT NEW EQUATIONS WILL SEE THE LIGHT OF DAY...
...IMAGINED BY THE COMING GENERATIONS, FULL OF TRUTH, OF BEAUTY AND PERHAPS EVEN OF... POETRY.
ALL FOR THE GOOD OF HUMANITY. ADIEU, MICHELE, AND THANK YOU.

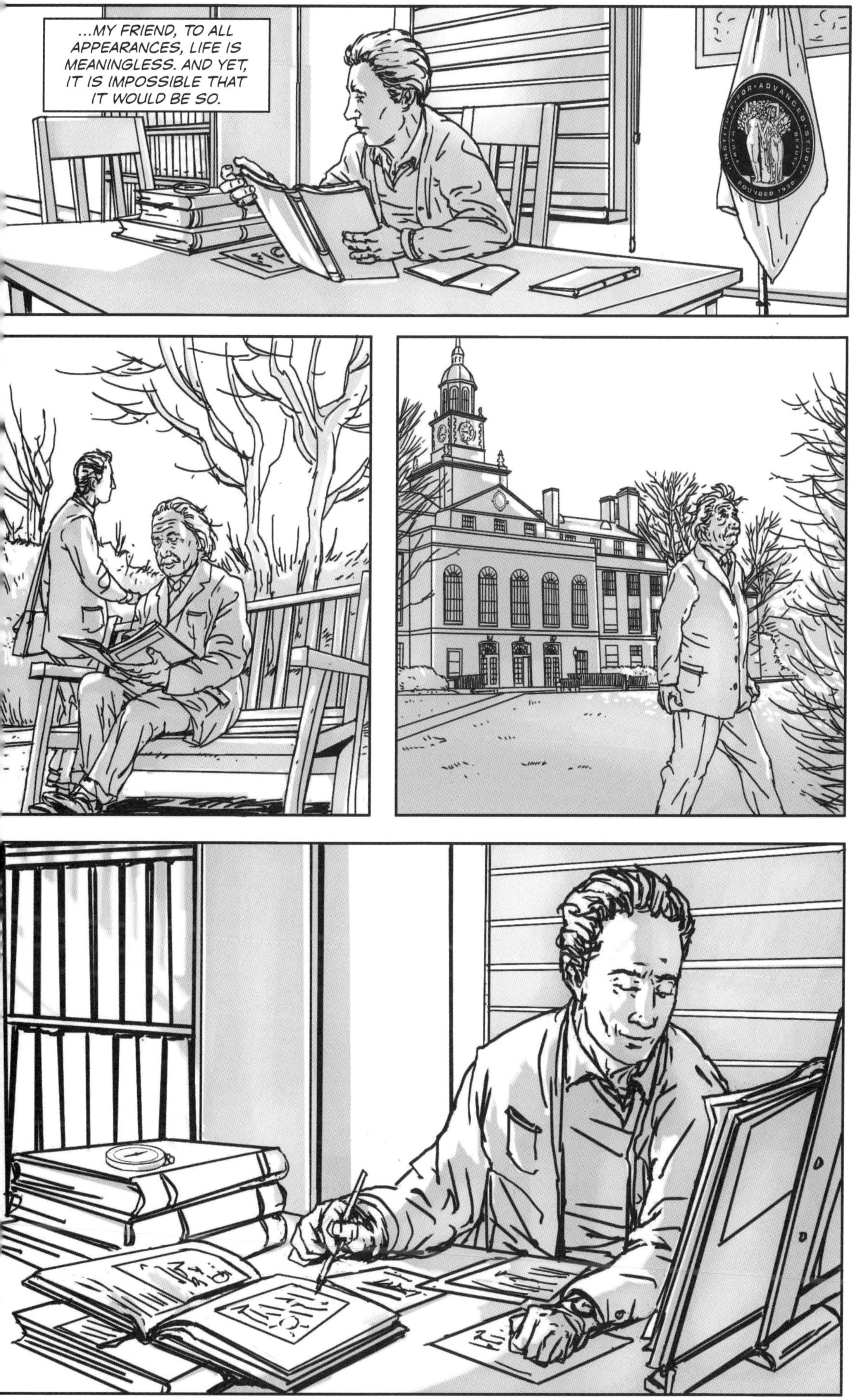
...MY FRIEND, TO ALL APPEARANCES, LIFE IS MEANINGLESS. AND YET, IT IS IMPOSSIBLE THAT IT WOULD BE SO.

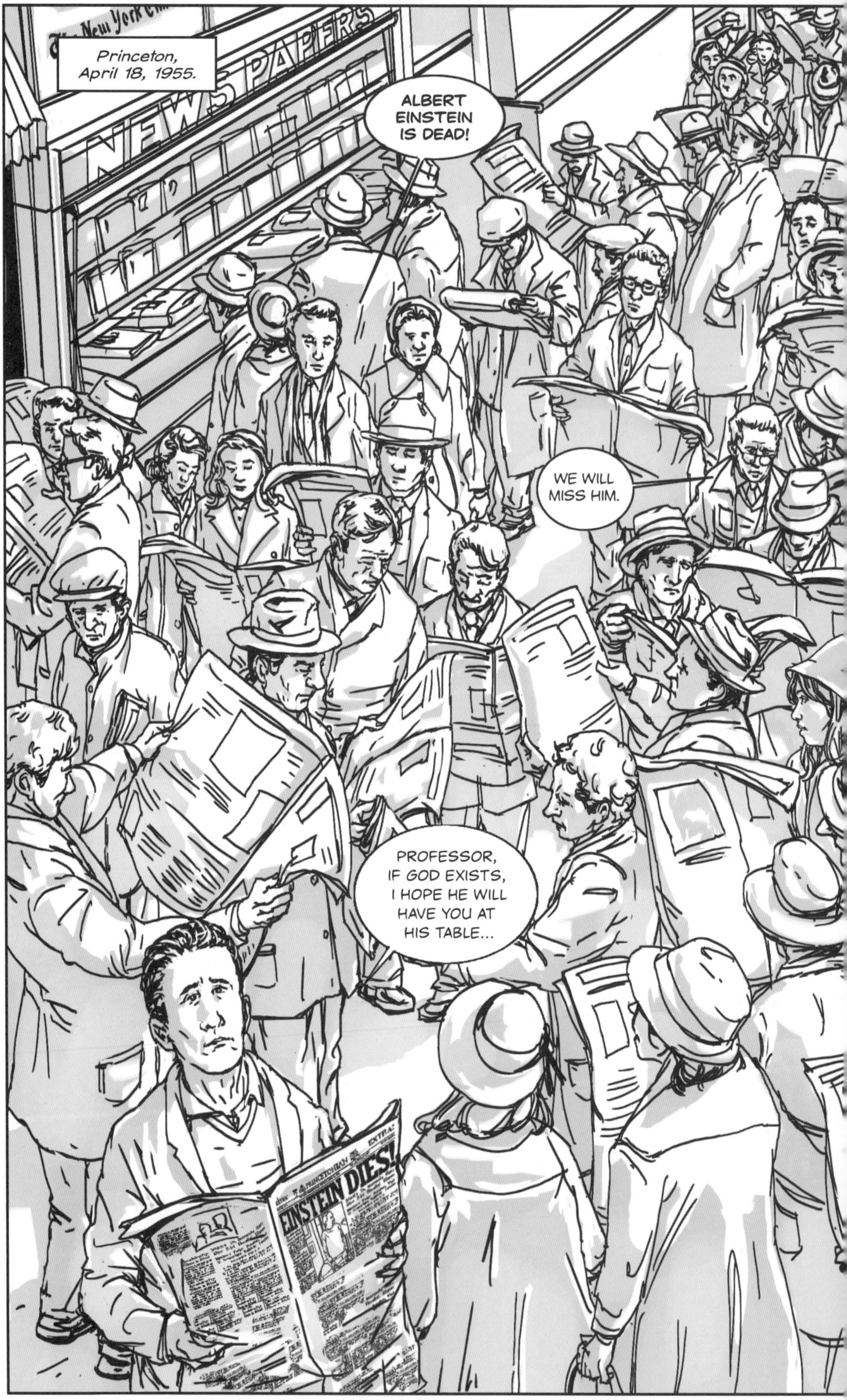
Princeton, April 18, 1955.
NEWS PAPERS
ALBERT EINSTEIN IS DEAD!
WE WILL MISS HIM.
PROFESSOR, IF GOD EXISTS, I HOPE HE WILL HAVE YOU AT HIS TABLE...
EINSTEIN DIES!
EXTRA!

EPILOGUE

"THE MOST BEAUTIFUL THING WE CAN EXPERIENCE IS THE MYSTERIOUS. IT IS THE SOURCE OF ALL TRUE ART AND SCIENCE. HE TO WHOM EMOTION IS A STRANGER, WHO CAN NO LONGER PAUSE TO WONDER AND STAND WRAPPED IN AWE, IS AS GOOD AS DEAD–HIS EYES ARE CLOSED." ALBERT EINSTEIN

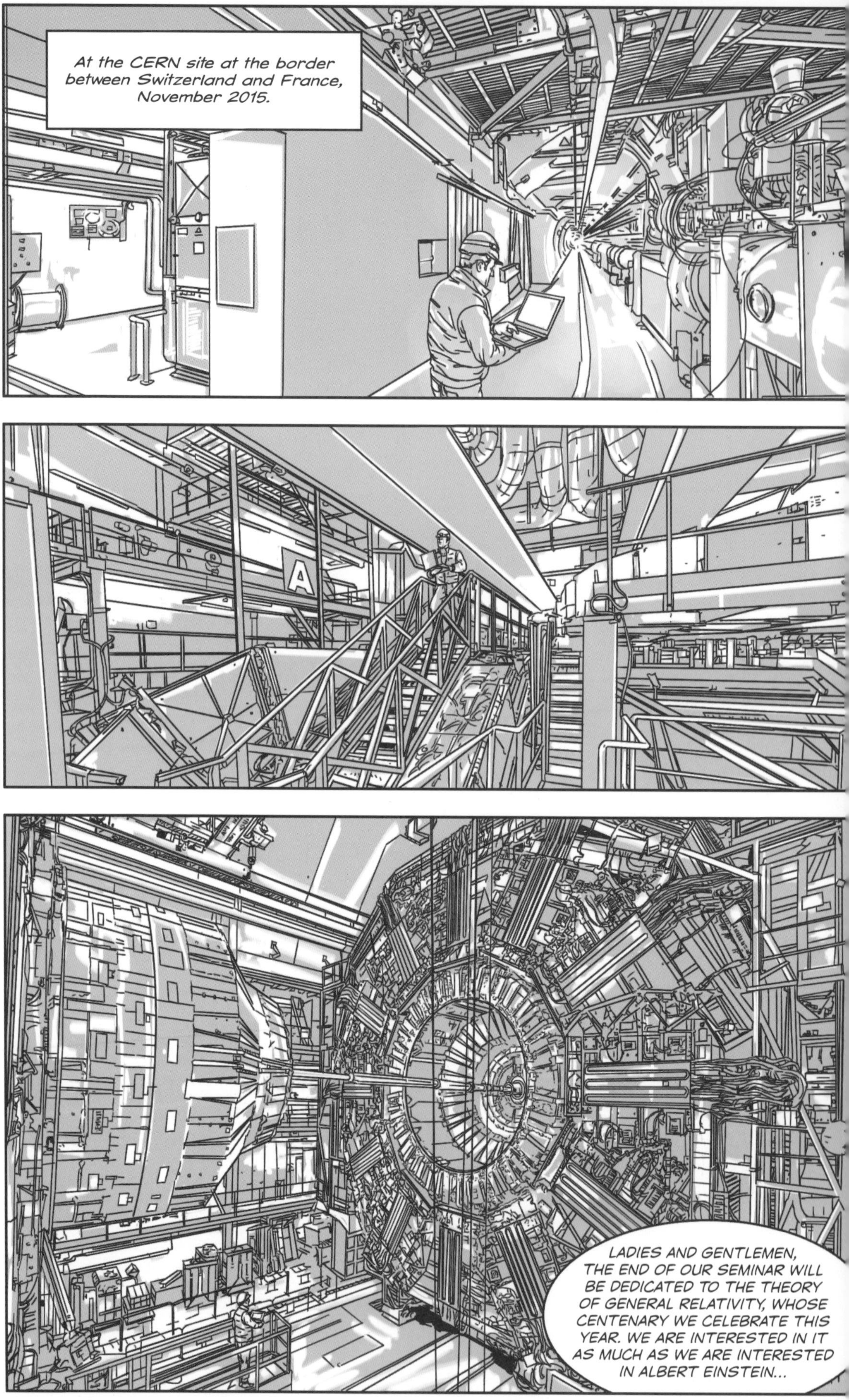
At the CERN site at the border between Switzerland and France, November 2015.
A
LADIES AND GENTLEMEN, THE END OF OUR SEMINAR WILL BE DEDICATED TO THE THEORY OF GENERAL RELATIVITY, WHOSE CENTENARY WE CELEBRATE THIS YEAR. WE ARE INTERESTED IN IT AS MUCH AS WE ARE INTERESTED IN ALBERT EINSTEIN...

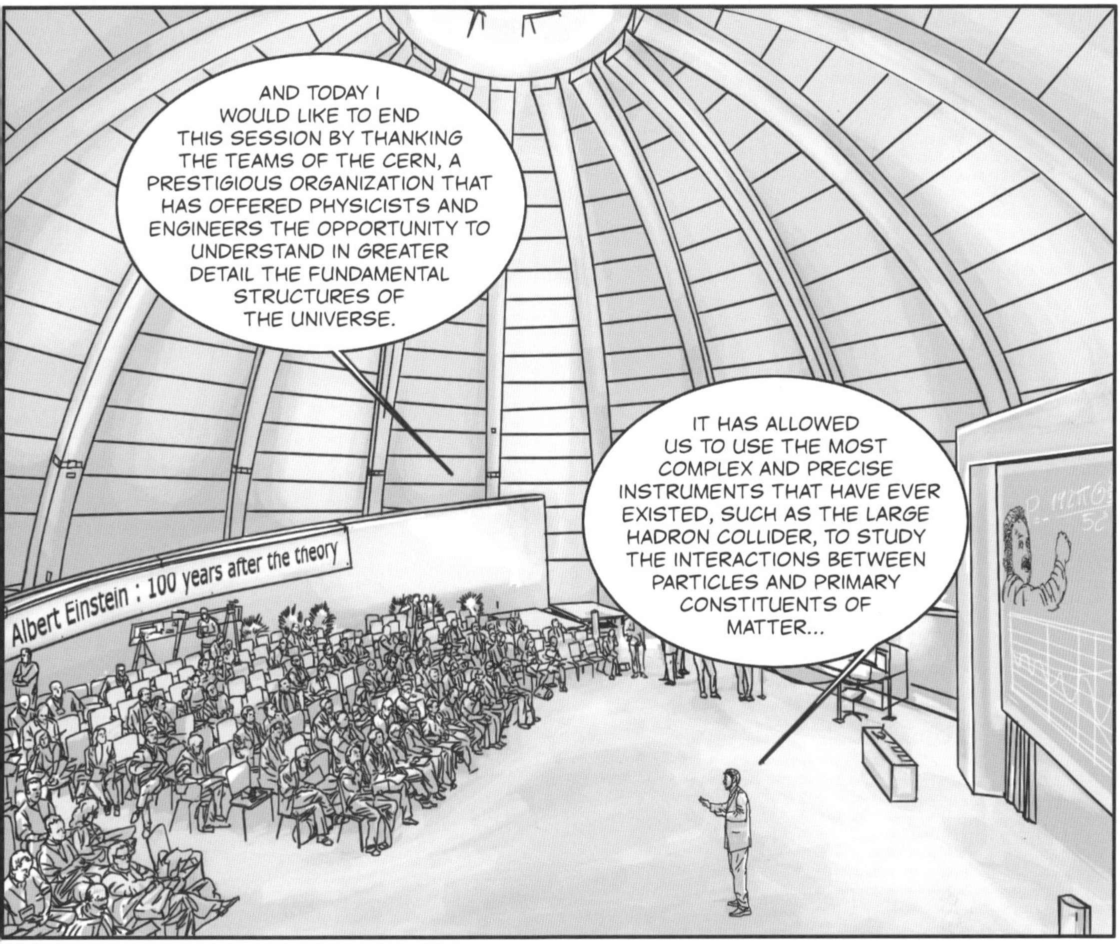
AND TODAY I WOULD LIKE TO END THIS SESSION BY THANKING THE TEAMS OF THE CERN, A PRESTIGIOUS ORGANIZATION THAT HAS OFFERED PHYSICISTS AND ENGINEERS THE OPPORTUNITY TO UNDERSTAND IN GREATER DETAIL THE FUNDAMENTAL STRUCTURES OF THE UNIVERSE.
IT HAS ALLOWED US TO USE THE MOST COMPLEX AND PRECISE INSTRUMENTS THAT HAVE EVER EXISTED, SUCH AS THE LARGE HADRON COLLIDER, TO STUDY THE INTERACTIONS BETWEEN PARTICLES AND PRIMARY CONSTITUENTS OF MATTER...
Albert Einstein : 100 years after the theory

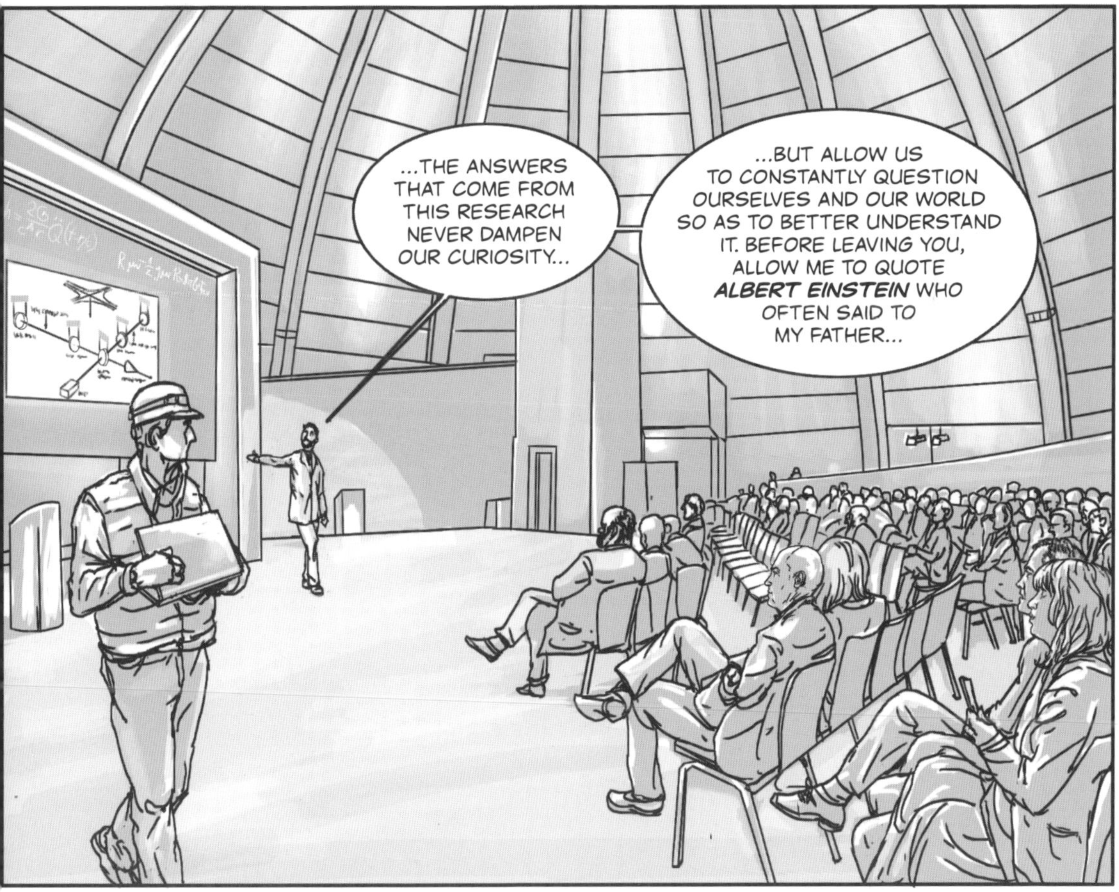
...THE ANSWERS THAT COME FROM THIS RESEARCH NEVER DAMPEN OUR CURIOSITY...
...BUT ALLOW US TO CONSTANTLY QUESTION OURSELVES AND OUR WORLD SO AS TO BETTER UNDERSTAND IT. BEFORE LEAVING YOU, ALLOW ME TO QUOTE ***ALBERT EINSTEIN*** WHO OFTEN SAID TO MY FATHER...

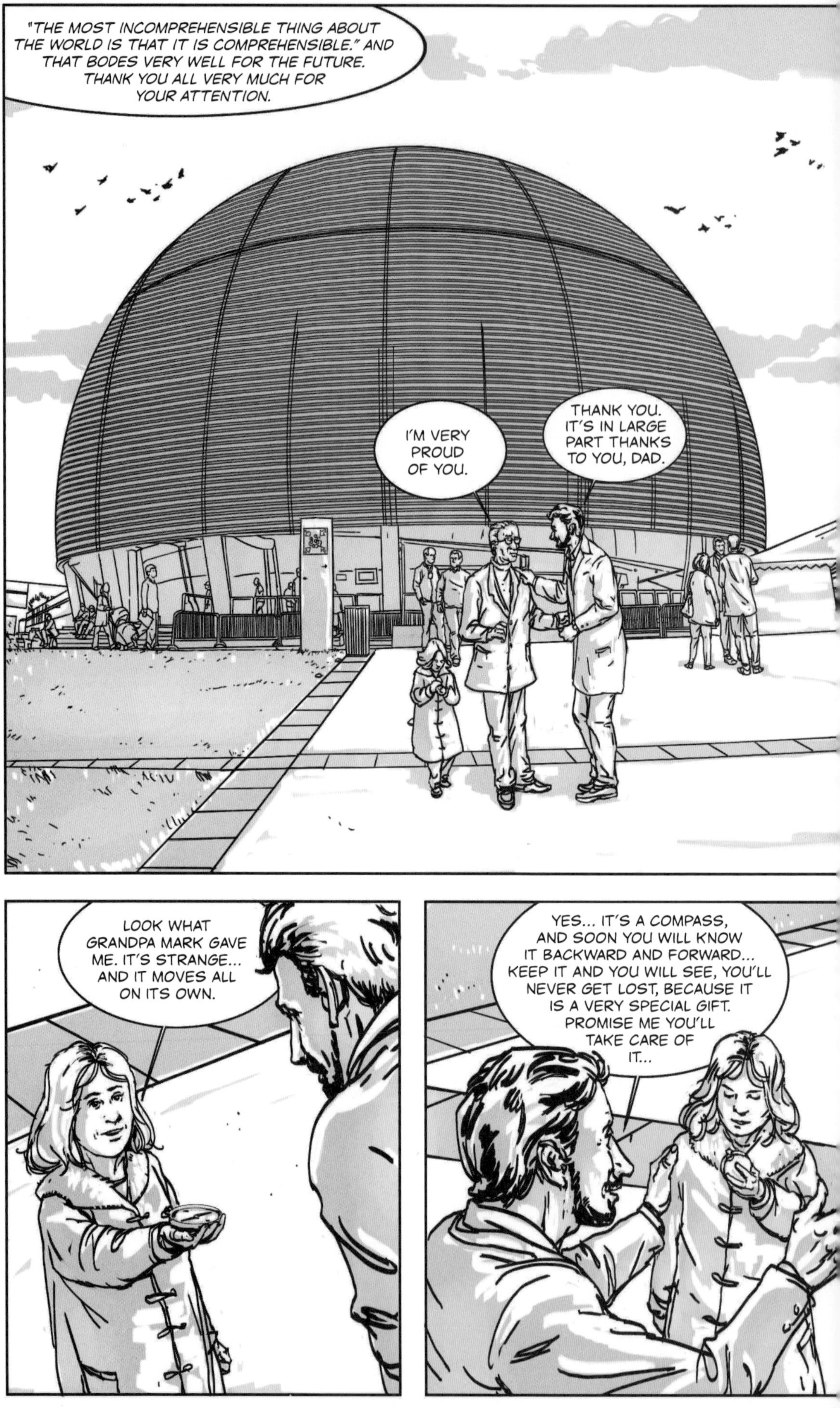
"THE MOST INCOMPREHENSIBLE THING ABOUT THE WORLD IS THAT IT IS COMPREHENSIBLE." AND THAT BODES VERY WELL FOR THE FUTURE. THANK YOU ALL VERY MUCH FOR YOUR ATTENTION.
I'M VERY PROUD OF YOU.
THANK YOU. IT'S IN LARGE PART THANKS TO YOU, DAD.
LOOK WHAT GRANDPA MARK GAVE ME. IT'S STRANGE... AND IT MOVES ALL ON ITS OWN.
YES... IT'S A COMPASS, AND SOON YOU WILL KNOW IT BACKWARD AND FORWARD... KEEP IT AND YOU WILL SEE, YOU'LL NEVER GET LOST, BECAUSE IT IS A VERY SPECIAL GIFT. PROMISE ME YOU'LL TAKE CARE OF IT...

I PROMISE!
CERN SERVICE DE RECRUTEMENT
CERN BUILDING 868
BUILDING 2051
CERN RECRUITMENT SERVICE
FRANCE
SCHWEIZ
CERN- SITE ...
CERN-POINT 6
CERN
CERN BUILDING 867
CERN BUILDING 180
GENEVE
BELGIC
LUXEMBURG
SWITZERLAND
FRANCE

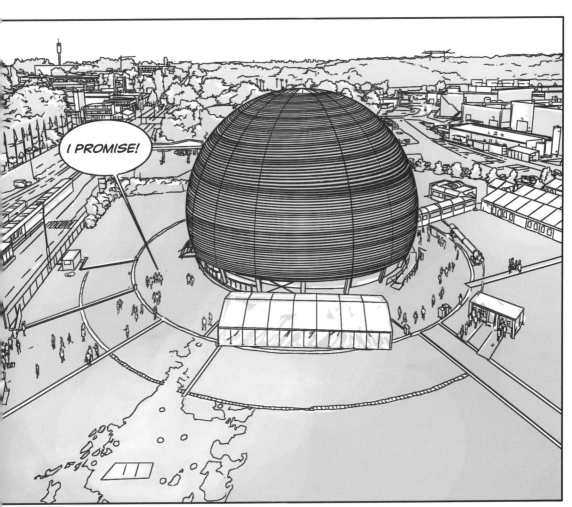

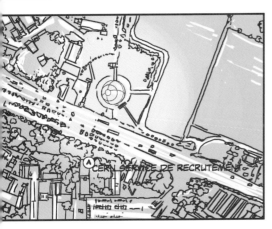

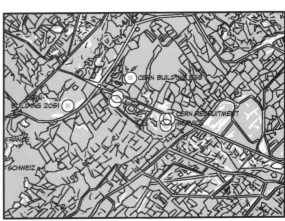

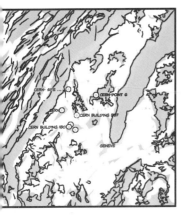

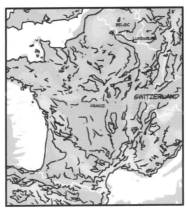

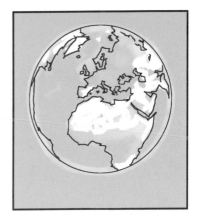

Key Dates in the life of Albert Einstein

March 14 1879

Birth of Albert Einstein in Ulm in the German Empire. His father and his uncle create an electrical engineering association in 1880.

1881

Birth of his sister, Maja.

Maja

1883

Albert is fascinated by the compass gifted to him by his father. He begins studying the violin at the age of 6.

1889

Albert Einstein meets **Max Talmud** who will later introduce him to philosophy.

1894

His father goes bankrupt. The family leaves Munich for Italy.

1895-1900

After first being rejected, he is successful in entering the Polytechnikum Zürich in Switzerland. There he meets **Michele Besso** and **Marcel Grossmann**, his great friends. He also meets **Mileva Maric**.

Michele & Marcel

1901-1902-1903

When Mileva Maric fails her final series of exams, the couple wishes to marry. The Einstein family refuses. With his friends' help, Albert moves to Bern and finds a job as an assessor at the patent office. He had previously searched all over Europe to find a position as a teacher without success. During this period, his father dies. Albert is only 22 years old and one of his first articles is published in "Annalen der Physik." Mileva is pregnant, it would appear as though the couple gave away the little girl

Mileva

for adoption. Nevertheless, Albert marries Mileva in 1903.

1905 Annus Mirabilis

When he is 26 years old, Albert Einstein successfully collects his thoughts and announces his work in four articles : a revolution is underway. They are published in the "Annalen der Physik" throughout this miraculous year. The famous equation $E = mc^2$ comes to light while **Henri Poincaré** of France and **Hendrik Lorentz** of the Netherlands had approximated the same results. They will, along with Einstein, become the fathers of relativity.

1906 – 1914

Starting in 1906, thanks to his thought experiments, he has a feeling that going into freefall cancels out the effect of weight, calling into question Newton's propositions. Meanwhile, in 1909, he receives his first doctorate "honoris" and leaves the patent office.

From this point onward, he dedicates more time to just causes including pacifism. In 1910, he is, with Mileva, the father of two sons, Hans and Eduard. Nevertheless, the couple separates in 1914 and Mileva leaves for Zurich with the children. War breaks out. He marries Elsa, his cousin.

1915

Albert Einstein announces the **Theory of General Relativity**. A new and spectacular revolution that still shakes the world of physics to this day. This relativist theory of gravity describes an influence on the movement of the stars, the presence of matter, and more generally energy when keeping in mind the principles of special relativity. This theory replaces the theory of universal gravitation put in place by Sir Isaac Newton.

Isaac Newton

1919

The eclipse photographs taken by **Eddington** provide experimental proof of the Theory of General Relativity. Albert Einstein becomes an international star.

1921

The Nobel Prize in Physics is awarded to Einstein for his contributions to theoretical physics, particularly for his discovery of the photoelectric effect.

1933

Albert Einstein leaves Germany once and for all. He will never return to Europe. The Nazis are in power, he resigns from the Bavarian Academy of Science and Humanities and accepts a position at the Institute for Advanced Study at Princeton. He is named to the Collège de France the same year.

1939

At the instigation of **Leo Szilard**, Albert Einstein signs a letter to President Roosevelt warning him of the risk of "extremely powerful bombs of a new type may thus be constructed" by the Nazis. This letter brings the Manhattan Project to life. Einstein, suspected of having communist sympathies, will not take part in the project.

April 18, 1955

Albert Einstein dies of an aneurysm. Against the wishes expressed in his last will and trust, his brain was removed by Dr. Harvey. At Princeton Hospital, in the final moments of his life, Albert Einstein asked for pen and paper so he could write down his final calculations.

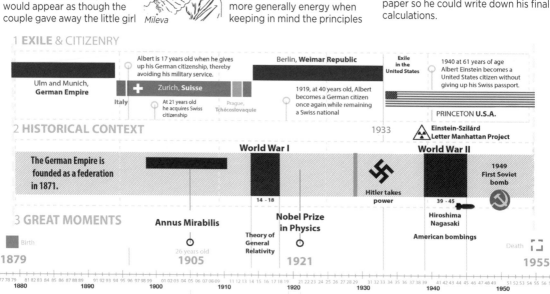

1 EXILE & CITIZENRY

Ulm and Munich, **German Empire**

Italy

Albert is 17 years old when he gives up his German citizenship, thereby avoiding his military service.

Zurich, **Suisse**

At 21 years old he acquires Swiss citizenship

Prague, Tchécoslovaquie

Berlin, **Weimar Republic**

1919, at 40 years old, Albert becomes a German citizen once again while remaining a Swiss national

Exile in the United States

1940 at 61 years of age Albert Einstein becomes a United States citizen without giving up his Swiss passport.

PRINCETON **U.S.A.**

2 HISTORICAL CONTEXT

1933

Einstein-Szilárd Letter Manhattan Project

The German Empire is founded as a federation in 1871.

World War I

14 - 18

Hitler takes power

World War II

39 - 45

Hiroshima Nagasaki

American bombings

1949 **First Soviet bomb**

3 GREAT MOMENTS

Birth

Annus Mirabilis

26 years old

Theory of General Relativity

Nobel Prize in Physics

Death

1879

1905

1921

1955

76 77 78 79 **1880** 81 82 83 84 85 86 87 88 89 **1890** 91 92 93 94 95 96 97 98 99 **1900** 01 02 03 04 05 06 07 08 09 **1910** 11 12 13 14 15 16 17 18 19 **1920** 21 22 23 24 25 26 27 28 29 **1930** 31 32 33 34 35 36 37 38 39 **1940** 41 42 43 44 45 46 47 48 49 **1950** 51 52 53 54 55 56 57

Bibliography and Sources

The life of Albert Einstein, his work and their influence on the world today have been the subject of thousands of books, articles, and documentaries.
The authors, like Newton, were fortunate enough to stand, with humility, on the shoulders of the giants that preceded them.

To name a few:

Books

Einstein, Albert, and Max Born. *The Born-Einstein Letters, 1916-1955: Friendship, Politics and Physics in Uncertain Times*. Macmillan, 2005.

Einstein, Albert, and John J. Stachel. *The Collected Papers of Albert Einstein*. Princeton University Press, 1987.

Fölsing, Albrecht, and Ewald Osers. *Albert Einstein: A Biography*. Penguin Books, 1998.

Isaacson, Walter. *Einstein: His Life and Universe*. Simon & Schuster, 2008.

Jerome, Fred. *The Einstein File: J. Edgar Hoover's Secret War Against the World's Most Famous Scientist*. St. Martin's Griffin, 2003.

Neffe, Jurgen. *Einstein: A Biography*. Trans. by Shelley Frisch. Johns Hopkins University Press, 2009.

Rigden, John S. Einstein 1905: *The Standard of Greatness*. Harvard University Press, 2005.

Robinson, Andrew. *A Hundred Years of Relativity*. Princeton University Press, 2015.

Rowe, David, and Robert Schulmann. *Einstein on Politics: His Private Thought and Public Stands on Nationalism, Zionism, War, Peace, and the Bomb*. Princeton University Press, 2013.

Film

Moffat, Peter and Philip Martin. *Einstein and Eddington*: BBC Two, 2008.

TV Series

Pink, Noah, and Ken Biller, creators. *Genius*, season 1. National Geographic, 2017.

Radio Documentary

Hart-Davis, Adam, narrator. "1905." *The Eureka Years*, series 3, episode 4, BBC Radio 4, June 2, 2009, https://www.bbc.co.uk/programmes/b007yvyq.

Documentary and Video

Lochhead, Jamie E. "Inside Einstein's Mind: The Enigma of Space and Time." *Nova*, season 42, episode 23, 25 November 2015.

"Albert Einstein Warns of Dangers in Nuclear Arms Race." A, correspondent. NBC News. NBCUniversal Media. 12 Feb. 1950. NBC Learn. Web. 18 March 2015

Quotations

Some of the dialogue attributed to Albert Einstein in this book is based on interviews he gave or selections from his texts and articles. These texts are available in the following forms:

Einstein, Albert. *The World as I See It*. Trans. by Alan Harris. Philosophical Library, 1949.

Einstein, Albert. *Out of My Later Years*: Citadel Press, 1950.

To Reflect On...

Beginning in the 1920s, Albert Einstein was a sort of international star whose every word was reprinted in the media all over the world. This allowed him to draw interest to his field and also to spread his progressive ideals as an activist for peace.

"IMAGINATION IS MORE IMPORTANT THAN KNOWLEDGE."

"IF SOMEONE CAN ENJOY MARCHING TO MUSIC IN RANK AND FILE, I CAN FEEL ONLY CONTEMPT FOR HIM; HE HAS RECEIVED HIS LARGE BRAIN BY MISTAKE, A SPINAL CORD WOULD HAVE BEEN ENOUGH."

*"IT IS HARDER TO CRACK PREJUDICE
THAN AN ATOM."*

*"LIFE IS AN ADVENTURE; IT MUST
CONTINUOUSLY QUARREL WITH DEATH."*

*"I MAINTAIN THAT THE COSMIC RELIGIOUS
FEELING IS THE STRONGEST AND NOBLEST
MOTIVE FOR SCIENTIFIC RESEARCH."*

*"I DO NOT KNOW WHAT THE THIRD WORLD WAR
WILL BE LIKE, BUT I DO KNOW THAT THERE WILL
NOT BE MANY PEOPLE LEFT TO SEE THE FOURTH"*

"WHAT TRULY INTERESTS ME IS WHETHER GOD HAD ANY CHOICE IN THE CREATION OF THE WORLD."

"WE WILL HAVE THE DESTINY THAT WE DESERVE."

"IT IS NOT ENOUGH TO TEACH A MAN A SPECIALTY. THROUGH IT HE MAY BECOME A KIND OF USEFUL MACHINE BUT NOT A HARMONIOUSLY DEVELOPED PERSONALITY."

*"I CANNOT IMAGINE A GOD
WHO REWARDS AND PUNISHES
THE OBJECTS OF HIS CREATION."*

*"I DO NOT AT ALL BELIEVE IN HUMAN FREEDOM
IN THE PHILOSOPHICAL SENSE. EVERYBODY ACTS
NOT ONLY UNDER EXTERNAL COMPULSION BUT
ALSO IN ACCORDANCE WITH INNER NECESSITY."*

*"IT HAS BECOME APPALLINGLY OBVIOUS THAT OUR
TECHNOLOGY HAS EXCEEDED OUR HUMANITY."*

Also available from NBM Comics Biographies:

THE BEATLES IN COMICS!
Various authors, Michels Mabel

THE TRUE DEATH OF BILLY THE KID
Rick Geary

The Provocative COLETTE
Annie Goetzinger & Rodolphe

Philip K. DICK
A Comics Biography
Laurent Queyssi, writer, Mauro Marchesi, art

ELVIS
Philippe Chanoinat and Fabrice Le Henanff

GHETTO BROTHER- Warrior to Peacemaker
Julian Voloj, Claudia Ahlering

GIRL IN DIOR
Annie Goetzinger

GLENN GOULD: A Life Off Tempo
Sandrine Revel

BILLIE HOLIDAY
José Muñoz, Carlos Sampayo

MARIE ANTOINETTE, PHANTOM QUEEN
Annie Goetzinger & Rodolphe

MONET: Itinerant of Light
Efa, Salva Rubio

The ROLLING STONES in Comics!
Ceka and various artists

NIKI DE SAINT PHALLE
The Garden of Secrets
Dominique Osuch, Sandrine Martin

SARTRE
Mathilde Ramadier & Anais Depommier

THOREAU, A Sublime Life
A. Dan, Maximilien Le Roy

THE BEATLES
in comics
nbm
GRAPHIC NOVELS

The TRUE DEATH of Billy THE Kid
RICK GEARY

Annie Goetzinger
The Provocative
COLETTE
nbm
GRAPHIC NOVELS

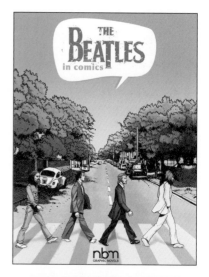

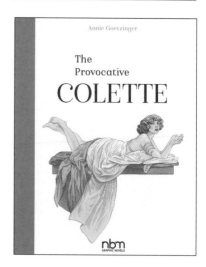

We have over 200 graphic novels
See more at:
NBMPUB.COM

NBM
160 Broadway, Suite 700, East Wing
New York, NY 10038
Catalog upon request

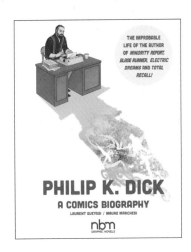

THE IMPROBABLE LIFE OF THE AUTHOR OF *MINORITY REPORT*, *BLADE RUNNER*, *ELECTRIC DREAMS* AND *TOTAL RECALL!*

PHILIP K. DICK
A COMICS BIOGRAPHY
LAURENT QUEYSSI / MAURO MARCHESI

nbm
Graphic Novels

Le Hénanff · Chenoinat

Elvis

nbm
Graphic Novels

Julian VOLOJ · Claudia AHLERING

GHETTO BROTHER

WARRIOR TO PEACEMAKER

nbm
Graphic Novels

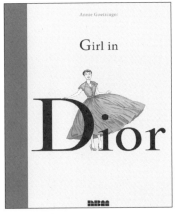

Annie Goetzinger

Girl in
Dior

NBM

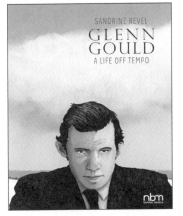

SANDRINE REVEL
GLENN GOULD
A LIFE OFF TEMPO

nbm
Graphic Novels

MUÑOZ & SAMPAYO
BILLIE HOLIDAY

nbm
Graphic Novels

Rodolphe & Annie Goetzinger
MARIE ANTOINETTE
Phantom Queen

NBM

EFA - RUBIO
MONET
Itinerant of Light

nbm
Graphic Novels

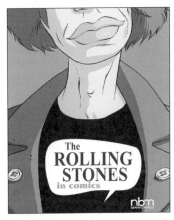

The ROLLING STONES
in comics

nbm
Graphic Novels

DOMINIQUE OSUCH · SANDRINE MARTIN
NIKI
DE SAINT PHALLE
THE GARDEN OF SECRETS

nbm
Graphic Novels

Mathilde Ramadier & Anaïs Depommier
SARTRE

nbm
Graphic Novels

A. DAN - LE ROY
THOREAU
A Sublime Life

NBM

Albert Einstein and his second wife Elsa in Washington (1923)
Harris & Ewing – Library of Congress